The Georgetown Guide to Arabic–English Translation

The Georgetown Guide to **Arabic–English** Translation

MUSTAFA MUGHAZY

Georgetown University Press / Washington, DC

Library of Congress Cataloging-in-Publication Data

Mughazy, Mustafa, 1974– author.
The Georgetown manual of Arabic-English translation / Mustafa Mughazy.
pages cm
Includes bibliographical references and index.
ISBN 978-1-62616-292-1 (hardcover : alk. paper) —
ISBN 978-1-62616-279-2 (pbk. : alk. paper) —
ISBN 978-1-62616-280-8 (ebook)
1. Arabic language—Translating into English. 2. Translating
and interpreting—Philosophy. I. Title.
PJ6403.M84 2016
428'.02927—dc23
2015022046

∞ This book is printed on acid-free paper meeting the requirements
of the American National Standard for Permanence
in Paper for Printed Library Materials.

17   16   9 8 7 6 5 4 3 2   First printing

Cover design by Beth Schlennoff

Printed in the United States of America

In memory of Dr. Souad Hussein Sobhy

Contents

Acknowledgments

This book would not have been possible without the inspiration, support, and guidance of many people, especially Jeffery Angles, Cynthia Running-Johnson, Devin Stewart, David Wilmsen, and Mai Zaki. I am deeply indebted to many former students at Western Michigan University, whose questions, discussions, and criticisms helped shape this book. Of these, I must mention Ashleigh Ali, Ashley Aubermann, Kristin Horitski, Marissa Icabone, Emily Napier, Margaret Petersen, Margaret Proctor, Lindsey Reyes, Jacob Rogers, Martina Roland, Daniel Schipp, Jacob Tardani, and Emily Woodard. I would like to thank Ingie Zakaria and Nihad Heliel for their thoughtful discussions and comments on various drafts of the book. I would particularly like to thank my wife, Lesley Yuill-Mughazy, for seeing me through the process of writing this book and for patiently responding to my endless questions as every possible translation example in the book was discussed, challenged, and debated. Finally, I would like to thank the editors and reviewers of Georgetown University Press, particularly Hope LeGro, for their valuable insights and for patiently guiding me through the process.

Introduction

Who Needs a Manual for Arabic–English Translation Anyway?

Translation is often seen as something that anyone who is fluent in two languages can do; one simply reads a text in the source language and somehow comes up with an equivalent text in the target language. Common misconceptions of translation such as this can go as far as to treat it as an art form, a view that chooses to ignore the fact that art also requires extensive training and deep knowledge of methods and techniques. It only takes a few minutes of trying to translate a text to make one realize that such views could not be further from the truth. Translation, as we will see in this book, is a complex process that follows a scientific method, whereby we analyze the source text to determine its communicative functions; to identify functional equivalence problems; to apply translation strategies to generate target language candidates, or hypotheses; and to finally test them to assess their validity.

Translation is like a reverse-engineering process whereby, say, we might take apart a clock made of metal parts in order to build a functioning replica made entirely of plastic. Our final product will not look the same as the original clock, and it would be impossible to simply copy the designs of its inner workings, because plastic and metals have very different properties. For example, we cannot make small, plastic springs or very thin gears of plastic. But these changes do not matter; the only thing that matters is that our replica will tell the time correctly. This process involves identifying the pieces and mechanisms in the original clock, determining their functions, and figuring out how they work together to achieve the main goal of telling the time. Then, we need to experiment with different strategies to

make the pieces of plastic work together to achieve the same goal. Sometimes, the original clock may have additional functions, such as an alarm,
a night-light, or even artistic features for aesthetic effects. These functions
should also be performed by our plastic clock. Translating from Arabic to
English follows a similar path, but it is of course a much more complicated
process because there are so many more linguistic features in any language
than there are pieces in a clock; and given the generative nature of grammar, there are infinite numbers of possible combinations of linguistic forms.
However, these complications do not make translation impossible, because
there are constraints that guide our work.

Let us take the sentence الساعة الرابعة والثلث فجرا as an example of how this
process works. It is a rather simple sentence, made up of the subject الساعة *the
hour*, the conjoined predicate الرابعة والثلث *the fourth and a third*, and the adverb فجرا. The word الساعة is lexically and functionally ambiguous—it could
be a noun meaning *clock*, *watch*, or *hour*; or it could be an adverb meaning
now. Our knowledge of Arabic grammar tells us that it is used in this sentence as a noun serving as a subject, and our understanding of the function
of this sentence as a whole tells us that the intended reading is *hour*. Note,
however, that *the hour* cannot be used as the subject of an English sentence
that tells the time; it needs to be replaced with *it* or *the time*. The adverb فجرا
also poses a lexical problem; it is derived from the noun فجر *dawn*, but there
are no English adverbs derived from *dawn*. Therefore, we need to find a modifier phrase that can serve the same grammatical function, such as *at dawn*.
Now we have an English counterpart for every word in the Arabic sentence,
but the combination *the hour/time is the fourth and a third at dawn* does
not sound natural in English. Here is what we just did: We analyzed the linguistic structure of the Arabic source sentence, and we identified what it says
and what it does: It tells the time in a natural way in Arabic. We also tested
the literal candidate (i.e., what it says) against our internalized database of
English time expressions, and we decided to rule it out.

We now need to look into other English time expressions to see if there is
a true functional equivalent. There are several candidates to test including,
among others, *It is twenty past four in the morning*, *It is twenty after four in
the morning*, and *It is 4:20 a.m.* The choice of the successful candidate will
depend on the following criteria: (1) It needs to include all the information
encoded in the source text, (2) it needs to achieve the discourse functions
of the source text, and (3) it needs to sound natural in the same contexts as
the source text. The three candidates in question meet the first two criteria,

but we do not have enough contextual information to make a final decision with respect to the third criterion. For example, we need to know whether the tone of the source text is conversational or formal. Fortunately, we rarely translate isolated sentences, and there is usually enough information about the context to help us select the optimal translation candidate.

Because language is itself an expression of culture, we expect to encounter words and expressions in the source language that either have no counterparts in the target language or have counterparts that are used differently. This is why we need to pay special attention to the cultural references in the texts we translate. For instance, in addition to the linguistic information encoded in the sentence we analyzed above, there are two cultural references that are encoded in the noun الثلث *the third* and the adverb فجرا *at dawn*. These references have to do with the fact that Arabic uses the third as a fraction of the hour, and that it makes temporal references using the intervals associated with Muslim prayer times. Obviously, these references do not apply to English-speaking cultures, but this is not a very serious problem, because these references do not affect the function of the source sentence, which is to tell the time in a natural way. There are, of course, many other cases in which cultural references pose more interesting challenges. Think of culture-specific expressions, such as عقدة الخواجة *lit. the foreigner's complex* (i.e., the preference among many Arabs for European and American products and ideas over their local counterparts); of traditional professions, such as المسحراتي (the man who walks the streets at night during Ramadan singing and beating a drum to call on people to wake up for their predawn meal); and of celebrations, such as العقيقة (a Muslim practice in which a sheep is slaughtered and given to charity to celebrate the birth of a child). Such terms are not impossible to translate because we are not matching up words from different languages. Our goal is to achieve the communicative function of the source text, even if we need to add definitions, paraphrase expressions, or, in some cases, delete them altogether—as we will see in the following chapters.

The approach I adopt in this book is a functional one, whereby a translation candidate is considered optimal if it achieves the same communicative functions as the source text. But what are these functions? Let us think of the clause as the smallest linguistic unit that provides a complete description of a situation: The verb tells us what kind of event is described, whereas the subject and the object(s) identify the participants in this situation. Modifiers, such as adverbial phrases, provide additional information about the internal structure of the situation in question, such as its location in time and space and the manner in which the event takes place. Functional categories, such as negation, case, mood, tense, and modality, provide external information about this situation. In other words, they tell us whether it is a past, present, or future situation; whether it is a real situation or a hypothetical one; and whether it is true or not. Although clauses can be used as independent sentences, we often see clauses combined through coordination and subordination to encode logical relations, such as conditionals and conjunctions, and temporal relations, such as simultaneity, overlap, and sequence. The resulting constructions are compound or complex sentences that describe how events relate to each other, thus creating more complex event descriptions. Every word and every grammatical construction in a clause contributes to the clause's referential function, and subordinate clauses also contribute to achieving the sentence's referential function. A successful translation candidate provides a description of a situation that is as faithful as possible to the one described in the source text. In other words, it needs to include all the information encoded in the source text, unless we have good reasons to exclude or add some information items.

Just as we expect lexical mismatches between Arabic and English, we expect some Arabic grammatical constructions to have no equivalents in English or to have counterparts that are used differently. This is not a serious problem, because we can still identify different English constructions that achieve the same referential functions. For example, الساعة الرابعة والثلث فجرا is a nominal sentence that does not have a verb, a structure that would be obviously ungrammatical if maintained in our translation. Moreover, the predicate phrase الرابعة والثلث *the fourth and a third* has an adjective conjoined to a noun, which is ungrammatical, suggesting that the adjective الرابعة *the fourth* actually modifies a deleted noun that is a copy of the subject phrase. These are language internal issues, and their role in the translation process is to help us identify the source text's referential functions. An optimal translation candidate does not need to use the same grammatical structures as the source text; it only needs to fulfill the same referential functions. In fact, as we will see in chapters 2 and 3, there are cases in which we need to translate a negative sentence as an affirmative one or a sentence in the active voice as a passive one, as long as the translation provides a situation description that is as faithful as possible to the one in the source text.

In addition to their referential functions, sentences have pragmatic functions. This is when a sentence (or an utterance) is used to do something beyond describing a situation. For example, شكرا is an expression of grati-tude that literally means *thankfully*, whereas the response عفوا is an adverb derived from the verb عفا *to forgive*. Their linguistic content does not tell us much about their functions; therefore, we cannot translate them literally as *thankfully* and *forgivingly*. These expressions do not report on situations. Rather, they are used to carry out actions. To translate these utterances, we need functional equivalents that are conventionally used to carry out these same actions regardless of their linguistic structure, as in *Thank you* and *You are welcome*, respectively. Pragmatic functions, such as express-ing gratitude, issuing warnings, making promises, and offering condolences, usually have social and cultural attributes, such as formality, intensity, and appropriateness. For example, the sentence كان عندي سؤال *lit. I had a question* can be used as a polite way to make an indirect request rather than reporting on a past situation. A successful translation candidate needs to achieve the pragmatic function of the source sentence while maintaining its politeness and indirectness, even if we need to use different linguistic structures.

We also see some discourse markers and grammatical constructions that are conventionally associated with certain discourse functions. For ex-ample, the sentence أما الميدالية الفضية فقد حصل عليها محمود جابر *lit. As for the silver medal, Mahmoud Jabir got it* has the discourse marker أما *as for*, which encodes two discourse functions. It signals contrast between the ref-erent of the noun phrase that immediately follows it and a similar referent in the preceding discourse, another medal in this case. The other function is to signal discourse prominence. The object noun phrase الميدالية الفضية *the silver medal* is used as the first noun phrase in the sentence following أما in a construction known as topicalization. Compare this sentence with أما محمود جابر فقد حصل على الميدالية الفضية *lit. As for Mahmoud Jabir, he got the silver medal*. This structure tells the reader that the sentence is about the referent of the first noun phrase. In other words, it is more salient than the referents of the other noun phrases in the sentence. Just like referential functions, discourse functions need to be maintained in translation because they are an integral part of the message encoded in the source sentence. To keep the noun phrase referring to the medal in the topic position, which has the same discourse function in English, we can use a different verb, as in *the silver medal went to*. Of course, this substitution comes at the expense of referential faithfulness.

Quite often, we find ourselves in situations in which we cannot main-tain both referential and discourse/pragmatic functions at the same time, which is to be expected because we are dealing with different linguistic and cultural systems. As a result, we sometimes need to make decisions about which functions to maintain in our translation. Generally speaking, if there is a conflict between faithfulness to the referential functions of a sentence and faithfulness to its pragmatic and discourse functions, we compromise on referential faithfulness. This is what I have done in all the examples discussed thus far. For example, we undermined referential faithfulness to the phrases *the fourth* and *a third* in our translation of الساعة الرابعة والثلث فجرا. In other words, if we must choose between what the source text literally says and what it does, we need to make sure that our translation maintains the what-it-does part. There are also times when we need to undermine some pragmatic and discourse functions. For example, Arabic business letters and e-mails usually use the frozen expression أما بعد *lit. as for after* to signal the transition from pleasantries and preliminary remarks to the main body of the text. The frozen expression *without further ado* serves the same function, but it would sound rather odd in an English business letter or e-mail. For our translation to sound natural in the same context as the source text, we need to leave out this expression. Of course, this does not mean we can change the information content of the source text as we please—just some wording, and only when necessary.

We now turn to the question of what it means for a translation candidate to sound natural in the same context as the source text. Naturalness here refers to the frequency of the words and expressions in our translation relative to a genre. For example, the word ذراع *arm* is used in Arabic as a measurement unit (18 inches), which is equivalent to the obsolete *cubit*. If we are translating an advertisement about office space for lease and we use *cubits*, it would sound odd because it is a low-frequency word in this genre. We should instead use feet or other measurement units that are common in this genre. However, if we are translating a novel about medieval knights, *cubit* would fit well in this context. The same pattern applies to multiword expressions. For instance, the phrase وقد نقلت وكالة أنباء الشرق قوله *lit. Al-Sharq News Agency reported his saying* can be translated using the phrase *quoted him as saying* or *reported him as saying*. Both candidates are grammatical, and both have the same discourse functions. The only difference is that *quoted him as saying* has a much higher frequency in English news than does *reported him as saying*. Therefore, we can conclude that the former candidate sounds more natural in this context. We often rely on our intuitions to determine the frequency of our translation candidates, but we can use specialized online tools, such as genre-specific language corpora, to get a more accurate frequency assessment. For information about these online tools, and for further reading on translation techniques, see the bibliography at the back of the book.

This book adopts a bottom-up linguistic approach, starting with morphemes and words, and building up to discourse-level translation problems and strategies. Every linguistic concept is presented, with definitions and examples from both Arabic and English. Translation issues and strategies are discussed in detail, and translation patterns are established wherever applicable. As you go through the chapters, make sure to familiarize yourself with the linguistic concepts before attempting to translate the examples. Then, analyze the examples and describe the translation problems using the linguistic terms you have learned. Make a list of your translation candidates, and go through them to decide whether they should be ruled out and why until you identify an optimal candidate. The appendices provide lists of expressions similar to the ones discussed in the chapters. You can use these lists to find other texts to translate using the same principles. It is very important that you analyze the examples, identify and describe the problems, generate translation candidates, and select the successful ones. Our goal is not only to choose successful translation candidates but also to be able to explain and defend our choices.

as words
(dependently)   ① free morphemes

(non "   ② bound

verb change
adverb   derivational + "functional"
③   ④   ↓
grammatical
info

Getting Words Across
Word-Level Translation Problems and Strategies

Words are often assumed to be the building blocks of language; they have specific meanings that we can find in dictionaries, and they can be combined according to the rules of grammar to form meaningful phrases and sentences, which in turn can be combined to form paragraphs and extended discourses. However, when we look closely at the structures of words, we realize that they are in fact made up of smaller units of meaning, or morphemes. For example, when we compare the words *break*, *breakable*, and *unbreakable*, we realize that affixes (i.e., suffixes and prefixes) add new components of meaning. The suffix *-able* changes the verb *break* into an adjective (*break → breakable*), whereas the prefix *un-* adds negation (*breakable → unbreakable*). The word *unbreakable* is actually made up of three morphemes: the stem *break*; and the two affixes, each of which contributes to the word's meaning. Therefore, in order to translate words, we first need to deconstruct their meanings by analyzing their morphological structures.

In order to analyze the morphological structures of words, we need to distinguish two types of morphemes: free morphemes, which can be used independently as words, such as the stem *break*; and bound morphemes, which cannot be used as words. Bound morphemes are suffixes and prefixes, and thus they must be attached to stems, such as *en-* in *enrich* and *-less* in *homeless*. We also need to establish a distinction between derivational and functional morphemes. Derivational morphemes typically change a stem's part of speech. For instance, the suffix *-ness* derives nouns from adjectives (e.g., *happy → happiness*), whereas the prefix *-ize* generates verbs from adjectives (e.g., *modern → modernize*). Derivational morphemes sometimes contribute to the meanings of words without changing their part of speech. For example, the prefix *re-* is attached to verbs to indicate repeated action (e.g., *rewrite* and *redo*), whereas the prefixes *un-*, *im-*, and *dis-* add negation (e.g., *unimportant*, *imperfect*, and *dislike*). Functional morphemes, conversely, provide grammatical information, including tense (e.g., the past tense *-ed*), number (e.g., the plural *-s*), and person (e.g., the third person *-s* in *He speaks*). Once we have identified the functions of the morphemes that make up a word, we can start looking for equivalents in the target language that can achieve these same functions.

Derivational morphemes play a critical role in generating words, but there are also other word formation strategies. Words can be formed by combining already-existing stems (e.g., *mailbox* and *bathroom*) or by blending them (e.g., *smog* from *smoke* and *fog*, and *brunch* from *breakfast* and *lunch*). The initial letters of the words that make up a phrase can be used together to form either a new word (e.g., *laser—light amplified by [a] stimulated emission of radiation*) or an abbreviation or acronym (e.g., *USA—United States of America*). Sometimes, an already-existing word is clipped or shortened to create a new one, such as *ad* from *advertisement* and *phone* from *telephone*. Generating new words is not strictly a process that is internal to one particular language, because words can be borrowed from other languages, such as *chef* from French and *spiel* from Yiddish. Understanding how word formation strategies work is essential to the translation process because they tell us how the source language's words are generated and help us identify or generate equivalents in the target language.

There are important differences in the ways words are structured in Arabic and in English. Notably, most Arabic words are built from roots rather than stems. For example, the words كتب *wrote*, كتاب *book*, كاتب *writer*, مكتوب *written/letter*, and مكتبة *library* are all derived from the root ك ت ب, which is associated with writing. Most Arabic content words, such as nouns, verbs, and adjectives, are generated by applying roots to specific templates. Active participles, for instance, are derived from basic roots by inserting the three root consonants into the template فاعل, resulting in words such as كاتب *writer*, صانع *manufacturer*, and لاعب *player*, all of which have the same vowel melody. Arabic also makes use of prefixes, such as the definite article الـ, as well as some suffixes, including dual and regular plural morphemes. Each morpheme—whether it is a root, a template, or an affix—carries a certain component of meaning; and accordingly, it plays a crucial role in our understanding of Arabic words and how we can translate them into English.

Although most Arabic content words are generated through root and pattern derivation, other word formation processes are available. For example, there are relatively few Arabic acronyms, such as م in م ٢٠١٥ سنة *AD 2015*, in which م stands for ميلادية *Anno Domini (the Year of Our Lord)*, and ق. م., which stands for قبل الميلاد *Before Christ* (*BC*). Compound words are rare in Arabic, but we can find a few recent examples, such as الرأسمالية *capitalism*, which is based on رأس *head* and مال *money*. In Modern Standard Arabic, the most productive word formation process, other than root and pattern derivation, entails borrowing words from other languages and modifying them to comply with the sound system of Arabic, as in الديموقراطية *democracy* and استراتيجية *strategy*.

Knowledge of word formation rules is fundamental to the process of translation. As a first step, we need to analyze the morphological structures of the words we are translating to identify the information encoded in each morpheme. Then, we need to make sure that this information is maintained in the translation. This chapter describes the main problems that translators often encounter when dealing with words, along with strategies that can help resolve them.

1 Word-Level Translation Problems

1.1 *Lexical Gaps*

It is not unusual for a speech community to have concepts with no words that describe them. For example, English has different words for people who lose family members—such as *orphan*, *widow*, and *widower*—but there is no word for a mother who loses her child. This is a lexical gap. When it comes to translation, we often encounter crosslinguistic lexical gaps. These are words that exist in the source language but have no equivalents in the target language. The source language's culture-specific semantic fields are prime grounds for lexical gaps, simply because the concepts or cultural practices to which they refer do not exist in the target language's culture. For instance, السبوع refers to a traditional ceremony that many Arab families hold seven days after the birth of a baby. There is no such celebration in

English-speaking cultures; therefore, السبوع is considered a lexical gap that is difficult to translate.

Crosslinguistic lexical gaps can be found in all culturally biased semantic fields—including terms of address, such as حاج, which literally means *someone who performed the Muslim pilgrimage to Mecca*; religious practices, such as سحور, *the predawn meal in Ramadan*; and culture-specific material products, including food items and articles of clothing. A few such terms have developed equivalents that can be found even in English–English dictionaries. These are either transliterated borrowings, such as *jihad* and *sheikh*, or standardized counterparts, such as *Qur'anic verse* for آية and *The Night of Power* for ليلة القدر. The problem is that the majority of Arabic words that constitute lexical gaps in English do not have standardized equivalents. Even already-existing equivalents do not always work, because some have changed certain aspects of their meaning in English, as in the case of *jihad*, or they require specialized knowledge that the intended readers might not have, as in the case of *The Night of Power*.

Lexical gaps are by no means limited to culture-specific concepts. In fact, most of them are the result of word-formation processes that work differently in Arabic and English. Here is a case in point: The adjective علمي *scientific*, which is derived from the noun علم *science*, feeds into a derivational process that generates the noun علمية in (1). English has similar morphological derivations, but there is no word for *scientificness* or *scientificity*; hence the lexical gap.

(1) مجلة الفوانيس (المغرب)، ١١ فبراير ٢٠٠٨.
لم تكن هذه الأيديولوجيات الدينية تنسب نفسها إلى العلم أو تدعي **العلمية**.
These religious ideologies did not associate themselves with
science or claim to be scientific.

Another example is denominal verbs, which are verbs derived from nouns, such as *to house (someone), to hand (something over)*, and *to chair (a committee)*. Arabic allows deriving these verbs in a more productive way than English, and as a result, many such verbs in Arabic have no equivalents in English. For instance, there is no English verb that means *to carry something under one's armpit* as the Arabic verb يتأبط in (2). Sometimes, English has a similar derivation process, but the resulting word means something different from the source word, as in the case of ترجل *dismount/get off*, which is derived from رجل *leg*.

(2) جريدة الحياة (السعودية)، ٩ مارس ٢٠٠٥.
ثم ترجل بعد ذلك حمود وكان يرتدي الزي العربي وهو **يتأبط** مسدسا من نوع
«كولت سمث».

Then, Hammoud got out of the car dressed in Arab garb, with a
Colt Smith gun tucked under his arm.

When we say that a word in the source language has an equivalent in
the target language, we tend to assume that these words are of the same
category or part of speech, which is quite often the case. However, there is
nothing unusual about having an Arabic word with an English equivalent
that belongs to a different part of speech. The preposition عند *at* is probably
the most obvious case, because it can express possession, but no English
preposition has the same meaning. This is why the verb *to have* is considered a functional equivalent of the preposition عند in contexts such as عندي
سؤال *I have a question*.

Cases of part-of-speech mismatches are plentiful in the verbal category.
Many Arabic verbs that describe properties or attributes rather than actions,
such as يستحيل *to be impossible* in (3) and يبعد *be far* in (4), do not have
verbal equivalents in English.

(3) جريدة الرياض (السعودية)، ٢٣ مارس ٢٠١٣، العدد ١٦٣٤٣.
يستحيل معرفة ما إذا كانوا في مكان قريب أو على بعد مئات الكيلومترات.
It is impossible to tell whether they are nearby or hundreds of
kilometers away.

(4) جريدة السفير (لبنان)، ٩ نوفمبر ٢٠١٣، العدد ١٢٤٠٢.
هناك في موريتانيا ذهب، وخاصة في منجم «تازيازت» الذي **يبعد** ٣٥٠ كلم
عن العاصمة شمالا.
There is gold in Mauritania, especially in the Tazyazit Mine 350
kilometers north of the capital.

Some Arabic verbs correspond to English modals, such as يستطيع *can*
and يجب *must/have to*, whereas others correspond to adverbs, such as كاد,
which translates as *almost*. Although these pseudo-equivalents have similar meanings, they have different grammatical properties that should be
taken into consideration when translating. We look at these in some detail
in chapter 3.

Despite the idiosyncratic nature of many lexical gaps, some patterns are relatively systematic. For instance, Arabic adverbs can be derived from nouns and adjectives by adding the *tanween* suffix, such as سريعا *quickly* from سريع *quick*, and صباحا *in the morning* from صباح *morning*. Many Arabic adverbs that are derived from nouns constitute lexical gaps in English, especially if they are derived from nouns that refer to events, such as تفاديا in (5). This adverb is derived by adding the *tanween* suffix to the noun تفادي *avoiding/avoidance*, but there is no such adverb as *avoidingly* in English.

(5) جريدة السوداني (السودان)، ١٧ ديسمبر ٢٠١٤.
أمر الشيخ زايد المهندس المشرف على تنفيذ أحد المشاريع الرئيسية في مدينة أبو ظبي بأن يغير مسار الشارع **تفاديا** لقطع الشجرة.
Sheikh Zayed ordered the engineer in charge of a major project
in Abu Dhabi to reroute the street to avoid cutting down the tree.

How we translate Arabic adverbs depends on their context. Some of them can be paraphrased as prepositional phrases, such as صباحا *in the morning*, whereas others can be translated as adverbial clauses, such as تفاديا *to/in order to avoid*, among other possibilities.

Although lexical gaps seem challenging, there are several ways of dealing with them. Whether the lexical gap is the result of cultural or linguistic differences, we can paraphrase it to explain what it means. There is no rule that says we must translate a word as a word; we can translate a word as a phrase, or even as a sentence. The crucial point here is that we need to understand the source and nature of the difficulty in order to come up with viable translation candidates from which to choose.

1.2 False Equivalents

The meaning of a word can go beyond its referential potential to include social attitudes and valuations. These nonreferential types of meaning can be problematic if the source word has a counterpart in the target language that does not share all these aspects—that is, if they are not true functional equivalents. Let us take social meaning as an example. Some words are conventionally associated with culture-specific attitudes that range from taboo or inappropriate to politically correct or positive. Because these attitudes are culture-specific, we expect them to vary from one language to the other. For instance, the Arabic nouns السود *Blacks* and الهنود الحمر *Red culture*

Indians in (6) are used only as neutral descriptions of these ethnic groups, but their English counterparts are unacceptable racially charged terms. Note that these terms were introduced into Arabic by translating them literally from English. Because the author of the Arabic text in (6) uses these terms neutrally, we should avoid the English literal counterparts and instead use neutral terms that are culturally appropriate, such as *African Americans* and *Native Americans*.

(6) جريدة الوطن (السعودية)، ١٨ فبراير ٢٠٠٩، العدد ٣٠٦٤.
قام العقيد القذافي بتذكير الأمريكان كيف أنهم كانوا يحملون صورا نمطية
سلبية عن فئات من داخل المجتمع الأمريكي نفسه مثل **السود** أو **الهنود الحمر**.

Colonel Qaddafi reminded the American people how they used to have negative stereotypes of certain ethnic groups within American society itself, such as African Americans and Native Americans.

Words with different interpretations can further complicate the issue of crosslinguistic equivalence. For example, the noun مرافق refers to any individual who is designated to provide company in some official capacity. It can be used to describe someone staying in a hospital with a sick relative, a chaperone, or a bodyguard accompanying celebrities or dignitaries, among other possibilities. In the context of (7), المرافق describes a person whose job it is to accompany foreign guests during business meetings and interviews. Note that the person described as مرافق is not the host, but someone who represents the host. The English counterpart listed in most Arabic–English dictionaries is *escort*. Although both words have the same referential meaning—namely, *someone whose job it is to provide company*—they have very different social meanings. As a result, they are not true functional equivalents in this context. Fortunately, this sentence provides a description of the duties associated with this job, which justifies translating it as *interpreter*. In this way, we can avoid the potential confusion of the ambiguous *escort* as well as the inaccuracy of translating مرافق as *bodyguard*, *chaperone*, or *guide*.

(7) عبد الوهاب مطاوع، ٢٠٠١، "اندهش يا صديقي"، دار الشروق، القاهرة،
ص ١٩.
شيئان كرهتهما في رحلاتي للخارج [...] هما **المرافق** الذي تفرضه علي الجهة
الداعية ليصاحبني في زياراتي، ومهمة **المرافق** هي أن ييسر لي زياراتي
ويترجم لي محادثاتي مع من لا يعرفون الإنجليزية.

Two things I hated about my trips abroad: One is the interpreter that the host agency would impose on me during my visits. The interpreter's job was to facilitate my visits and translate my conversations with those who did not speak English.

Social meaning also involves religion-based attitudes and perspectives. Arab writers quite often use terms that have roots in religious discourse, even in nonreligious texts. That is because these words already carry the implied attitudes they wish to convey without making them explicit. The noun بدعة in (8) is synonymous with اختراع and ابتكار, all of which mean *innovation/invention*. The only difference is that بدعة has a negative social meaning, whereas the other two are associated with positive attitudes. The negative attitudes associated with بدعة stem from a saying by the Prophet Muhammad in which he uses this word to describe unorthodox religious practices. By using بدعة in (8), the author is strongly suggesting that President Muhammad Morsi's visit to Israel should not be seen as a new, yet unacceptable or aberrant political decision. The challenge is to make sure that this negative attitude does not get lost in the translation.

(8) جريدة الوفد (مصر)، ١ سبتمبر ٢٠١٢.
قالت الدكتورة نورهان الشيخ، أستاذة العلوم السياسية بجامعة القاهرة، إن
زيارة الرئيس مرسي لإسرائيل ليست **بدعة** سياسية.

Dr. Norhan Al-Shaykh, professor of political science at Cairo
University, said that President Morsi's visit to Israel is no
political heresy.

Connotations are a different type of nonreferential meaning, whereby words have implied or suggested associations that are distinct from their denotations or referential meanings. The difference between connotations and social meanings is that social meanings are consistent, whereas connotations are context-specific. In other words, a word with either a negative or positive social meaning maintains this association across discourse types, but a word can have either positive or negative connotations, depending on the context. In the context of (9), the adjective المتحررة *lit. liberated/freed* has negative connotations, namely, that these television programs are liberal; that is, they present content that some would consider inappropriate, but in the context of (10), there are no such connotations. The sentence positively describes a woman who has freed herself from illiteracy. These two instances of the same word need to be translated differently to reflect their different connotations.

(٩) جريدة الدستور (الأردن)، ٢ يوليو ٢٠١٣، العدد ١٦٥١٥.
ويقول حسين جبر إن المشكلة هي انتشار الفضائيات والقنوات **المتحررة** التي تبث البرامج "اللاأخلاقية".

According to Hussein Jabr, the problem is the widespread availability of permissive satellite television channels that air "immoral" programs.

(١٠) جريدة الأهرام (مصر)، ٢٦ سبتمبر ٢٠٠٥، العدد ٤٣٣٩٣.
هذه هي قصة نجاح **متحررة** من الأمية روت تفاصيلها في الاحتفال باليوم العالمي لمحو الأمية.

This is the success story of a woman freed from illiteracy as she told it at the celebration of International Literacy Day.

Proper nouns, or names, are probably the least complicated words to translate. In fact, they are not even translated; they are simply transliterated. This is because they have no semantic content; a person named كريم *Karim* does not need to be generous, even though that is the meaning of the generic Arabic word *karim*, just as a person named Smith does not need to be an actual blacksmith. Proper nouns are discussed in the semantic literature as "rigid designators," which are words whose function is restricted to referring to particular individuals. There are, however, some minor issues related to Arabic proper nouns. First, they are not orthographically distinguished from other words because there are no capital letters in Arabic. Some contemporary writers use quotation marks or parentheses to single them out but there are usually enough contextual clues that tell us whether a word is being used as a proper noun or a content word, such as كريم, which could be a name or an adjective. Second, some places and individuals have different names in Arabic and English, such as القاهرة *Cairo*, المغرب *Morocco*, and أفلاطون *Plato*. There are not that many of these kinds of words, and we can find most of them in dictionaries. With non-Arabic names, there is of course the issue of spelling variations, such as طام, طوم, and توم for *Tom*, and مارجاريت, مرجريت, مارقريت, and مارغريت for *Margaret*.

The real difficulty with proper nouns is that sometimes they have communicative functions other than referring to individuals. For example, if I say *John thinks he is Superman*, I am not accusing John of being delusional;

I am simply describing his belief that he has Superman-like properties, such as extraordinary strength. Names like *Romeo, Sherlock, Einstein, Joe Schmoe,* and *Jane Doe* break the barrier between proper nouns and content words because they are associated with certain social meanings and connotations that should be maintained in translation. When dealing with Arabic names of this kind, there are certain complications that we need to bear in mind. First, many such names are completely foreign to the target language's culture; therefore, transliterating them does not constitute successful communication. For example, most native speakers of English are not familiar with the two medieval Arab grammarians mentioned in (11) or with the connotations associated with their names.

(11) عبد الوهاب مطاوع، ٢٠٠١، "اندهش يا صديقي"، دار الشروق، القاهرة، ص ٢٣.

وفي رومانيا جاؤوا لنا بمرافق شاب تعلم العربية في جامعة موسكو ويتحدثها بلغة **الزمخشري وسيبويه.**

In Romania, they got us a young interpreter who learned Arabic at Moscow University. He spoke an archaic form of Classical Arabic that can be found only in medieval grammar books.

Second, we need to identify the communicative functions that motivate using such names, especially those whose connotations can vary from one context to another. For instance, the name of عنترة بن شداد, the pre-Islamic warrior poet, is associated with bravery and defiance, as in (12), but in (13) the same name has the connotations of quixotic futility. Names with connotations pose a significant challenge, and thus we need to be creative in finding ways to express their connotations in the target language.

(12) جريدة الرأي (الكويت)، ٤ نوفمبر ٢٠١٣، العدد ١٢٥٤٤.

وأضاف العدساني «نحن نقتدي بسيدنا أيوب عليه السلام، لكن لدي شجاعة **عنترة** وأستطيع الرد».

"We are trying to be as patient as Job, but I also have the courage of a lion, and I can answer back," added Al-Adsani.

(13) علي الوردي، ١٩٩٦، "خوارق اللاشعور"، دار الوراق للنشر، لندن، ص ٢٤٠.

فمثلما يتغير المجتمع وتتحول النظم الاجتماعية تتغير الأفكار وتتحول القيم. ومن يقف أمام التيار تجرفه أمواجه كمن يريد محاربة الصاروخ بسيف **عنترة بن شداد!**

Just as societies and their structures change, ideologies and values also change. Anyone who stands in the way of change gets swept away. It is like fighting windmills.

[handwritten: tilting]

The examples above demonstrate that understanding the meaning of a word is not limited to recognizing its referent, whether it is an individual, a thing, a property, or an action. To truly understand a word, we also need to recognize its social meanings and connotations. Therefore, the notion of crosslinguistic equivalence is not just about the referential potential of words or the information found in dictionary entries. For two words from two different languages to be true functional equivalents, they must share all their aspects of meaning. If they are not true functional equivalents, we need to find alternative ways to maintain their referential meanings as well as their social meanings and connotations in our translation.

1.3   Borrowings

[handwritten: When borrowing often the meaning shifts]

Borrowing is a natural sociolinguistic phenomenon that comes about as a result of language contact. When speech communities interact, they adopt words from each other's languages, either to fill lexical gaps in their native language or to gain the prestige associated with these foreign words. Lexical borrowings undergo phonological and morphological alternations to fit into the linguistic systems that acquire them. Modern Standard Arabic is no exception; it has adopted many words from different languages, especially English and French. For example, استراتيجية *strategy*, ديموقراطية *democracy*, and تكنولوجيا *technology* are all borrowings that have been Arabized. In most cases, borrowings from English pose no difficulties to us because they can simply be back-translated.

Borrowings become problematic when they are actually false friends—that is, when they are borrowings that sound like English words but have different meanings. The words رجيم and أوكازيون are perfect examples. They sound like *regime* and *occasion* but, respectively, they actually mean *diet* and *sale/discount*. The differences in meanings between these words and their English counterparts are attributed to their origins, given that they were borrowed into Arabic from French. More serious problems are encountered when a borrowing changes its meaning in one language but not in the other. For example, the Arabized borrowing كازينو has lost the sense of *casino* (i.e., a gambling establishment), and now it only means *outdoor café*. Examples like these indicate that we should not take borrowings for granted.

[handwritten: Casino ملهى للقمار]

We often see borrowings from colloquial dialects in contemporary Standard Arabic writing, even when Standard Arabic alternatives are available. Writers purposefully choose to use colloquialisms to better achieve their communicative goals. In (14), for instance, the writer is expressing his disapproval of religious media with fundamentalist agendas that try to appeal to young audiences by using a contrived, youthful style. The noun الروشنة *acting cool* is a colloquialism, if not a slang word, that is used by young people to describe this attitude. By using the contrast between الروشنة *acting cool* and the adjective الدينية *religious*, the writer emphasizes what he views as a contradiction underlying this approach to preaching.

(14) جريدة الأهرام (مصر)، ٧ أغسطس ٢٠٠٧، العدد ٤٤٠٧٣.
ورويدا رويدا تكشف تلك **الروشنة** الدينية المصطنعة عما وراءها، فإذا به *الروشنة*
نفس الوجه القبيح للتطرف.   *Coolness*

Gradually, this religious "cool attitude" mask falls to reveal the same old ugly face of extremism.

This example demonstrates that, in addition to referential meanings, borrowings are associated with attitudes toward the donor language or dialect. Looking up a colloquialism in a dialectal Arabic dictionary is not the problem. The real challenge is to figure out the author's intentions behind choosing a particular colloquialism or borrowing and to make sure that these intentions are reflected in the translation.

1.4   Word Frequency

Sometimes we encounter Arabic words with perfect referential English equivalents, but these words are common in one language, whereas their counterparts are low-frequency words that are rarely used, if not archaic. For example, the noun شبر in (15) is equivalent to *span*, which is an obsolete measurement unit: the distance between the end of the thumb and tip of the little finger of an open hand (approximately 9 inches). The problem is that if we translated أشبار as *spans*, most readers would not recognize this archaic use. Therefore, the literal translation candidate *although he was not even five spans tall, it was not easy to interview him* is not a valid option. Fortunately, the phrase describing the height of the interviewee is used metaphorically in this particular sentence, and we can avoid dealing with the archaic word by ignoring the metaphor altogether.

(knee high to a grasshopper)

(15) جريدة المصري اليوم (مصر)، ٢٠ نوفمبر ٢٠٠٨، العدد ١٦٢١.
رغم أن طوله لا يتعدى الـ ٥ أشبار، فإن الحوار معه لم يكن سهلاً.
Although he is only a child, he was not easy to interview.

We cannot posit a rule that says: Do not use low-frequency words, because writers sometimes use such words on purpose. The word حكماء *sages/
wise men* in (16) is a Classical Arabic word that is not used often in contemporary Standard Arabic discourse, which is exactly why it was chosen in
this context. The author sarcastically uses it to imply that those individuals
are not really that wise and that their ideas are outdated. In this case, we
can translate حكماء as "*sages*" or "*wise men*," because the English counterparts have the same connotations. The quotation marks are clues that can
help readers recognize the sarcasm.

(16) أمين هويدي، ١٩٩٧، "التحولات السياسية الخطيرة: البيروسترويكا
وحرب الخليج الأولى"، دار الشروق، ص ١٢.
كان الرجل يصر على تسميته بالخليج "الفارسي" وبعض العرب كانوا
يصرون على تسميته بالخليج "العربي" مما كان يثير غضبه، وتفاديا للمأزق
فكر بعض **حكمائنا** بأن يكتفوا بتسميته "بالخليج".
The man insisted on calling it "the Persian Gulf," whereas some
Arabs insisted on calling it "the Arabian Gulf," which provoked
his anger. To avoid the problem, some of our "wise men" decided
to call it just "the Gulf."

Words such as شبر *span* and حكيم *sage* suggest that the issue of crosslinguistic equivalence goes beyond referential meanings and connotations.
If a common Arabic word has a perfect English referential counterpart that
is archaic, we cannot consider them true functional equivalents. Words
from different languages are considered functionally equivalent only if they
mean the same thing and they are used the same way. It is important to
note here that frequency needs to be assessed relative to a genre. For example, a search in the "Corpus of Contemporary American English" yields
more than five hundred instances of the "wise person(s)" sense of *sage*
and *sages* in science fiction stories, but only six in newspaper articles on
national news. This pattern suggests that if we are translating a science fiction story, *sage* would be viable translation for حكيم, but not in newspaper
articles. Of course, these results need to be looked at closely to avoid counting the frequencies of other senses of the word *sage*. We will return to the

issue of word frequencies in section 2.2, in which I discuss translation by substitution.

1.5 Ambiguity

When we look up words in a dictionary, we rarely find a word that has only one meaning or sense; some entries are even a page or more long. An ambiguous word can have multiple related senses—such as *good*, which could mean *favorable*, as in *good news*; or *substantial*, as in *a good amount of.* In other cases, the senses associated with one word are not immediately related, such as *bat*, which can be used to describe a baseball bat or the nocturnal animal. Examples like these can be easily found in Arabic or any other language, and disambiguating them is a basic reading comprehension strategy that provides essential input for the translation process. The issue of ambiguity in Arabic is further complicated by homographs, which are words that are spelled the same way but have different meanings, especially in authentic texts in which vowel diacritics are kept to a minimum, if used at all.

Lexical ambiguity can be problematic when the immediate context does not help us identify the intended meaning. For example, the word خط could mean *line*, *path*, *track*, or *font*, among other senses, but the context of (17) can help us discard most of these senses in favor of *freeway lane*. We can assume that this is the intended meaning because a painted demarcation line on the freeway cannot be designated for cars with two or more passengers; it is the space between two lanes that can be designated as such.

(17) غازي عبد الرحمن القصيبي، ١٩٩٧، ''العودة سائحا إلى كاليفورنيا''، دار
الساقي، ص ١٧.
خصص خط خاص من «الفري وي» للسيارات التي تحمل أكثر من راكب واحد.
A freeway lane has been designated for cars with two or more
passengers.

There is another instance of ambiguity in this sentence, namely, راكب, which could mean *a passenger* or *anyone who is in a vehicle (including the driver)*. On the restrictive reading of *passenger*, a car cannot use the carpool lane if there are only two people inside it—the driver and one rider—there must be a minimum of three people in the car to comply with the law. On the nonrestrictive reading, only one person in addition to the driver is enough to use the carpool lane legally. Fortunately, this ambiguity does not apply in English, and we can safely translate راكب as *passenger*. Note that our background knowledge of carpooling and its regulations is essential to our understanding of this sentence and, consequently, for our ability to translate it accurately. The consequences of misinterpreting ambiguities can be as serious as mistranslating laws.

We can also find semantic ambiguities at the morphological level, because some morphemes have dual functions. To illustrate this point, let us look at the semantic functions of the Arabic definite article ال. This prefix attaches to nouns to encode definiteness—that is, the writer expects readers to know the specific referent of that noun, either because it is part of the assumed shared background knowledge or because it was recently mentioned in the discourse. However, ال also has another function, namely, to mark generic nouns, which are nouns that do not refer to any particular individuals or entities, but to types. For example, the definite noun الشاب *lit. the young man* in (18) does not refer to a specific young man but to the generic type of young people, regardless of gender. English generic nouns are often bare plurals without the definite article. Thus, Arabic definite singular generic nouns need to be translated as bare plural nouns or collective nouns, such as *young people* or *youth* in (18). Before translating this sentence, we need to first decide whether its ambiguous definite noun phrase is generic or specific.

(18) عزت حجازي، ١٩٨٥، ''الشباب العربي ومشكلاته''، سلسلة عالم المعرفة، الكويت، ص ٦٩.

في مثل هذه الظروف، يحس **الشاب** بأنه وحده لا يجد عونا من المجتمع.
In such circumstances, young people feel all alone, with no help from the community.

English generics are sometimes bare singular nouns, but their Arabic equivalents are still definite, such as الدين *lit. the religion* in (19). If the Arabic definite article is automatically translated as *the*, our translation would be about a specific religion. But this is not what the Arabic source sentence is about; it is about the abstract concept of religion as a social construct. Of course, we need to decide whether to translate the Arabic generic noun as a plural or a singular bare noun, and this decision is completely dependent on the context of the sentence under consideration. Note that we can also translate الدين *religion* as *church*, but this candidate can skew the cultural content of the translation.

(19) موقع قناة العربية الإخبارية، ١٧ أبريل ٢٠٠٥.

وبطبيعة الحال لا يمكن فصل **الدين** عن الدولة في أي حال من الأحوال.

Naturally, religion cannot be separated from the state under any circumstances.

Lexicographers try to include as many senses as possible for each word in their dictionaries, but we often encounter words used to mean things other than what we find in dictionary entries. Translators need to rely on their knowledge of both the source and target languages' cultures and on all the available contextual clues to determine the intended meanings of ambiguous words.

1.6   Semantic Complexity

Languages with rich morphology allow the outputs of derivational processes to function as inputs to other such derivations, resulting in morphologically complex words. For example, the root ن ض ب generates the verb نضب *to run out*, as in *Oil might run out soon*. This verb feeds into another derivation process that produces the Form IV causative verb أنضب *to make something run out*, and consequently the Form X استنضب *to do something that causes something to run out*. Finally, the output of this derivation chain feeds into yet another process, to derive the noun استنضاب *doing something to cause something to run out* in (20). There are various translation candidates to consider here, including *using up*, *consuming*, *depleting*, and *exhausting*, among others. The issue is which of these possible translation candidates expresses the meaning of indirect causation that is encoded in the Arabic source word's complex semantic structure.

(20) نادر فرجاني، ١٩٨٣، ''الهجرة إلى النفط''، مركز دراسات الوحدة العربية، بيروت، ص ١٩.

لقد أصبح **استنضاب** النفط في بعض أجزاء الوطن العربي وسيلة للثراء غير المترتب على نشاط منتج.

Oil depletion in some parts of the Arab world has become a means of accumulating wealth without engaging in productive activities.

In addition to morphological complexities and lexical gaps, semantic complexity involves fine semantic distinctions between words that express subtle

Constituent   *reciprocal*

shades of meaning. This issue has to do with the structure of the lexicons of the target and source languages, given that one language might make a fine distinction between two similar meanings but the other might not. We find many such cases in the Arabic verb system. For instance, the verbs راسل and تراسل both mean *to send letters*, but they differ in how they describe this type of situation. The Form III verb راسل provides a unidirectional description—that is, one person is sending a letter to someone else—but the Form VI reciprocal verb تراسل describes a situation in which two or more people write letters to one another. This difference can be easily reflected in the translation by adding modifying phrases, as in *send letters to each other*, or by using a different word that entails the difference, such as *correspond*.

The problem is that such easy answers are not always available. The difference between the verbs قاسم and تقاسم, both of which mean *to divide something and share it*, is also one of directionality. The Form VI verb تقاسم describes a reciprocal event during which two or more people share the same thing—that is, all participants contribute—whereas the other, more basic verb form indicates that the sharing was the result of the actions of one individual. The outcome of both types of event descriptions is the same: The concerned individuals share the same thing, but the crucial difference is whether this sharing was done willingly. Using قاسم in (21) indicates that the Lebanese politician Walid Jumblatt did not want to share the representation of the Druze constituency with Prince Talal Arslan; it is the latter who imposed this sharing. In (22), conversely, the verb يتقاسمون emphasizes that Iraqi Sunnis and Shiites willingly shared food and drink with each other.

(21) جريدة الحياة (السعودية)، ١٦ يناير ١٩٩٦، العدد ٣١٧٤٠.
أما جنبلاط فسلم بأن **يقاسمه** الأمير طلال أرسلان التمثيل الدرزي منذ البداية.
As for Jumblatt, he conceded from the beginning that Prince
Talal Arslan would share the representation of the Druze
constituency with him.

(22) جريدة عكاظ (السعودية)، ٢٤ ديسمبر ٢٠٠٦، العدد ٢٠١٦.
استطاع موسم الحج أن يوحد صفوف العراقيين الذين وصلوا إلى مكة المكرمة.
الشيعة والسنة تجدهم في سكن واحد **يتقاسمون** الأكل والشرب.
The hajj season has unified the Iraqis who arrived in Mecca,
where you find Sunnis and Shiites in the same lodgings sharing
food and drink.

The problem with semantically complex words is not just whether they constitute lexical gaps. These subtle differences in meaning provide valuable information about the situations described in the source sentences, and it is the translator's duty to make sure they survive the translation process.

All the translation problems we have discussed thus far stem from the issue of crosslinguistic equivalence, especially when we define meaning in a way that includes social attitudes and connotations in addition to the referential potential of words. Basically, there is no one-to-one correspondence between all form–meaning pairs across languages; crosslinguistic equivalence issues form a continuum. At one end of this continuum, we have lexical gaps, whereby one language has a word that describes a culture-specific concept but there is no word to describe this concept in the target language. At the other end, we have perfect equivalents that share all the aspects of their meaning, referential and otherwise. In between, we have word pairs that share only some aspects of their meanings. When translating a text, we need to identify all the aspects of meaning associated with the source language's words while analyzing the writer's motivations for using them. After all, words are used to guide readers' thinking, and as translators, our task is to use the target language to guide readers in the same direction.

2 Translation Strategies

2.1 Translation by Deletion

When we compare professionally translated texts with their original Arabic sources, we often find Arabic words and morphemes that have simply been left out of the translation. Leaving out words or morphemes initially seems to go against the very purpose of translation, because it necessarily entails the loss of certain components of meaning. However, when we take a closer look at these omitted elements, we realize that leaving them out is more helpful to readers than incorporating them in the translation. In fact, in certain contexts, leaving out certain words or morphemes is unavoidable.

To understand why omission is sometimes necessary, let us take a look at the feminine suffix when it is attached to adjectives (e.g., كبيرة *big-feminine*), and at nouns with the feminine suffix that refer to inanimate objects (e.g., طاولة *table-feminine*). In such cases, the feminine suffix gives information about the word rather than its referent—that is, the word has a "feminine" gender, but its gender does not apply to its referent (i.e., the property of being big and a table, in these examples). Grammatical gender is not a semantic feature but a structural one that helps establish grammatical relations between words, such as subjects and verbs or nouns and their modifying adjectives. Therefore, it should be ignored when translating. In fact, any morpheme that encodes a linguistic feature of a word rather than its referent should be left out.

[margin note: natural gender]

When it comes to natural gender, however, there is no rule that tells us whether we should delete or maintain the feminine marking. We need to analyze the context to decide whether specifying the referent's gender is relevant. In (23), for instance, the feminine gender marking needs to be incorporated in our translation because Madeleine Albright is not the first person to ever hold the position of secretary of state; she is only the first woman to do so. Because we cannot add feminine marking suffixes, such as -ette and -ess, to the noun phrase *secretary of state*, our best option is to add the adjective *female* and to translate the phrase أول وزيرة للخارجية as *the first female secretary of state*.

(23) جريدة أوان (الكويت)، ٣٠ أكتوبر ٢٠٠٨، العدد ٣٤٥.
مادلين أولبرايت أصبحت العام ١٩٩٧ أول **وزيرة** للخارجية.

In 1997, Madeleine Albright became the first female secretary of state.

In (24), conversely, gender marking needs to be left out, even though it encodes natural gender. This is because if we incorporate it, the translation would suggest that at least one man who held the position of secretary of state visited Libya during the past fifty years, which is not what the source sentence means. In other words, we need to choose between describing the referent of أول وزيرة للخارجية as the first secretary of state, or as the first among the women who have held this position.

(24) جريدة الشرق الأوسط (السعودية)، ٢٣ أغسطس ٢٠٠٧، العدد ١٠٤٩٥.
تعتزم كوندوليزا رايس **وزيرة** الخارجية الأميركية زيارة العاصمة الليبية
طرابلس في أكتوبر (تشرين الأول) المقبل لتكون بذلك أول **وزيرة** خارجية لدى
واشنطن تزور ليبيا منذ أزيد من نصف قرن.

Secretary of State Condoleezza Rice plans to visit the Libyan capital, Tripoli, in October, thus becoming the first American secretary of state to visit Libya in more than half a century.

Translation by omission can also be applied to content words, but only if using their equivalents would sound redundant in English. The main targets of elimination are words whose meanings are lexically entailed—that is, their meanings are already encoded somewhere else in the text. In (25), for instance, we have the adjective أعزب *single*, which is modified by the reduced relative clause لم يتزوج *did not get married*, both of which mean the same thing. Translating this phrase as *a single man who did not get married* is superfluous; therefore, we need to delete either the adjective or the modifying clause. This kind of apparent redundancy is not uncommon in Arabic, because it is used as a rhetorical technique that signals emphasis. To make sure we do not lose the source phrase's emphasis function, we can make up for the deletion by using the negation adverbial *never* instead of *did not*.

(25) جريدة الجزيرة (السعودية)، ١٩ نوفمبر ٢٠٠٧، العدد ٢٢٣.
وهو **أعزب** لم يتزوج وكانت والدته رحمها الله هي التي ترعى شؤونه.
He never got married, and it was his late mother who used to
take care of him.

Repetition is another phenomenon of Arabic discourse that calls for omission when translating. The use of multiple clauses and/or modifying phrases sometimes results in long sentences or complex constructions that can disrupt the discourse's flow. As a way of compensation, Arabic allows one to repeat a word or a phrase to maintain textual cohesion; hence, the second instance of the verb بدأ *started* in (26), which reconnects the text after the appositive clause marked with the hyphens. English, conversely, does not allow this type of repetition; consequently, the verb must be used only once in the translation. Note that eliminating the second instance of بدأ *started* is only one step in translating this sentence. We still need to make a few other changes to the translation's structure to accommodate the deletion.

(26) زكي نجيب محمود، ١٩٨٧، "هذا العصر وثقافته"، دار الشروق،
القاهرة، ص ١٩٤.
بدأ هيكل – بمناسبة صدور كتاب عن «قصص البردي» (١٩٢٦)– **بدأ** في
ربط الصلة بين مصر الحديثة ومصر القديمة.
Following the publication of a book about the Papyrus Tales
in 1926, Haykal started making connections between modern
Egypt and ancient Egypt.

Using synonyms—that is, words that mean the same thing—is another emphasis technique that is commonly used in contemporary Arabic writing. For example, the adjectives البعيدة *far* and النائية *remote* in (27) mean the same thing, more or less; therefore, it is safe to ignore one of them when translating, because a literal translation, such as *the distant and remote village*, would be considered redundant in English. The phrase هذه القرية البعيدة النائية can be translated as *this remote village*, because the adjective *remote* is higher on the scale of distance than the generic *far*. However, if we want to maintain the translation's emphasis, we can compensate for the deletion by using an emphasis technique that is acceptable in English. In this particular sentence, we can add *such* and translate هذه القرية البعيدة النائية as *such a remote village*. The demonstrative هذه *this* also needs to be left out because English does not allow noun phrases with multiple determiners, such as *this such a remote village*.

(27) جريدة الأهرام (مصر)، ٢٤ يوليو ١٩٩٩، العدد ٤١١٣٧.
لماذا اختار الله لمبعث الإسلام هذه القرية **البعيدة النائية** في شبه الجزيرة العربية؟
Why did God choose such a remote village in Arabia to be the birthplace of Islam?

For a word to be redundant, it does not need to be repeated or lexically entailed; sometimes, the meaning of a word is made readily available through contextual clues. For instance, in (28) the noun صحيفة *newspaper* and the adjective الأمريكية *American* describe the *New York Times*, which is obviously an American newspaper. However, this assumption is valid only if readers are themselves American or are at least quite familiar with American media outlets. Therefore, these words صحيفة *newspaper* and الأمريكية *American* are included in the source text to define the *New York Times* for Arab readers, some of whom might not be familiar with the newspaper. But because here we are interested in an English-speaking audience, we can justifiably assume that they know of the *New York Times* and leave out both the noun صحيفة *newspaper* and the adjective الأمريكية *American*. Thus, the phrase صحيفة نيويورك تايمز الأمريكية is better translated as *the New York Times* instead of the redundant *the American newspaper the New York Times*.

(28) جريدة الرياض (السعودية)، ١٧ مارس ٢٠٠٥، العدد ١٣٤١٥.
ذكرت **صحيفة** نيويورك تايمز **الأمريكية** نقلا عن مسؤولين عسكريين أن ٢٦ سجينا توفوا أثناء احتجازهم من جانب القوات الأمريكية في العراق وأفغانستان منذ عام ٢٠٠٤.

The *New York Times* quoted military officials as saying that twenty-six detainees have died in American custody in Iraq and Afghanistan since 2004.

One must be very careful when deciding whether a word is truly redundant or not, because seemingly superfluous words can sometimes be used for specific discourse functions, such as signaling emphasis or triggering certain emotions or attitudes. The challenge is to identify the discourse functions of these seemingly redundant words and to make sure they are maintained in the translation.

2.2 Translation by Substitution

The translation strategy of substitution is particularly helpful when one deals with cases of less-than-perfect equivalence. When an Arabic word and its English counterpart have the same referent, but they either have different connotations or are used differently, one can simply look for another English word that can be used in similar contexts, even if it does not have the same referent. The most obvious cases in which we need substitution involve words with specialized functions, such as time expressions, units of measurement, and other words of this nature. These can be translated according to the conventions of the target language's culture rather than those of the source language. The sentence in (29) is a straightforward example. The Arabic way of telling time involves using the third as a fraction of the hour as well as adverbs such as ليلا *at night* and فجرا *at dawn*, none of which are standard use in English. These words have perfect English referential equivalents, but we cannot use them in the translation. The solution is quite simple: We use the English way of expressing time, and thus translate من التاسعة والثلث ليلا إلى الثانية عشرة والنصف فجرا as *from 9:20 p.m. to 12:30 a.m.*, or other acceptable conventions of telling time, instead of the literal translation *from the ninth hour and a third at night to the twelfth hour and a half at dawn*.

(29) جريدة الحياة (السعودية)، ٢١ مارس ١٩٩٧، العدد ١١٨٧٤.
استمرت الحفلة من التاسعة **والثلث** ليلا إلى الثانية عشرة والنصف **فجرا**.
The party went on from 9:20 p.m. until 12:30 a.m.

Translation by substitution is especially helpful when dealing with words that have specific functions but no suitable equivalents in the target

[handwritten margin notes: Lexical gaps = no equivalent in English therefor, we use Substitute]

language. Consider the nouns فدان, قيراط, and سهم in (30). The noun فدان refers to a unit of area (1.038 acres), and thus we can use *acre* as a rough equivalent. But the other two units constitute lexical gaps that have no equivalents in English; a قيراط is 1/24 of a فدان, whereas a سهم is 1/24 of a قيراط. In a case like this, we are better off doing the math and converting the Arabic measurement units into common English ones; thus, the phrase describing the land in question is best translated as *2.498 acres*. Of course, if small fractions are important, as in legal texts such as this one, the conversion needs to be precise. Otherwise, we can round up the numbers—here, to *2.5 acres*. Note that قيراط has been adopted into English as *karat*, which is a unit of the purity of gold, and *carat*, which is a unit of mass for gemstones; but neither unit can be considered a functional equivalent, because they are used to measure different properties. Also, فدان has been borrowed into English as *feddan*, but it is rather archaic, and thus it is used only in very restrictive contexts.

(30) جاد الحق علي جاد الحق، ١٩٩٨، "فتاوى دار الإفتاء المصرية"، ج ٣، القاهرة، ص ١٧٥.
والباقي وهو **فدانان** و ٩ **قراريط** و١٨ **سهما** من **قيراط** يقسم بين ابنيه الاثنين وبناته الخمس.

The remaining land, which is 2.498 acres, is to be divided
among his two sons and five daughters.

Translation by substitution is also useful if the English counterpart is archaic, as in the case of شبر in (31). As mentioned above, this is a unit of length equivalent to the obsolete English span, the distance between the tip of the thumb and the tip of the little finger of an open hand (approximately 9 inches). This unit should be converted into inches or feet, but not translated as a *span* because most readers would not recognize this archaic term. The same applies to ذراع *cubit*, which is also an obsolete unit of length, the distance between the elbow and the end of the middle finger (approximately 18 inches). The phrase أربعة أذرع وشبر *lit. 4 cubits and a span* is better translated as *81 inches*, *6.75 feet*, or other acceptable ways of measuring length in English.

(31) جريدة الحياة (السعودية)، ٥ نوفمبر ١٩٩٦، العدد ٧٧٧٦.
ورفع عتبة الباب الشرقي بمقدار أربعة **أذرع وشبر**، وهكذا أرجع الكعبة إلى ما كانت عليه قبل عمارة ابن الزبير.

He raised the threshold of the eastern door by 6.75 feet, thus restoring the structure of the Ka'aba to what it used to be before Ibn Al-Zubayr's renovations.

The choice of an appropriate substitute is always dependent on the function of the source word relative to the context of the sentence we are trying to translate. For example, in the example above, we converted شبر *span* into inches because the source word is used to describe actual measurements. In (32), however, شبر *span* is used metaphorically; therefore, we cannot just convert it and translate الانسحاب من شبر as *withdrawal from 9 inches*. This is because *9 inches* does not have the same metaphorical reading as the Arabic source phrase. In this particular case, we can substitute *span* with *inch*, which is the minimum English unit of area used metaphorically in the same way as the Arabic شبر *span*. Moreover, we can maintain the emphasis associated with the Arabic metaphor by adding a modifier phrase of emphasis, as in *a single inch*. Although the substitutions in both sentences are motivated by the archaic nature of the English counterpart, we translate the same word differently in each case because it has different functions in the two sentences.

(32) جريدة الحياة (السعودية)، ٤ ديسمبر ١٩٩٦، العدد ١٤٠٤٧.
عجزت قرارات الأمم المتحدة عن إجبار إسرائيل على الانسحاب **شبرا** واحدا من تلك الأراضي.

The UN resolutions failed to force Israel to withdraw from a single inch of those territories.

The availability of referential equivalents across languages does not guarantee the viability of a literal translation because, quite often, words with the same denotations cannot be used to describe the same situations. Because translation is about describing the same situations in a different language rather than matching up words, one must find words in the target language that are best suited for the context. For example, the passive verb خصص in (33) is derived from a causative verb that means *causing something to become special*; therefore, it can be translated as *was specialized*. However, it would be rather odd to say *a highway lane was specialized for vehicles with more than one person*. What we need for this particular sentence is an English predicate that is commonly used to describe selecting an already-existing highway lane and changing or delimiting its function. Note that we are now thinking about English, not Arabic. Candidates for this description include *was set aside*, *was dedicated*, *was assigned*, and *was designated*, with the last one being the most suitable substitute.

(33) غازي عبد الرحمن القصيبي، ١٩٩٧، "العودة سائحا إلى كاليفورنيا"،
دار الساقي، ص١٧.
خصص خط خاص من الفري وي للسيارات التي تحمل أكثر من راكب واحد. هذا الخط يساعد هذه السيارات على التحرك بسرعة أكثر. **والحكمة** هي تقليل عدد السيارات بتشجيع أصحابها على المشاركة.

= designated

A freeway lane has been designated for cars with two or more passengers to help traffic move faster. The idea is to reduce the number of cars on the road by encouraging people to carpool.

Figuring out what writers try to do with words is an ongoing task for translators, because the output of the translation process needs to achieve the communicative goals intended in the source text. The noun الحكمة *wisdom* in (33) indicates that the author is trying to provide an explanation for having carpool lanes. It has a perfect referential equivalent in English, but it is rather awkward in this particular context to describe the reasons for carpooling as wisdom. Instead, one might substitute *wisdom* with a more suitable word or phrase that is commonly used in justification contexts, such as *the objective*, *the goal*, or, even better, *the idea*.

Before leaving this sentence, we should take another look at lexical borrowings. The best way to deal with borrowings from English is to back-translate them, which is quite straightforward if the borrowed word is only transliterated, such as فري وي *freeway*. In other cases, borrowings involve extensions of meaning—that is, an already-existing Arabic word develops a new meaning to describe a foreign concept. This is when one needs to use contextual clues and cultural knowledge to identify the original English word and use it rather than attempting to find a referential equivalent. For instance, in the context of (33), خط and المشاركة should be translated as *lane* and *carpooling* instead of the referential equivalents *line* and *sharing/participating*. In other words, we are substituting referential equivalents with words that better suit the context.

The same strategy can be applied to borrowings from colloquial dialects; we can identify the communicative purpose for using the colloquialism and find an alternative English word or phrase that serves the same function, even if it is not a referential equivalent. In (34), the writer is engaging in a

dialogue with the reader. The author indicates that he has nothing worthy
of writing about in his monthly column, and the imaginary reader makes
the cynical comment that the author never really has anything interesting to
say. In the next exchange, the author accepts the joke to establish a casual
tone. This is the communicative function of the colloquialism قفشة, which
literally means *a catch*. The problem is that literal translations, such as
good catch and *funny catch*, are not used in English to respond positively to
jokes. It is more natural to use *good one*, which achieves the communicative
function of قفشة; hence the substitution.

(34) عبد الوهاب مطاوع، ٢٠٠١، "اندهش يا صديقي"، دار الشروق، القاهرة،
ص ٥.
لا تتوقع مني شيئا مفيدا هذا الشهر. تقول: ومتى كان فيه شيء مفيد؟ **قفشة**
ظريفة!

Do not expect anything useful from me this month. You might
wonder, "Since when do you have anything useful to say?"
Good one!

Translation by substitution provides a perfect solution to the problem
of culture-specific connotations. If the source language's word and its target language's referential counterpart have different connotations or social
meanings, one needs to find a substitute that has the same cultural value,
even if it does not have the same referent. The sentence in (35) presents an
interesting case, but first it is important to provide the cultural background.
This sentence is about a young woman whose family and friends would like
to see her get married. If she is interested, they would identify potential
suitors, tell her about them, and arrange social events at which she could
meet them. This social practice is basically a form of matchmaking that is
viewed positively in Arab societies.

(35) أنيس منصور، ١٩٨٣، "ألوان من الحب"، دار الشروق، القاهرة، ص ٢٠٦.
عرضوا عليها طبيبا في الثلاثين من عمره، فرفضت الطبيب. قالوا لها إنه
وحيد أبويه وعنده عشرون فدانا وله سيارة فخمة، ولكن الفتاة رفضت الطبيب.

They suggested a thirty-year-old doctor as a suitor for her, but
she rejected him. They told her that he is an only child who
owns twenty acres and a luxury car. Still, she rejected him.

The problem in (35) is that the verb used to describe this situation in the
source sentence—namely, عرض—is referentially equivalent to *offer*, *show*,

demonstrate, and *display*, all of which would have negative or derogatory connotations if used with a human direct object—namely, the doctor. If any of these verbs were to be used in our translation, it would connote a misleading description of the situation. Instead, we need to find a substitute that describes this activity without invoking any connotations that are not intentionally implied in the source sentence. Possible translation candidates include *introduced, match her with, hook up, set her up with*, and *get her a blind date with*. There is nothing in the context to indicate that the young woman got to meet the doctor; she simply rejected the idea. This rules out *introduced*. Expressions such as *hook up, set her up*, and *get her a blind date* are not appropriate for this context. The phrase *tried to match her with* is actually an accurate description, but it might suggest that she had little say in the process, especially given that it would be used as a passive verb. Perhaps the best translation candidate is *suggested* in the active voice—which, just like the Arabic source word, is neutral and has no indications that she met him, started a relationship with him, or was pushed into anything; he was only mentioned to her by a friend or a relative.

Experienced translators recognize some culturally motivated substitution patterns. One such pattern has to do with first-person reference, which many Arab writers try to avoid because it can be considered arrogant and inappropriate. This is why we sometimes see writers talking about themselves in the third person, using such expressions as العبد لله *lit. the worshipper of God* in informal discourse, as in (36), and الباحث *the researcher* in academic discourse, as in (37). Note that the switch in reference from the third to the first person requires reconstructing *the source got lost from him* to *I lost the reference*. Other third-person expressions used to avoid first-person references include الكاتب *the writer*, الفقير إلى الله *lit. the pauper to God*, and أخيكم *your brother*. Maintaining the self-referential third person in our translation—say, by using *yours truly*—is not only misleading but also can trigger negative attitudes. Therefore, all instances of third-person references to oneself should be substituted with first-person references.

(36) جريدة الأهرام (مصر)، ١٤ نوفمبر ٢٠٠٠، العدد ٤١٦١٦.
في الوقت الذي يعاني فيه كثيرون من المواطنين مشقة الحصول على شقة تتناسب مع قدراتهم المحدودة فإن **كاتب** هذه السطور يمتلك شقتين في محافظة واحدة! والحكاية أن **العبد** لله حصل على مسكن من المحافظة عن طريق الاستبدال.

While many people are struggling to find an apartment they can afford, I happen to have two in the same province. The story started when I got an apartment from the provincial government through an exchange.

(37) نبيل علي، ٢٠٠١، "الثقافة العربية وعصر المعلومات"، عالم المعرفة ٢٦٥، الكويت، ص ٦٥.

ورد هذا التعبير في إحدى الدراسات التي صادفها **الباحث** إلا أن المصدر قد تاه **منه**.

This term occurred in a study I came across, but I lost the reference.

Substitution is probably the most commonly used word-level translation strategy because it provides ways of resolving a wide range of equivalence problems. Although there are many reasons for substitution, it is always motivated by the desire to make sure that the translation achieves the communicative goals of the source text. This is why substitution is constrained by the text and the context. We need to make sure that the substitute sounds natural when used with other words in the same sentence and that it fits with the discourse type and the tone of the text as a whole. These are issues that I discuss in detail in the subsequent chapters.

2.3 *Translation by Morphological Unpacking*

We saw in the discussion above of lexical gaps that Arabic morphological derivation chains sometimes generate words that have no equivalents in English. Some of these gaps are the result of differences in the productivity of morphological rules across languages. For example, the verb اخضر has no equivalent in English because the adjective *green* does not undergo the morphological processes that derive verbs from adjectives. One way of dealing with lexical gaps of this nature is to unpack the structure of the Arabic word and spell out its semantic content in English. Thus, the verb اخضر can be unpacked as *to turn green*. In other cases, the relevant English morphological processes are productive, but the outcome does not mean the same thing or cannot be used in the same way as the Arabic source word, as in the case of المنتظرين in (38). The Arabic active participle is equivalent to many English agent nouns that end with the suffixes *-er* and *-ant*, such as معلم *teacher* and مساعد *assistant*. The participle منتظر describes someone who is waiting, but the English counterparts *waiter*, *anticipant*, and *expectant* have very different meanings; therefore, they can be ruled out as successful translation candidates. Instead, we can unpack the morphological structure of المنتظرين as *those who are waiting*.

(38) جريدة الشرق الأوسط (السعودية)، ١ نوفمبر ٢٠٠٨، العدد ١٠٩٣١.
وبعض هؤلاء **المنتظرين** لفرصة الشراء لديهم الاستعداد لدفع أي مبلغ.

Some of those waiting for an opportunity to buy are willing to
pay any price.

Unpacking is a useful strategy when it comes to translating morphologically complex words. We can use it to deal with nouns inflected for natural gender (e.g., طبيبة *female doctor*), causative verbs (e.g., أضحك *to make someone laugh*), and many other derived lexical categories. However, it is not the solution to all lexical gaps, because meaning is always dependent on the context. Let us take locative nouns as an example of how and when morphological unpacking can be applied as a translation strategy. Locative nouns constitute a morphological category of derived nouns that denote places, such as مرصد *observatory*, مكتبة *library*, and مختبر *laboratory*. Most Arabic locative nouns have lexicalized or derived English equivalents, but that does not mean we can always use them. For instance, when translating the locative noun مستقر in (39), we need to analyze the context to choose between the derived counterpart *settlement* and the unpacked equivalent *settling place*. Because the sentence under consideration is about refugees and immigrants rather than settlers, we opt for *settling place*, which fits better in this context.

(39) جريدة العرب (المملكة المتحدة)، ٣ يوليو ٢٠٠٧، العدد ٧٧٢٩.
وفي عام ٢٠٠٦ وحده وصل أوروبا تسعة آلاف عراقي وتوجهوا نحو السويد
كمستقر نهائي.

In 2006 alone, 9,000 Iraqis arrived in Europe and headed for
Sweden as a final settling place.

The sentence in (40), conversely, concerns a ship; therefore, we cannot use *settling place* or *settlement* to describe the location where its voyage ends. Instead of a literal translation or morphological unpacking, we need substitution to translate مستقر as *destination*.

(40) جريدة القدس (فلسطين)، ١١ نوفمبر ٢٠٠٨، العدد ١٤٠٩٥.
تبحر السفينة الشهيرة كوين إليزابيث ٢ اليوم من ميناء ساوثهامبتون في
طريقها إلى **مستقرها** الأخير في دبي.

The famous cruise ship *Queen Elizabeth II* sails today from the
Port of Southampton on its way to its final destination, Dubai.

We should not think of morphological unpacking as the only solution to
any particular kind of translation problems. Just like any other translation
strategy, it is only a way of generating translation candidates for us to examine before deciding on the optimal translation output.

2.4 *Translation by Paraphrasing*

Translation by paraphrasing is an umbrella category of various translation
substrategies that involve providing additional information to help readers
recognize the referents of the source words in the absence of direct equivalents. This approach is similar to word games in which we try to get someone to recognize a concept or a thing without us saying the word that refers
to it. Basically, we use examples, definitions, descriptions, and the like to
facilitate comprehension. For example, الخماسين in (41) refers to the sandstorms that blow over Cairo during a fifty-day season in the spring. Because
other translation strategies—such as morphological unpacking, substitution, and deletion—would not yield acceptable solutions, we can translate
الخماسين by providing a definition, as in *the spring sandstorms*.

(41) جريدة الجمهورية (مصر)، ٥ مايو ٢٠٠٧.
أجل عودته لمصر حاليا بسبب سوء الأحوال الجوية التي تشهدها حاليا وموجة
الخماسين التي من الممكن أن تؤثر على حالته الصحية.
He postponed his return to Egypt for the time being because of
the bad weather there and the wave of spring sandstorms that
might affect his health.

Paraphrasing is not a translation strategy of last resort that we should
employ only when everything else fails. There are many cases in which referential equivalents are available, but the information they provide is not sufficient for our readers to understand the context of the sentence. In (42), we
have the noun الرؤية *sighting*, but *sighting* by itself is not a successful translation candidate because readers are not likely to recognize what was sighted
and how it relates to this context. In this sentence, الرؤية describes seeing
the new moon that marks the beginnings of the lunar months of the Islamic
calendar. The intended readers of the Arabic source text will be quite familiar
with this concept. This is why the author can use الرؤية without specifying

its object—that is, it is assumed shared knowledge. Most English-speaking readers, however, are not likely to have this kind of background information; therefore, our translation needs to elaborate on the term to explain the context.

(42) جريدة الشرق الأوسط (السعودية)، ٥ ديسمبر ٢٠٠٢، العدد ٨٧٧٣.
أعلن المركز الثقافي الإسلامي في لندن اعتبار اليوم هو الأول من شهر شوال بعد ثبوت الرؤية.

Following confirmation of the sighting of the new moon, the
Islamic Cultural Center in London announced that today marks
the beginning of the lunar month of Shawwal.

Ambiguity is another translation problem that can be dealt with using paraphrasing. The word النيروز describes the Persian New Year and spring festival, but it also refers to the Coptic Christian New Year celebration in Egypt; hence the ambiguity. Although the Persian and the Coptic New Year celebrations are both called النيروز, they have very little in common; they have different histories, they mark the beginnings of two different calendars, and they occur at different times of the year. The Arabic-speaking reader of (43) is not likely to be confused as to which new year is being celebrated; it is the Coptic New Year. There are enough clues in the text that help resolve the ambiguity. If we transliterate النيروز as *Noruz* or just translate it as *the New Year*, we are confusing our readers because they might not know what Noruz is or which new year is being celebrated. However, if we paraphrase it as *the Coptic New Year*, there is no room for confusion.

(43) جريدة الأهرام (مصر)، ٢٨ أغسطس ٢٠٠١، العدد ٤١٩٠٣.
قررت القيادة السياسية أن يكون الاحتفال الرئيسي بجمعية التوفيق وأن يكون خطيب الحفل هو الزعيم سعد زغلول، كما كان أيضا خطيب حفل **النيروز** عام ١٩٢٣م.

The political leadership decided that the main celebration would
be held at the Al-Tawfiq Association, and that the keynote
speaker would be Saad Zaghloul, who was also the speaker at
the Coptic New Year celebration in 1923.

Paraphrasing can be used with Arabic names that are associated with special connotations, such as the names of the medieval Arab grammarians الزمخشري and سيبويه in (11), repeated below as (44). Transliteration, which is the conventional way of dealing with proper nouns, is of no use

here. That is because most English-speaking readers have probably never
heard of these individuals and are not familiar with the connotations associated with their names. In other words, even if we transliterate the names
and add a brief explanation—for example, *the medieval Arab grammarians Sibawayh and al-Zamakhshari*—we end up losing their connotations.
Instead of using these names, one can use paraphrasing to spell out the
intended connotations; thus, the phrase لغة الزمخشري وسيبويه *lit. the language of Sibawayh and al-Zamakhshari* can be translated as *an archaic
form of Arabic*. This translation maintains the author's negative attitude
toward the variety of Arabic used by the interpreter, which is not normally
used in conversation. The added clause at the end ensures that readers will
recognize the author's cynical attitude, which would be lost if we just used
Classical Arabic.

(44) عبد الوهاب مطاوع، ٢٠٠١، "اندهش يا صديقي"، دار الشروق، القاهرة،
ص ٢٣.
وفي رومانيا جاؤوا لنا بمرافق شاب تعلم العربية في جامعة موسكو ويتحدثها
بلغة الزمخشري وسيبويه.

In Romania, they got us a young interpreter who had learned
Arabic at Moscow University. He spoke an archaic form of
Classical Arabic that can be found only in medieval grammar
books.

Paraphrasing as a translation strategy is by no means restricted to lexical gaps or culture-specific concepts. We can actually use it with almost
any word, as long as the additional information we provide is helpful. We
can add a modifying phrase, a clause, or even a sentence to make some
connotations or social meanings explicit, or to explain the significance of
word choice. We only need to make sure that we do not add too much extra
information that is not available in the source text, because such additional
material could disrupt the rhetorical structure of the translation or change
the original message.

2.5 Translation by Transliteration

Transliteration basically entails writing the source Arabic word in English
letters, just as we do with most foreign names. This strategy amounts to lexical borrowing, and many Arabic words have entered the English language

this way—for example, *alcohol, algebra, algorithm*, and, more recently, *jihad* and *hijab*. Translators have license to borrow from the source language when dealing with some lexical gaps, especially technical terminology and culture-specific concepts. Transliteration by itself does not lead to successful communication, because readers are not likely to recognize the concepts described by the transliterated words; they are still foreign words. It takes time for a transliterated borrowing such as *jihad* or *hijab* to become widely understood. This is why transliterated words should be accompanied by definitions. This strategy is very similar to paraphrasing. The only difference is that we include the transliteration of the source words, provided we have good reasons for doing so.

For example, الحكشة in (45) refers to an Egyptian traditional team sport with which most English-speaking audiences are not likely to be familiar; therefore, transliteration by itself does not amount to successful communication. This game is similar to hockey, but we cannot substitute الحكشة with *hockey* because this translation candidate is both inaccurate and misleading—it is a different game. Deleting the problematic word would render the sentence completely incomprehensible, whereas morphological unpacking would not yield any candidates; the word is a very old borrowing that goes back to ancient Egypt, and its derivational morphology is not analyzable. If we paraphrase الحكشة as *an Egyptian traditional hockey-like game*, the sentence becomes a bit awkward because we have lost the definite subject noun, as in *In an Egyptian traditional hockey-like game, Hawwaret Adlan Youth Center came in first place*. This leaves us with only one option: Provide the transliteration of الحكشة followed by the definition, which guarantees successful communication.

(45) جريدة الجمهورية (مصر)، ١٤ يناير ٢٠٠٣.
وفي **الحكشة** احتل المركز الأول مركز شباب هوارة عدلان.
In *hoksha*, an Egyptian traditional hockey-like game, Hawwaret Adlan Youth Center came in first place.

Of course, this translation is less than perfect, but at least our readers would know the defining characteristics of the game based on their previous knowledge of hockey: It has two competing teams, it involves kicking a ball with sticks, and players score points by getting the ball into the other team's goal net. This is the same strategy that has introduced many words describing foreign sports into English—such as judo, sumo, and kung-fu—but until *hoksha* becomes widely known in English-speaking parts of the world, we need to include the definition.

Sometimes we need to add definitions to transliterated names to make sure that readers can recognize the significance of their referents. We have already agreed that proper nouns, such as the names of people and places, should not be translated but instead should be transliterated because they do not have semantic content. However, if we think that our readers might not be able to identify the referent—say, because they are not familiar with the named individuals or locations—we can provide helpful background information. For example, السلوم in (46) is the name of a small Egyptian town near the eastern border with Libya. The intended readers of the source text are expected to know enough about the town to recognize it once its name is mentioned, but the readers of the translation might not have heard about it; they might not even know that it is a town. This is why adding some information along with the transliteration can be valuable, especially if the source text presupposes knowledge of the referent and provides no contextual clues that can help.

(46) جريدة الأهرام (مصر)، ٣٠ مارس ٢٠٠٦، العدد ١٦٨٢٩.
قدموا من أنحاء العالم لمشاهدة الكسوف الكلي للشمس في **السلوم**.
They came from all over the world to watch the total solar
eclipse in Al-Sallum, a small Egyptian town on the eastern
border with Libya.

Finally, we sometimes see content words transliterated and defined, even though they have referential equivalents in the target language. Typically, this strategy is used when the source word has developed a sense that is genre-specific. In religious discourse, for example, we often encounter the word الأمة *the community*; but if translated as such, our readers might not understand to which community we are referring. We can paraphrase الأمة as *the world community of Muslims*, thus guaranteeing successful communication and avoiding ambiguity. The only purpose of transliterating الأمة as *ummah* is to familiarize the readers with the word that is used in such contexts as jargon or terminology. Therefore, we can even use it as a proper noun, namely, *the Ummah*. The problem with this strategy is that it might give readers the false impression that the target word refers to a concept that is completely alien to their culture. This is quite often misleading, because it can change the original message by adding the translator's attitudes toward that concept. For example, if we transliterate and define علماء as *ulama or religious scholars*, we are giving the readers the impression that these religious scholars are different from the religious scholars in their culture, say, they have different social roles or status. As translators, we should not try to influence readers' attitudes by stressing the foreignness of certain concepts. Perhaps, it is better to follow George Orwell's rule in his famous 1946 essay "Politics and the English Language": "Never use a foreign phrase, a scientific word, or a jargon word if you can think of an everyday English equivalent."

Exercises

Exercise 1: Identifying Translation Problems

Identify the difficulties that might arise when translating the underlined words. What translation strategies can you use?

(1) جريدة العرب (قطر)، ٧ فبراير ٢٠٠٧، العدد ٧٥٤٥.
وأصر والدي حينها على شرط إكمال تعليمي في عقد الزواج ليكون كل شيء واضحا **وجليا** أمام الطرفين قبل الزواج.

adverb from noun
obviously
Lexical gap
emphasis

(2) عباس محمود العقاد، ١٩٦٣، 'يوميات العقاد'، نهضة مصر للطباعة والنشر والتوزيع، ص ٣٤.
لقد تركت الساعة على مكتبي خطابا أعددته لإرساله إليك **وضمنته** بعض المعلومات عن شرشل بك.

ambiguity
put
I Included / Contain
passive/active

(3) جريدة عكاظ (السعودية)، ١٠ مارس ٢٠٠٨، العدد ٢٤٥٨.
كتبت مرارا مؤكدا أن تشارلس **داروين** صاحب نظرية البقاء للأصلح وكتاب ''أصل الأنواع''، والذي يلخص **العوام** فحواه بأن أصل الإنسان قرد.. **داروين** هذا توصل إلى نتيجة مقلوبة.

general people / Commoners
He Himself

(4) جريدة الشرق الأوسط (السعودية)، ٣٠ أبريل ٢٠٠٤، العدد ٩٢٨٥.
تناول من جهة أخرى الوضع السائد في الأراضي الفلسطينية والقضية العراقية، مؤكدا في هذا الإطار أنه جدد التأكيد على موقف المغرب في ضرورة أن يحتفظ العراق بوحدته **الترابية**.

Territorial Integrity

(5) جريدة الأهرام (مصر)، ١٠ أكتوبر ٢٠٠٢، العدد ٤٢٣١١.
لا يوجد مكتب لقطع التذاكر أو لحضرة الناظر، وبالرغم من ذلك فطبقا لأحكام **قراقوش** فمن يركب منها بلا تذكرة يدفع غرامة!

unjust judge / arbitrary decisions
lexical gap

Exercise 2: Definiteness

How would you translate the underlined definite noun phrases? Justify your translations.

(١) جان الكسان، ١٩٨٢، ''السينما في الوطن العربي''، سلسلة عالم المعرفة، الكويت، ص ٩٢.
أما قصة الفيلم فكانت مستوحاة من قصة حقيقية، وقعت أحداثها في دمشق أبان حكم
الملك فيصل.

Transliteration name   *King Faysal*

(٢) نادر فرجاني، ١٩٨٣، ''الهجرة إلى النفط''، مركز دراسات الوحدة العربية، ص ٤٣.
نقدم في هذا **الفصل** من الكتاب دراستي حالة وبعض **الملاحظات** العامة على وضعية
الهجرة في **بلدان المنشأ.**

chapter, general notes, countries of Origin

(٣) جريدة السياسة (الكويت)، ١٩ أبريل ٢٠٠٧.
وأضافت الجسار أن **الرجل** أخذ حقه بحكم أيديولوجيا الممارسات التي أتيحت له وعليه أن
يعرف أن **المرأة** تستحق فرصا مماثلة وهي ليست منافسة له على الإطلاق.

man, woman

(٤) جريدة الرياض (السعودية)، ٢ سبتمبر ٢٠٠٣، العدد ١٢٨٦٥.
وقد حصلت على **الطلاق** على أساس وجود خلافات غير قابلة للحل مع زوجها.

Divorce

(٥) جريدة الأهرام (مصر)، ٦ سبتمبر ٢٠٠٤، العدد ٤٣٠٠٨.
يمنحك **الشاي** ابتسامة ناصعة ـ عكس ما تعتقدين ـ فهو مصدر طبيعي **للفلورايد.**

Tea, Floride

Exercise 3: Adverbs

How would you translate the underlined adverbs? State the translation problems and the strategies you use.

morphological

(١) جريدة أخبار اليوم (مصر)، ١٤ أبريل ٢٠٠٧، العدد ٣٢٥٨.
قررت الحكومة السويسرية المضي **قدما** في خطتها المثيرة للجدل لمكافحة الإرهاب.

move forward

(٢) جريدة الثورة (سورية)، ٨ فبراير ٢٠٠٥، العدد ٤٥٦٨٧.
كان شديد الحزن على أم كلثوم، ولعله وجد في نشره الكتاب نوعا من الوفاء لصوتها الذي
أمتعه **أبدا.**

to do her voice justice   *Substitute always*

(٣) جريدة الرياض (السعودية)، ٢٠ مارس ٢٠٠٨، العدد ١٤٥١٤.
تقول نورة الزهراني أنها لم تحلم **يوما** أنها ستصبح سيدة أعمال تدير عملا كبيرا.

Substitute or paraphrasing   *never not for a single day*

Presiding *heading* *Substituting*

(4) جريدة الصحافة (السودان)، ١٨ مارس ٢٠٠٨، العدد ٥٢٩٧.

وصل الرئيس عمر البشير إلى العاصمة البرتغالية لشبونة، **مترأسا** وفد السودان في القمة الأوروبية الأفريقية التي بدأت أعمالها مساء أمس.

as the head
leading the delegation

(5) مصطفى محمود، ١٩٩٧، ''ألعاب السيرك السياسي''، دار أخبار اليوم، القاهرة، ص ١٢٠.

وأذكره بالدكتور لويس عوض حينما كان يجمعنا حوله في الأهرام يعلمنا كيف نفكر **ماركسيا**.

as Marxists
to think like a Marxist

Exercise 4: Lexical Gaps

The underlined words constitute lexical gaps in English. How would you translate them?

(1) جريدة الرياض (السعودية)، ٢٣ نوفمبر ٢٠٠٢، العدد ١٢٥٧٣.

يرى المراقبون أن هذه الخطوة من الولايات المتحدة الأمريكية مؤشر قوي على فشلها وشركائها في منظمة تنمية الطاقة في شبه القارة الكورية (كيدو) على **تدجين** كوريا الشمالية.

taming, subdue,

(2) جريدة المستقبل (لبنان)، ١٣ مارس ٢٠٠٧، العدد ٢٦١٢.

كان الصراع الدموي بين اليسار التركي ويمينه القومي منذ أواسط الستينات **يبطن** بعدا مذهبيا دينيا وكذلك بعدا قوميا.

religious! nationalist

Conceal *undertone*
hiding

(3) مجلة الفرات (العراق)، ١٧ مايو ٢٠٠٨.

حينما اتخذت عشائر الديوانية والناصرية وكربلاء قرارها على سبيل المثال بأن تغرم العشيرة التي يقتل أحد من أبنائها أو يفتك بالناس مئة مليون دينار فضلا عن **دية** القتيل نفسه.

blood money
restitution

(4) جريدة الأهرام (مصر)، ٢٦ مارس ٢٠١١، العدد ٤٥٤٠٠.

الدعم ذلك **الغول** المفترس الذي يلتهم ميزانية مصر إلى أين يذهب ولمن يذهب وهل يصرف ماديا أم يصرف عينيا؟ تلك هي المشكلة التي تؤرق كل رؤساء الوزارات السابقة والحالية والقادمة.

Savage,
Predatory
ravenous
beast
(monster)

materially in cash/kind

(5) جريدة المصري اليوم (مصر)، ٢٩ أكتوبر ٢٠٠٩، العدد ١٩٦٤.

يعود الأستاذ هيكل عبر فكرته ليضع وصايته ويفرض أسماء ويتركنا نتحدث عنه بينما يقول بكل ثقة **العارف** بما ستؤول إليه الأمور «أنا أقول ذلك وأنا رجل عمري ٦٨ سنة، ولا أطمع في منصب، وراض بما وصلت إليه».

Knowledgeable

as one who knows how
things will shake out

Exercise 5: Advanced Translation

Translating the underlined words in the sentences below can be rather challenging. What problems do they pose, and what strategies can be employed to translate them?

(1) مجلة أدب ونقد (مصر)، ٢٠٠٦، العدد ٢٥١.

عندما أعلن **الميرزا** حسين علي نوري (الذي حصل على لقب بهاء الله فيما بعد) وسط جماعة من أتباعه في بغداد في العام ١٨٦٣م أنه **المهدي** الذي جاءت بمهدويته البشارة على لسان من ادعى المهدوية قبله، ويقصد به الباب الذي كانت طهران قد شهدت إعدامه قبل ذلك بسنوات، فإن أحداثا **للفتنة** كانت تجري آنذاك على ساحة الإسلام الواسعة.

(2) علي الراعي، ١٩٩٩، "المسرح العربي"، سلسلة عالم المعرفة، الكويت، ص ٥٤.

ومن يزر اليوم سوق جامع الفناء بمراكش يجد هذه الصورة التي نتخيلها حقيقة واقعة. يجد مسرح الحلقة في أشكال متعددة، ويجد مسرح الممثل الفرد الذي يقوم وحده بجميع الأدوار، ويجد تمثيلا عاديا يتعدد فيه المؤدي، ويشبه من قريب تمثيل **المحبظين** كما يجد ألعابا مختلفة **للحواة** والمشعوذين.

(3) جريدة أخبار الخليج (البحرين)، ٦ مارس ٢٠٠٧، العدد ١٠٦١٩.

انتظر الشباب وصول **الحاج** خلف كي يقص عليهم **شلخة** من شلخاته المعهودة لكنه تأخر عن الموعد.

(4) مجلة الكورة والملاعب (مصر)، ٨ مارس ٢٠٠٩، العدد ١٤٣٦.

الخلاصة هي أن الزمالك لا يعتمد على شخص بعينه لأنه مؤسسة رياضية ضخمة ولها تاريخها كما أنه ليس مأوى أو **تكية** لبعض الذين يحاولون الاستفادة منه.

(5) أمين هويدي، ١٩٧٧، "التحولات السياسية الخطيرة" دار الشروق، القاهرة، ص ٢٤.

والولايات المتحدة ـ التي تحاسب الدول المدينة حساب الملكين عن طريق **ناكر ونكير** وهما البنك الدولي وصندوق النقد الدولي على التوالي ـ هي أكثر الدول مديونية.

Harshly Judges

And the US that stands in judgment over debtor nations through the World Bank & the International Monetary Fund – is in more debt than any other state

Putting Words Together

Phrase-Level Translation Problems and Strategies

doing packaging

translating Sentence نص into one word (packaging)

We saw in chapter 1 that individual words can sometimes pose translation problems even if they have referential counterparts in the target language. I also discussed some strategies that can help resolve these problems, but they do not cover all the issues that translators must address. People normally do not speak or write in isolated words, and as translators, we usually work with paragraphs and extended stretches of discourse. Words are put together according to the rules of grammar to form phrases (noun phrases, verb phrases, prepositional phrases, etc.), and these phrases combine to form clauses, sentences, and paragraphs. The processes involved in forming phrases often lead to changes in the meanings of individual words; therefore, the meaning of a word is almost always dependent on the meaning of the surrounding words and the context. For example, the word *monkey* refers to a well-known primate, but knowing its equivalent in Arabic—namely, قرد— does not help us translate phrases such as *monkey business, grease monkey,* or *to have a monkey on one's back*. Word-for-word translations—such as قرد الشحم ,على ظهره قرد, and شغل قرود—quite often do not make sense in the target language, or they may mean different things idiomatically, even though all the individual words have perfect referential counterparts in the target language.

Trying to match up phrasal structures across languages does not always work, either. Consider, for example, the structure of noun phrases. Adjectives in Arabic follow the nouns they modify, and the adverbs that modify these adjectives come at the end of the phrase, as in اختبار صعب جدا *a very difficult test*. In English, conversely, adjectives precede nouns, and adverbs precede adjectives. Moreover, possessive constructions in Arabic have the noun referring to the possessor in the second position, as in سيارة منى *Mona's car*; but in English, the possessor noun comes first. Structurally speaking, Arabic and English noun phrases are almost mirror images of each other. Therefore, we cannot rely on word-for-word translation.

We can easily make a list of all the phrase structure rules in Arabic and English and feed them into a computer, along with a tagged lexicon (a dictionary). The computer can be programmed to translate phrases according to these rules. For example, it would switch the order of nouns and adjectives and place possessor nouns at the beginning of possessive noun phrases. However, we will still get many output phrases in which the translation is inaccurate or garbled because phrase structures do not always line up across languages; there are phrasal types in Arabic that have no equivalents in English. There are also many phrases whose meaning is not compositional—that is, the meaning of the individual words does not add up to the meaning of the phrase. These include idioms, such as *dirt poor* and *quitting cold turkey*, as well as frozen expressions, such as *by and large* and *every now and then*. This is where translators need to do more linguistic calculations than current computers can handle. In this chapter we look at the problems that come up when dealing with phrases, along with strategies that can help resolve them.

1   Translation Problems

1.1   Structural Mismatches

Some phrase-structure rules are identical in Arabic and English, such as having nouns following prepositions, but many are different, such as the (in)definiteness requirement on nouns with demonstratives. In English, only a bare noun with no article can follow a demonstrative (e.g., *I read this book* vs. the ungrammatical *I read this the/a book*). Arabic noun phrases with demonstratives, however, require definite nouns (e.g., قرأت هذا الكتاب vs. the ungrammatical قرأت هذا كتاب). This kind of structural mismatch does not pose any serious problems, for we can easily posit a rule that deletes the Arabic definite article when translating this phrasal construction. We can have similar rules that switch the order of nouns and their modifying adjectives or adjectives and their modifying adverbs.

Problems come up when we encounter structural gaps. These are source language phrasal constructions that have no structural equivalents in the target language. For instance, Arabic allows adjectives and participles in possessive constructions, as in محدود السلطة and بعيد النظر in (1) and (2), but there is no parallel construction in English. We can translate بعيد النظر as *farsighted*, which is a complex adjectival phrase—in this case, which actually forms a single word—made up of an adjective followed by an adjectival passive. This pattern works with other similar phrases/words, such as متفتح العقل *open-minded* and طيب القلب *kindhearted*. We cannot, however, posit a rule that applies this pattern to all Arabic adjectival possessive constructions. For example, we cannot reconstruct محدود السلطة as *limited authorized* or translate it word for word as *limited the authority*. In this particular case, we can reconstruct محدود السلطة as a verb phrase to get *has limited authority*. Alternatively, we can further reconstruct the whole sentence as *his authority is limited*.

(1) جريدة الشرق (قطر)، ٥ يناير ٢٠٠٩، العدد ٧٥٠٨.
السادات لم يكن مجنونا بل كان محللا سياسيا **بعيد النظر**.
Sadat was not a madman, but a farsighted political analyst.

(2) جريدة الجريدة (الكويت)، ٣٠ يونيو ٢٠١٣، العدد ٢٠١٣.
لن تكون مهمة الرئيس الجديد سهلة لأنه **محدود السلطة**.
The new president will not have an easy job because his authority is limited.

The problem of adjectives in possessive constructions is not an exception; there are many Arabic phrasal constructions that are not permissible in English, and vice versa. Some such structural mismatches need to be dealt with on a case-by-case basis, as we just saw. Others can be resolved by establishing rules that translate phrasal constructions directly, even if the grammatical structures of the translation outputs are different from the ones in the source phrases. This is the case with Arabic superlative adjectives in possessive constructions with relative clause complements, as in أخشى ما أخشاه in (3). What is special about this construction is that the verb in the relative clause and the superlative adjective are derived from the same root. Note that the superlative adjective is not derived from a common attributive adjective; it is derived directly from the root specifically for this construction. We cannot translate أخشى ما أخشاه word for word because we would end up with *the most fearful of what I fear*, which is not a valid translation; but we can rephrase it as *what I fear most*, in which *most* maintains the superlative function. The important thing here is that the translation is not based on the structure of the Arabic source phrase but on its semantic function.

(3) جريدة عكاظ (السعودية)، ١٨ مايو ٢٠١٤، العدد ٤٧١٨.
تسير السيارات التي تنتهي لوحاتها برقم فردي يوما وتتوقف يوما، والسيارات
ذات الأرقام الزوجية تسير في يوم وتتوقف في يوم.. لكن **أخشى ما أخشاه** أن
يدفعنا مثل هذا الإجراء إلى شراء سيارتين لكل واحد منا بدلا من سيارة واحدة.

Cars with license plates ending with an odd number would
alternate on the road with those with even numbers every other
day, but what I fear most is that such a decision would make
each of us buy two cars instead of just one.

Translation rules are not stipulations that translators should somehow
know; they are generalizations based on their examining several cases. We
start by analyzing the meaning of the Arabic construction. For example, the
relative clause ما أخشاه *what I fear* in (3) represents a list, or an ordered set,
of all the things the writer fears, whereas the superlative adjective singles
out the one thing that is feared most. This is the exact function of the English superlative free relative clause construction *what . . . most*. Now that we
have established the functional equivalency of أخشى ما أخشاه and *what I fear
most*, we can examine other instances of the source language construction
to see if this pattern holds. It works for أحب ما أحبه *what I love most* and
أسعد ما أسعدني *what pleased me most*, and for almost all similar phrases.
The fact that other phrases with the same structure can be translated in a
similar way indicates that we can treat this pattern as a rule. This example
demonstrates that there are systematic ways of dealing with some structural
mismatches.

1.2 Functional Mismatches

Whereas structural mismatches concern Arabic phrasal structures that are
not permissible in English, functional mismatches have to do with Arabic
phrasal constructions with English equivalents that are used differently. For
example, some English prepositional phrases are used as adverbial modifiers, such as *with care*, *with love*, and *by hand*. Arabic, conversely, allows
more prepositional phrases to be used as adverbial modifiers, such as ببطء
lit. with slowness and بسرعة *lit. with speed* in (4), but such morpheme-by-
morpheme translation candidates are not acceptable in English. Because we
are interested in the function of the Arabic prepositional phrases rather than
their structure, we can translate them using English phrases of different
types as long as they have the same function. The Arabic source phrases are

used as manner modifiers; therefore, we can use the manner adverbs *fast* and *slowly* as English functional equivalents.

(4) جريدة الأهرام (مصر)، ١ سبتمبر ١٩٩٩، العدد ٤١١٧٦.

عندما استمعت إلى تسجيلات لأحاديثها وخطبها لاحظت أنها تتكلم **بسرعة**.
فراحت تتكلم **ببطء ووضوح**.

When she listened to recordings of her own interviews and
speeches, she realized that she speaks fast, and as a result, she
started speaking slowly and clearly.

Functional equivalence does not need to involve phrases with the same
grammatical structure. In other words, we do not need to translate all Arabic
adverbial prepositional phrases as adverbs. In fact, there are many cases in
which we cannot find suitable adverbs, as in the case of بكثرة *lit. with plentifulness* in (5).

(5) جريدة عكاظ (السعودية)، ١٠ مارس ٢٠٠٨، العدد ٢٤٥٨.

أود أن أخبركم بأنه ليس لدينا فنادق خمسة نجوم في حضرموت **بكثرة**.

I would like to inform you that we do not have many five-star
hotels in Hadramawt.

In this particular sentence, the prepositional phrase بكثرة is used to modify having five-star hotels in terms of quantity. Therefore, we can substitute
it with a quantifier, such as *a lot of* or *many*. There is no one way to translate بكثرة, given that it can be functionally equivalent to *a lot*, *much*, *quite*,
plentiful, *often*, *frequently*, *in large quantities*, and *in abundance*, among
several other possibilities. The choice of the optimal translation candidate
always depends on the context rather than the grammatical structure of the
source phrase.

We saw in the previous chapter that many Arabic adverbs are derived
from nouns by adding the *tanween* suffix, as in صباحا and أحيانا, which can
be translated, respectively, as *in the morning* and *sometimes*. Some adverbs
can be repeated to form new adverbial constructions, as in اسما اسما in (6)
and اثنين اثنين in (7). Obviously, we cannot translate these phrases as *name
name* and *two two* because English does not allow this kind of repetition.
Besides, the English adverb derived from *name* is *namely*, which has a very
different meaning and function from its Arabic counterpart. Also, there is
no English adverb lexically derived from *two*. Thus it is very important for

us to understand the function of this construction, not just the meaning of the repeated words, before attempting to translate it. This adverbial construction describes an event as a repeated action, but the problem is that the repeated action can be interpreted differently depending on the context. The sentence in (6) describes a situation in which the action of examining one name was repeated until all the names were examined. The repeated adverb construction here suggests that the examination is meticulous and thorough. Note that we cannot apply reconstruction and translate ستفحص أسماء السجناء اسما اسما as *it will reexamine the names of the prisoners* because the prefix *re-* suggests that all the names were already examined; this is a different kind of repetition. In (7), conversely, the repetition expresses a different kind of event individuation; each addition involves two eggs. This means that repeated adverbs cannot be translated in a uniform way, even though they have the same structure.

(6) وكالة الأنباء الكويتية كونا (الكويت)، ١١ ديسمبر ١٩٩٨.
ونقلت الإذاعة الفلسطينية عن الدكتور عريقات قوله إن اللجنة ستفحص
أسماء السجناء **اسما اسما**.

The Palestinian Broadcasting Service quoted Dr. Uraiqat as saying that the committee will examine each and every one of the prisoners' names.

(7) جريدة كل الوطن (السعودية)، ٨ يونيو ٢٠٠٦.
يوضع المحتوى في إناء آخر حتى يبرد تماما، وبعد ذلك يضاف البيض **اثنين
اثنين** مع التقليب المستمر.

Put the mixed ingredients in a different bowl until they cool completely. Then, add the eggs, two at a time, while stirring constantly.

Unlike the idiosyncratic nature of the functional mismatches associated with adverbial uses of prepositional phrases, there are systematic ways of translating repeated adverbs. First, we need to identify the communicative function of the Arabic adverbial construction, and then we need to look for an English construction that achieves the same function. The repeated adverb construction is a verb phrase manner modifier that specifies succession or thoroughness. The English constructions *at the time* and *each and every* are functionally equivalent to the Arabic repeated adverb construction. The Arabic repeated adverb construction has two communicative functions that correspond to two different constructions in English. We can generalize this pattern, and whenever we run into a repeated adverb within a verb phrase, we can use the one that is a true functional equivalent.

Another pattern of functional mismatches involves the cognate object constructions, in which a verb takes an event nominal derived from the same root as an object, often with an adjective, such as فشل فشلا ذريعا in (8). The function of this construction is to provide a grammatical context in which an adjective can indirectly modify the verb by modifying its cognate object. English cognate objects, as in *to die a horrible death* and *to laugh a bitter laugh*, are relatively few and nonproductive. In other words, we cannot generate new cognate objects, as in *failed a miserable failure*, to translate فشل فشلا ذريعا. Cognate object phrases need to be reconstructed as phrases with the same functions, regardless of their grammatical structure. Because cognate object phrases function indirectly as modifiers, most of them can be translated using adverbs—for example, *failed miserably*.

(8) جريدة عكاظ (السعودية)، ٨ أكتوبر ٢٠٠٦، العدد ١٩٣٩.
لم نكن بحاجة أصلا لنظام المشاركة بالوقت وقد **فشل فشلا ذريعا** في بعض البلدان المجاورة.

We had no need for the time-share system to start with, and it failed miserably in some neighboring countries.

Arabic also allows unmodified cognate objects, as in دمرها تدميرا *lit. destroyed it a destruction* in (9), where we do not have an adjective that would qualify the destruction. These unmodified cognate objects have a different function: They add emphasis. The cognate object in دمرها تدميرا stresses that the destruction would have been complete. To make sure that the emphasis is not lost, we can add the adverb *completely*, as in *would have destroyed it completely*. We can also substitute the whole phrase with a verb that lexically encodes the emphasis, such as *devastate* or *ruin*.

(9) جريدة الأخبار (العراق)، ٧ أبريل ٢٠٠٨.
من حسن حظ العراق أن الأثريين الألمان قاموا بنقل هذه الآثار وحفظها هنا.
لو بقيت في العراق لكان الإهمال قد **دمرها تدميرا.**

Fortunately for Iraq, the German archeologists brought those artifacts over for preservation. If they had stayed in Iraq, they would have been ruined by negligence.

The problems posed by phrase-level functional mismatches are in fact very similar to those we saw at the word level in chapter 1. Both types of problems have to do with source language forms that are used differently from their counterparts in the target language. They are also very similar in the ways we deal with them, as we can use different target language forms that have the same functions. The big picture that emerges here is that we are more concerned with the functions of the source language phrases than their structure. Our ultimate goal is a translation that achieves the same communicative functions as the source text.

1.3   Structural Ambiguity

Another source of translation problems is structural ambiguity, which we see when a phrasal structure in the source or the target language allows more than one interpretation. For example, there are two ways to read the noun phrase قرار الرئيس الجديد in (10): *the decision of the new president*, and *the new decision of the president*.

> (10) جريدة القبس (الكويت)، ٤ أكتوبر ٢٠٠٧، العدد ١٢٣٣٧.
> إن الوزير الذي يبقى أمامه يومان أو ثلاثة على رأس وزارته يتحاشى الحديث
> عن **قرار الرئيس الجديد** بإلغاء وزارة الثقافة. ففي أوساط الرئيس الجديد
> يجري الحديث عن تشكيل حكومة مصغرة مؤلفة من ١٥ وزيرا بينهم رئيسها،
> وستلحق وزارة الثقافة بوزارة التربية.
>
> The ministers who have only two or three days left in office
> are avoiding talking about the decision by the new president to
> eliminate the Ministry of Culture. Within the circles of the new
> president, there is talk about forming a small government of
> fifteen cabinet positions, including the prime minister, with the
> Ministry of Culture merged with the Ministry of Education.

When translating this phrase, one must first identify the intended reading by using structural and contextual clues. Otherwise, the translation could provide inaccurate and misleading information. In this sentence, the intended reading is *the decision of the new president* because there is an unambiguous noun phrase in the same text—namely, أوساط الرئيس الجديد *the circles of the new president*—that helps resolve the ambiguity. The key here is that أوساط *circles* is a feminine broken plural; therefore, the masculine adjective الجديد *new* can only modify the masculine noun الرئيس *the president*. Structural clues such as gender agreement are critical to resolving ambiguity. Because English allows the same kind of structural ambiguity, translating the phrase قرار الرئيس الجديد as *the new president's decision* would maintain the same ambiguity (*the new president* vs. *the new decision*). Reconstructing the translation as *the decision by the new president* eliminates the ambiguity.

Unlike lexical ambiguity, which we discussed in chapter 1, structural ambiguity is predictable. The structural ambiguity in (10) is not a random instance. In fact, whenever a possessive construction composed of two nouns with the same gender is followed by an adjective, we have ambiguity, because the adjective can modify either noun, as in كلب الولد الصغير, which could mean either *the little boy's dog* or *the boy's little dog*. Moreover, some phrases with special semantic functions, such as على الإطلاق, are polarity items that are inherently ambiguous; but we can identify the intended reading from the structure of the sentence. If the sentence is negative, as in (11), على الإطلاق is translated as *at all* or *never*; but if the sentence is affirmative, it is translated as *ever*, as in (12). The interpretation of ambiguous phrasal polarity items, such as على الإطلاق *ever/never* and في يوم من الأيام *someday /never*, is dependent on the structure of the sentence. Knowing the grammatical structures in which we expect ambiguities is quite helpful in identifying and resolving them, which in turn leads to more accurate translation.

(11) جريدة الأخبار (مصر)، ٢٧ أكتوبر ٢٠٠٦، العدد ١٧٠١٠.
نهائيات كأس العالم ٢٠٠٦ في ألمانيا لم تعجبني **على الإطلاق**.
I did not like the 2006 World Cup Finals in Germany at all.

(12) جريدة أخبار السيارات (مصر)، ١ يوليو ٢٠٠٧، العدد ١١٣.
أعلنت شركة رولز رويس البريطانية طرح طراز جديد من الفانتوم باللون الفضي، احتفالا بالعيد المئوي لتدشين Silverghost إحدى أفضل السيارات **على الإطلاق**.

British car maker Rolls-Royce announced the release of a new silver model of the Phantom to commemorate the one-hundredth anniversary of the launching of the Silver Ghost, which is one of the best cars ever.

Sometimes ambiguity has to do with the target language's phrase structure. For example, the phrase ذاهب ليحقق لشعبه حلمه in (13) has only one interpretation, which is equivalent to *Abbas is going (to Annapolis) for the purpose of realizing his people's dream*. Translating ذاهب ليحقق as *is going to realize* is accurate, but it results in unnecessary ambiguity. That is because *going to* has a future reading with the connotations of determination and high probability, which are not available in the Arabic source sentence. The difference between *Abbas is going to realize his people's dream* and *Abbas is going (somewhere) in order to realize his people's dream* is obvious, because the former does not necessarily involve travel, whereas the latter does. Moreover, *going to* indicates that Abbas is expected to make that dream come true, but *going in order to* only reveals his intentions with no commitment to the outcome. One way of avoiding such ambiguity is to apply substitution and to instead use an unambiguous construction.

(13) جريدة الشرق الأوسط (السعودية)، ٢٧ نوفمبر ٢٠٠٧، العدد ١٠٥٩١.
رغم ما قاله الرئيس الفلسطيني، محمود عباس، عند وصوله إلى واشنطن في
طريقه إلى مؤتمر أنابوليس إنه »**ذاهب ليحقق** لشعبه حلمه بدولة فلسطينية
مستقلة«، لا يثق الفلسطينيون بأن هذا المؤتمر سيحقق اختراقا تاريخيا.

Upon his arrival in Washington, on his way to the Annapolis Peace Conference, Palestinian president Mahmoud Abbas said that he is participating in the conference in order to realize his people's dream of an independent Palestinian state. However, Palestinians do not believe this conference will achieve a historic breakthrough.

Finally, we need to realize that ambiguity is a common linguistic phenomenon. We are so used to dealing with structural and lexical ambiguities that we do not even notice them most of the time. If the ambiguity has to do with the source language, we need to make sure that our translation reflects the intended reading. If our translation inevitably leads to ambiguity, we need to make sure that there are sufficient structural and contextual clues to help our readers identify the intended reading.

2 Noncompositional Meaning

When we look at a phrase such as *John's old house*, we find that every morpheme contributes to the meaning of the phrase as a whole. In fact, the meaning of this phrase is the sum total of the meanings of its parts—that is, the meaning of this phrase is fully compositional. This is the case with most phrases, but some phrasal types do not follow this generalization, such as frozen expressions, collocations, compounds, and idioms. These are phrases whose meanings cannot always be understood by looking at their constituents; therefore, we cannot translate them simply by using their referential counterparts. Semantically noncompositional phrases require a different approach to translation, as we try to find target language phrases or expressions that have the same discourse functions as the source phrases, regardless of whether their constituents are referentially equivalent.

2.1 *Frozen Expressions*

Frozen expressions are fixed phrases, such as *so be it, fair and square, by and large*, and *every now and then*. We can see from the way frozen expressions are used that they do not allow any change to their structure. We cannot switch the order of conjuncts, as in the odd expressions *square and fair* and *by crook or by hook*, and we cannot change their inflectional morphology, say, by making them plural, as in *so be they*. Some frozen expressions are not even grammatical, such as *by and large*, where two words that belong to different parts of speech are conjoined. Frozen expressions are usually relics from earlier stages of the language that have become lexicalized over time; therefore, they should be treated the same way we treat individual words.

Arabic, like any other language, has its share of frozen expressions. Sometimes we can guess their meanings from their constituent words, even though they are not strictly compositional. For example, the words that make up the phrase بادىء ذي بدء suggest that this expression has to do with getting started. However, this does not help us understand what the phrase as a whole means or how it is used. In other cases, the meaning of a frozen expression is opaque, as in أما بعد. We know that أما means *as for* and بعد means *after*, but this does not tell us what they mean when used together. Also, in some instances the words that make up a frozen expression are so archaic that most native speakers do not know what they mean by themselves, as in the case of وهلم جرا.

When translating frozen expressions, we need to use target language functional equivalents, because we cannot rely on the meanings of their constituent parts. We actually need to start the translation process by identifying the communicative functions associated with these expressions. Then, we need to look for target language expressions that are conventionally used to achieve these same functions. By "functional equivalents," I mean expressions from different languages that are used in the same contexts. For instance, English fairy tales typically start with *once upon a time*, whereas Arabic fairy tales start with كان يا ما كان; therefore, we can consider these two frozen expressions as functionally equivalent, even though they have very different grammatical structures and lexical contents. The frozen expression وهلم جرا can be translated as *and so on and so forth, and so on*, or *etcetera*. All we need to know is that it is an expression used at the end of a list to indicate that there are other items of the same category with which the readers are assumed to be familiar. With the expression بادىء ذي بدء, we need to recognize that it is used at the beginning of a discourse to describe something as being of primary importance in comparison with other, similar items; therefore, we can translate it as *first and foremost*. Unfortunately, only a few Arabic frozen expressions are functionally equivalent to English frozen expressions, but we do not need to translate Arabic frozen expressions as English frozen expressions.

Translating frozen expressions becomes challenging when the target language does not have true functional equivalents. For example, the expression أما بعد is used to mark the transition from introductory discourse to the core content of a text. Typically, it is used in official letters and formal speeches after greetings and introductory remarks. The only English expressions that have similar functions are *anyhow* and *anyway*, or the more direct expression *let's get down to business*. However, these expressions are not appropriate in formal discourse, and they cannot be considered true functional equivalents of أما بعد. We can simply omit أما بعد from the translation because its discourse function is usually unmarked in English discourse. Instead, we can achieve the same communicative goal by starting a new paragraph.

Finally, some frozen expressions have culture-specific discourse functions, as in the case of والله أعلم *lit. and God knows best* in (14). This phrase is used as a formulaic expression at the ends of texts in which writers issue religious edicts or give academic opinions. The purpose of using this expression in these particular contexts is to show humility, as writers try not to sound as if they know everything or that they have the final say. It is part of the religion-based cultural etiquette of academic pursuit, which stems from the view that human knowledge is inherently limited compared with divine knowledge. Using the English word-for-word translation *God knows best* would be quite odd, whereas *God only knows* does not achieve the same communicative function. Because the communicative function of والله أعلم is language specific, we can leave it out. After all, it is part of the discourse's form rather than its content.

(14) جريدة الأهرام العربي (مصر)، ٢ أغسطس ٢٠٠٨، العدد ٥٩٣.
وأما ملك الموت فليس بمصرح باسمه في القرآن، ولا في الأحاديث الصحاح،
وقد جاءت تسميته في بعض الآثار بعزرائيل، **والله أعلم**.

As for the Angel of Death, his name is not mentioned anywhere
in the Qur'an or the verified sayings of Prophet Muhammad, but
the name *Ezrael* occurs in some classical texts.

Note, however, that the same expression has other communicative functions in other discourse genres. In (15), والله أعلم is used to express the author's
doubts about the statement that follows; hence, it is translated as *who knows*.

(15) جريدة عكاظ (السعودية)، ٣١ مايو ٢٠٠٧، العدد ٢١٧٤.
والله أعلم فقد تكون ذبابة ديكارت كالتفاحة التي سقطت على رأس نيوتن.. قد
تكون مجرد قصص.

Who knows? Perhaps Descartes's fly is just like the apple that
fell on Newton's head, only a story.

We find many frozen expressions in religious discourse, such as صلى الله
عليه وسلم *lit. May God bless him and grant him peace*, عليه السلام *lit. Peace be
upon him*, رضي الله عنه *lit. May God be pleased with him*, and many others.
These are used after mentioning the names of prophets and prominent religious figures (e.g., عيسى عليه السلام, and محمد صلى الله عليه وسلم ,أبو بكر رضي
الله عنه). These formulaic expressions tend to be used with reference to particular individuals, depending on their status within the religious tradition:
Prophet Muhammad takes صلى الله عليه وسلم, other prophets take عليه السلام,
and early prominent figures in Islam take رضي الله عنه. These expressions can
be difficult to deal with because English does not have functionally equivalent terms. The good news is that some of these terms have been around for a
long time, and thus other translators have had to deal with them. Many such
terms have even developed standardized translations that are specific to religious discourse, such as *Peace be upon him*, or *PBUH*, for صلى الله عليه وسلم.

2.2 Collocations

Collocations are phrasal combinations of words that tend to occur together, *idioms*
such as *a flock of birds*, *commit a crime*, and *a heavy accent*. The defining
characteristic of collocations is that though they allow grammatical modifi-
cation, their lexical constituents are fixed. For example, we can say *a flock*

of birds and *filthy rich*, but not *a herd of birds*, *a flock of cows*, *dirty rich*, or *filthy poor*. They are so fixed that we cannot use close synonyms to replace their lexical constituents; thus we can say *strike a balance* but not *hit a balance*, even though *hit* and *strike* are very similar in meaning. The inflectional morphology of collocations, conversely, is rather flexible; because they occur in passive constructions (e.g., *a crime was committed*), they can be pluralized (e.g., *flocks of birds*), and they allow modifiers (e.g., *a very heavy Scottish accent*). The meanings of collocations are not always transparent, as they are not strictly compositional. For example, when we pay someone a visit, we do not give money, and when we strike a balance, nothing gets hit. Although collocations allow grammatical alternations, they need to be dealt with on a case-by-case basis, just like other semantically noncompositional expressions.

Arabic collocations vary considerably in their restrictiveness. Some collocations are open in the sense that they have one word fixed, whereas another word is semantically and/or grammatically specified but lexically variable. For example, the collocation منتهى السرعة *lit. the end of speed* has the word منتهى *end* fully fixed; but السرعة *speed* can be substituted by any singular definite attributive noun, as in منتهى السعادة ,منتهى الحب, and منتهى الجمال. Other collocations are partially constrained in terms of their lexical content, as one word is fixed, whereas the other word can be any of a limited set of words. For example, the verb اقترف *commit* collocates with ذنب *sin* and جريمة *crime*, but not with الانتحار *suicide*, even though suicide is considered both a crime and a sin in Arab cultures. The fact that the collocation اقترف انتحارا *commit suicide* is inadmissible in Arabic testifies to the arbitrary nature of collocations. Most Arabic collocations, however, have fully specified lexical content, and we cannot change any of their constituent words, as in ألقى القبض على *arrest* and ألقى خطبة *give/deliver a speech*, where we cannot substitute ألقى *throw* with رمى *throw* or قذف *throw*, even though they are all synonyms.

Some Arabic collocations have direct English equivalents, such as يعتمد على *depend on* and يأخذ استراحة *take a break*; thus, these can be safely translated word for word. However, there are very few of these, and word-for-word translation should not be considered a normal way of dealing with collocations because it often leads to inaccurate results. Other collocations, such as اتخذ القرار in (17), and جلس على طاولة المفاوضات in (16), cannot be translated word for word because they either have different meanings, such as the rather odd *sit on the negotiation table*, or they are simply unacceptable in

American English, as *take a decision*. In such cases, we need to identify the meaning of the collocation as a whole and use its English functional equivalent, if there is one. In (16) and (17), جلس على طاولة المفاوضات and اتخذ القرار are better translated as *sit at the negotiation table* and *make a decision*.

(16) جريدة الوقت (البحرين)، ٩ سبتمبر ٢٠٠٨، العدد ٩٣٢.
أتمنى أن **نجلس على** طاولة المفاوضات فورا، إنها الطريق الوحيد إلى سلام شامل.

I wish we would sit at the negotiation table immediately. It is the only way to reach a comprehensive peace.

(17) جريدة العلم (المغرب)، ١ فبراير ٢٠٠٩، العدد ٢١٢٦٧.
لا تعليق لدي على قرار الحكم لكن من المؤسف أن نتهمه بالتحيز، وأعتقد أنه **اتخذ** قرارا شجاعا.

I have no comments on the referee's decision, but it is unfortunate that he was accused of bias. I believe he made a brave decision.

When translating collocations, we need to pay special attention to their connotations and social meanings, just as we do with individual words. For example, the collocation رقيق الحال *lit. of a tender state*, in the context of (18), can easily mislead us into translating it as *a sensitive person*, whereas it actually means *poor*. Because the phrase رقيق الحال is a polite way of describing someone who is of a lower socioeconomic status, we can translate it as *from a humble background*, which has the same social meaning.

(18) جريدة الشرق الأوسط (السعودية)، ٢ سبتمبر ٢٠٠١، العدد ٨٣١٤.
بعد تخرجي التحقت بالعمل بشركة عمي .. أعجبت بموظف شاب متدين **رقيق الحال**.

After graduation, I got a job at my uncle's firm. I fell in love with a colleague who was a religious young man from a humble background.

Translating collocations is not a very complex process. Each collocation has a head word that is semantically more prominent; usually, it is the word that is used literally, such as *rich* in *filthy rich* and *a look* in *take a look*. What we need to do first is to identify the head word in the Arabic collocation.

Usually, if the collocation is a verb with a direct object, such as ضرب مثلا *lit. strike an example* and اتخذ قرارا *lit. take a decision*, the head word is the direct object. If the Arabic collocation is a possessive construction, the most prominent word is quite often the second noun, as in سرب أسماك *lit. a flock of fish* and سرب حمام *lit. a flock of pigeons*. The second step is to use our knowledge of the source language and the context to determine the meaning and the function of the expression as a whole. For instance, the collocation شاي ثقيل *lit. heavy tea* is made up of a noun and a modifying adjective, with the two words used together to describe strong tea. Finally, we can look for an English collocation that uses the equivalent of the head word to describe the same attribute or situation, as in *give an example, make a decision, a shoal/school of fish*, and *a flock of pigeons*.

Things get complicated when we deal with collocations that have no direct equivalents in English, such as the open collocations with منتهى followed by a singular definite attributive noun. The noun منتهى literally means *terminal point*. When it collocates with الأهمية *importance*, as in (19), the phrase metaphorically describes extreme importance; therefore, it is considered equivalent to the English collocation *of the utmost importance*. We can use this equivalence pattern to translate other collocations with منتهى, such as منتهى السرية *utmost secrecy* and منتهى الاحترام *utmost respect*. However, like other translation patterns, it does not work all the time, because we cannot translate منتهى الغرابة as *utmost strangeness*. The arbitrary nature of collocations makes it difficult to establish translation rules.

(19) جريدة الأهرام (مصر)، ٢١ يونيو ٢٠٠٨، العدد ٤٤٣٩٢.
إن التواصل بين المواطن المصري في الخارج وسفارته أصبح أمرا **في منتهى الأهمية**.

Communication between Egyptian citizens abroad and the
Egyptian embassies has become a matter of the utmost
importance.

The thing to remember is that when we translate collocations, we are dealing with phrases rather than individual words. Therefore, we need to focus on the meaning of the collocation as a whole, including its contextual connotations and social meanings. Just as with other semantically noncompositional phrases, we do not need to translate Arabic collocations as English ones, as long as the translation achieves the same communicative functions.

2.3 Phrasal Compounds

In our discussion of word formation strategies, I briefly mentioned compounds, which are words formed by combining two already-existing stems, such as *cupcake, hotdog,* and *homework.* True Arabic lexical compounds, such as الرأسمالية *capitalism,* are rather limited; most Arabic compounds are in fact function words—for example, كيلا *in order not to,* which is made up of كي *in order to* and لا *not.* The productive compounding strategy in Arabic involves using two separate words together to mean one thing. These include relatively fixed possessive constructions, as well as some adjectival phrases, whose meanings are not strictly compositional. For example, if the phrase رأس السنة in (20) was to be translated word for word, it would be *the head of the year,* but this is not what it means in actual use. We can easily guess from the context that the phrase رأس السنة means *the beginning of the year,* and thus translate ليلة رأس السنة as *New Year's Eve.*

(20) جريدة الأهرام (مصر)، ٢ يناير ٢٠٠٣، العدد ٤٢٣٥٩.
الألعاب النارية تنطلق فوق ميدان التايمز في مدينة نيويورك الذي تجمع فيه مئات الآلاف ليشهدوا تقليد إسقاط الكرة الذي يقام سنويا منذ ٩٩ عاما في **ليلة رأس السنة**.

Fireworks go off over Times Square in New York City, where hundreds of thousands have gathered to watch the New Year's Eve ball drop, an annual tradition that goes back ninety-nine years.

The meaning of compounds is sometimes not very transparent, as in the case of ناطحة سحاب in (21), which literally means *something that butts the clouds.* The intended meaning of the phrase—namely, *skyscraper*—is not immediately accessible from its constituents, just like its English equivalent.

(21) موقع وكالة أخبار البي بي سي، ٢٦ فبراير ٢٠٠٣.
كشفت إمارة دبي عن خطة لبناء أعلى **ناطحة سحاب** في العالم.

The Emirate of Dubai revealed a plan to build the tallest skyscraper in the world.

There are also some compounds that include archaic words, such as قوس قزح *rainbow,* which literally means *Quzah's bow.* Most native speakers of

Arabic do not know that قزح is the name of a pre-Islamic Arabian deity; they simply use the expression as if it were one word.

The problems we encounter when translating compounds are not limited to their noncompositional nature because, just like individual words, they can have multiple equivalents in the target language, as in the case of أمين السر. This compound, which literally means *the person entrusted with the secret*, is used as a professional title for various administrative leadership positions, including, among others, *executive director, chairperson, committee chair, secretary*, and, as in (22), *registrar*. Translating such a phrase requires not only knowing what the compound as whole means but also identifying the specific target language equivalent that fits the context. The context of (22) indicates that أمين سر المحكمة is a position within the Special Tribunal for Lebanon established by the United Nations following the assassination of former Lebanese prime minister Rafiq Hariri. Therefore, the best way to identify the official title in English is to do some research on this tribunal. In this particular context, أمين سر المحكمة is *the tribunal registrar*.

(22) جريدة أخبار الخليج (البحرين)، ١٧ يناير ٢٠١٠، العدد ١١٦٢٢.
ويقول روبن فينسنت **أمين سر المحكمة** إنه يتوقع أن يطلب المدعي العام من السلطات اللبنانية أن تنقل إلى لاهاي الضباط الأربعة.

Robin Vincent, the tribunal registrar, said that he expects
the prosecutor-general to request the Lebanese authorities to
extradite the four officers to The Hague.

Some phrasal compounds have technical and nontechnical equivalents in English. For example, أزمة قلبية *lit. a crisis of the heart* can be translated as *myocardial infarction* or *heart attack*. Both are valid equivalents, but the choice of the functional equivalent depends on the genre of the source text. If the compound is used as jargon in a specialized text—say, a medical report—we need to use the correct terminology; but if it is a text for nonspecialists, we are better off using the common expression.

Compounds that refer to culture-specific concepts can be rather challenging because, quite often, they have no equivalents in the target language, just like individual culture-specific words. The compound أهل الكتاب in (23), for example, is used only in historical and religious texts to refer to Christians and Jews in premodern times. The expression *(Fellow) People of the Book* was coined specifically to translate this compound. If the expected audience is not likely to be familiar with the term, or if we want to make sure the translation has no cultural biases, we can simply paraphrase أهل

الكتاب as *Christians and Jews*. Note that we used the compound *interfaith dialogue* to translate يحاور *debate* to maintain the connotation that it was a nonconfrontational exchange of ideas of an academic nature.

(23) جريدة الأهرام (مصر)، ٢٢ يناير ٢٠٠٧، العدد ٤٣٨٧٦.

وفي العصر العباسي كان القاضي الباقلاني (ت ٤٥٣) أهم العلماء الذين كانوا يحاورون **أهل الكتاب**.

During the Abbasid Era, Qadi Al-Baqillani (died 453 AH, or AD 1061) was one of the most prominent scholars who engaged in interfaith dialogue with Christians and Jews.

The culture-specific compound كتب الكتاب *lit. the writing of the book* in (24) describes a prenuptial ceremony that entails signing marriage documents before the actual wedding. Obviously, there is no such ceremony in English-speaking cultures; hence the lexical gap. In this case, we can apply word-level translation strategies, such as paraphrasing and providing definitions.

(24) جريدة الأهرام (مصر)، ٤ مارس ٢٠٠٦، العدد ٤٣٥٥٢.

وبدأنا نعد العدة للزواج وحددنا يوم **كتب الكتاب** وأرسلنا الدعوات للأهل والزملاء والأحباب ولكن . . .

We started preparing for the wedding, and we set a date for the party where we would have signed the marriage documents. We even sent out invitations to friends and family, but . . .

Although compounds are multiword phrases, they behave like individual words; they can constitute lexical gaps, and they can have multiple equivalents in the target language. The challenges of translating phrasal compounds have to do with their semantically noncompositional nature and their use as terminology or jargon. This is why they are best dealt with using word-level translation strategies.

2.4 Idioms

Idioms constitute a separate category of semantically noncompositional expressions. What distinguishes idioms from other such expressions is their figurative nature. In fact, idioms start out as new metaphors, but they lose their novelty and become fixed because of their consistent use over long periods of time. When we say that someone spilled the beans, we are not describing a situation in which someone actually spills beans. Rather, it is only a figurative expression that is conventionally used to describe a situation in which someone divulges information that is supposed to be kept secret. In most cases, people forget the origins of idioms and only maintain their functional meanings. Most English speakers do not know the relation between beans and secrets, but they know how to use the idiom. Common English idioms include *bark up the wrong tree, break the ice, bury the hatchet,* and *let the cat out of the bag.*

The main challenge in translating idiomatic expressions is identifying their intended meanings. Some idioms can be understood by relying on common knowledge, such as ريشة في مهب الريح *lit. a feather in the path of wind*. On the basis of our knowledge of feathers and wind, we can guess that this idiomatic expression means *being helpless*. With لبن العصفور *lit. bird milk* in (25), we know that there is no such thing as bird milk. However, we can guess that it describes things that do not exist, such as the Phoenix or unicorns. Although this idiom is rather opaque, we can infer its meaning from the context. This idiom describes a hypothetical situation in which someone attempts to please another by performing impossible tasks, which is similar to the contexts in which the English idiomatic expression *bend over backwards* is used.

(25) جريدة الشرق الأوسط (السعودية)، ٥ أبريل ٢٠٠٤، العدد ٩٢٦٠.
لو أن دمشق أعطت **لبن العصفور** للإدارة الأمريكية الحالية، فلن ترضى عنها علنا.

Even if Damascus bent over backward to please the current American administration, the administration would not express its pleasure publicly.

We should not risk mistranslating idioms by trying to guess their meanings all the time, because some of them describe situations that cannot be inferred from the metaphors, such as ابتسامة صفراء *lit. a yellow smile* in (26), which means *a fake smile*. If we only rely on our intuitions, we might erroneously translate it as *a cowardly smile* or *an ugly smile*.

(26) جريدة الخليج (الإمارات)، ١٢ نوفمبر ٢٠٠٨.
لا أتواجد في مكان إلا إذا كنت أرتاح إلى الموجودين فيه، فأنا لا أعرف رسم
ابتسامة صفراء على وجهي.

I do not go anywhere unless I feel comfortable with those around me, because I do not know how to wear a fake smile.

When it comes to translating idioms, the notion of equivalence can only be defined in functional terms, because translating idioms literally does not guarantee successful communication. For an English idiom to be functionally equivalent to an Arabic one, they do not need to use the same figure of speech, but they must be used to describe the same kinds of situations. For example, if عشم إبليس في الجنة in (27) was to be translated literally as *Satan's wish is to be in heavens*, it would lose its idiomatic function, and many readers might not even recognize what it is supposed to mean. Instead, we can use an equivalent English idiom that describes an impossible situation, such as *when pigs fly* or *when hell freezes over*.

(27) مجلة روز اليوسف (مصر)، ١٣ أبريل ٢٠١٣.
وقال لمن يحلمون بدخول الناتو مصر: عشم إبليس في الجنة!
He told those who dream of NATO intervening in Egypt, "When pigs fly!"

Functional equivalence is not limited to situations in which we have idioms from two different languages that can be used to describe the same situations. Idioms, like words, have social meanings that we need to consider when translating. For example, the idiomatic phrases في ذمة الله *lit. in God's trust* and انتقل إلى رحمة الله *lit. moved into God's mercy* in (28) are used to describe death in a respectful way. English idioms such as *croaked, kicked the bucket, six feet under*, and *pushing up daisies* also describe death, but they are not respectful or formal. When translating انتقل إلى رحمة الله and في ذمة الله, we cannot use any of these idioms because they have different social meanings, and as a result, they cannot be considered functionally equivalent to the Arabic idioms under consideration.

(28) جريدة الرياض (السعودية)، ١٢ نوفمبر ٢٠٠٧، العدد ١٤٣٨٥.
عبد الله العزاز **في ذمة الله: انتقل إلى رحمة الله تعالى** يوم أمس في ألمانيا
عبد الله بن عبد الرحمن العزاز نائب محافظ المؤسسة العامة لتحلية المياه.
Abdallah Al-Azzaz died; Abdallah Bin-Abdelrahman Al-Azzaz, deputy director of the Saline Water Conversion Corporation, passed away yesterday in Germany.

Moreover, functional equivalence is not only about appropriateness. Many respectful and appropriate English idioms that describe death, such as *asleep in Christ* and *in the arms of the Father*, cannot be used to translate في ذمة الله

and انتقل إلى رحمة الله because they are culture-specific and thus they have different religious associations. Even idiomatic expressions like *fallen* and *made the ultimate sacrifice* do not work in this sentence because they are reserved for the honorable deaths of soldiers. What we need for (28) is an idiom that describes the same situation with the same social meanings. Because this sentence is an excerpt from an obituary, we need to follow the English discourse patterns of obituaries. Thus, we need to avoid idioms in the heading, and we need to use a neutral idiom, such as *passed away* or *departed* to translate انتقل إلى رحمة الله and في ذمة الله. Of course, we lose the religious component of the Arabic idioms by using such neutral expressions, but the damage is minimal because these idioms are used as respectful formulas rather than actual religious invocations.

The diglossic situation of Arabic provides writers with another rich source of idiomatic expressions, namely, the spoken dialects. Just as we saw in our discussion of colloquialisms in written discourse, we often find colloquial idioms in Standard Arabic texts. These are borrowed from the dialects to achieve certain communicative functions that cannot be attained by Standard Arabic idioms. In (29), for example, the writer uses the colloquial Egyptian idiom اشترى دماغه *lit. he bought his head* to describe a member of the parliament who fell asleep during a heated debate over a new legislation. By using this idiom, the writer is suggesting that this politician is irresponsible, indifferent, disrespectful, and unworthy of this position. These connotations are directly related to the fact that this idiom started out as a stigmatized slang expression used by teenagers before it became a widely used colloquial idiom. The challenge is to find an English idiom that can be used in the same context while triggering all these connotations. One candidate is the idiom *he did not give a damn*, but it might be inappropriate for a newspaper article. Therefore, we can rule it out as a true functional equivalent. A better option is *he could not care less*, which is better suited for this genre.

(29) جريدة الوفد (مصر)، ٣١ أكتوبر ٢٠٠٦.

رغم العواصف داخل مجلس الشعب لإقرار قانون حبس الصحفيين إلا أن النائب عصام عبد الغفار **اشترى دماغه** وراح يغط في نوم عميق داخل المجلس أثناء إقرار مشروع قانون حبس الصحفيين!!

Despite the turmoil in the People's Assembly over the legislation that would sanction detaining journalists, Representative Issam Abdelghaffar could not care less; he was fast asleep during the vote.

Some Arabic idioms are borrowed from English, which makes them easier to translate. All we really need to do is to identify their English counterparts and back-translate them. One such idiom is نصيب الأسد in (30), which literally and metaphorically means *the lion's share*.

(30) جريدة الاقتصادي (السعودية)، ٢٦ نوفمبر ٢٠٠٧.
في ألعاب القوى حصل المنتخب السعودي على **نصيب الأسد** من الميداليات.
In track and field, the Saudi national team won the lion's share
of medals.

Borrowed idioms are sometimes slightly modified, but we can still identify their metaphorical meanings and their English counterparts. For instance, العودة إلى المربع الأول *lit. returning to the first square* is actually a translation of *back to square one*. It is the linguistic constraints of Arabic that induce these modifications, because the phrasal combination المربع واحد is not grammatical. Other borrowed idioms include دموع التماسيح, which is equivalent to *crocodile tears*, but the Arabic word for *crocodile* is a definite plural. We also find some idioms that exist in both languages with minor differences in their lexical content, such as أصاب/ضرب عصفورين بحجر واحد *lit. he hit two birds with one stone*, where the verb *to kill* is used in the English idiom instead of أصاب or ضرب *hit*.

We need to watch out for false equivalents when dealing with source language idioms that look like borrowings. Some Arabic idioms have English counterparts that use similar metaphors but mean different things. The English idiom *to come full circle* is used to describe a situation in which a series of events or changes takes place, but things end up the way they started. The Arabic idiom اكتملت الدائرة *lit. the circle was completed*, conversely, describes a situation in which a process takes its natural course to the end, which is a very different state of affairs from the beginning, as in (31). The circle metaphor lends itself to both interpretations; when drawing a circle, the pen ends up where it started (the English idiom), but only when the drawing process is complete do we have a full circle (the Arabic idiom). This shows that idioms should not be taken for granted, even if they use the same metaphor.

(31) جريدة الأهرام (مصر)، ٦ أبريل ٢٠٠٧، العدد ٤٣٩٥٠.
اكتملت الدائرة إذن من المقاومة إلى المواجهة المسلحة إلى التسوية السلمية،
غير أن التعايش السلمي لم يتحقق بين الشعب الإسرائيلي والشعب المصري.

> The conflict between Egypt and Israel has run its course—
> from resistance to armed confrontation, and finally a peaceful
> settlement; but peaceful coexistence between the two peoples
> has not been achieved.

Idioms, like other semantically noncompositional phrases, are indirect ways of describing situations. If we can identify functionally equivalent English idioms, we can use them in the translation, provided they fit the context and the genre. However, there is no rule that requires us to translate Arabic idioms as English ones. We can simply use nonmetaphorical expressions to translate idioms, as long as the translation achieves the same communicative goals as the source phrase.

3 Translation Strategies

3.1 Morphological Packaging

In our discussion of word-level translation strategies, we saw that some morphologically complex words can be translated by unpacking them into phrases—and the reverse is also possible. We often encounter Arabic phrases that are best translated as morphologically complex English words. Basically, we use the rich derivational morphology of English to construct words from the equivalents of the words that make up Arabic phrases. For example, the complex prepositional phrase على غير المتوقع in (32) is used as a manner modifier that describes how the unemployment rate has jumped. Translating this phrase word for word gives us *on that which is not expected*, but this phrase cannot function as a manner modifier in English. What we need is to identify the part of the source phrase that carries its semantic focus, and to use English morphology to derive a word that has the function of the whole Arabic phrase. The semantic focus of على غير المتوقع is the passive participle متوقع *expected*, whereas غير encodes phrasal negation; thus, we can translate غير متوقع as *unexpected* by adding the negation prefix. The preposition على is used in this phrase to provide the grammatical structure that allows using it as a modifier. We can do the same in English by using the adverbial suffix *-ly*, resulting in *unexpectedly*.

(32) جريدة الدستور (الأردن)، ٥ أغسطس ٢٠٠٦، العدد ١٤٠٢٧.
أظهرت بيانات وزارة العمل الأمريكية أن معدل البطالة قفز **على غير المتوقع**
ليصل إلى ٤٫٨ في المائة.

The US Department of Labor data show that unemployment has
jumped unexpectedly to 4.8 percent.

We can use this strategy with many types of phrases, depending on the
available English derivation rules. English nominal morphology allows the
derivation of agentive nouns by adding the suffix -er, as in *provider* and *con-
sumer*. This gives us the option of translating collocations such as صانع الفخار
and صاحب العمل, which literally mean *the maker of pottery* and *the owner of
work* as *potter* and *employer*, respectively. The prefix *re-* is attached to verbs to
add the meaning of repetition, which makes it possible for us to translate the
verb phrases أعاد بناء *lit. returned building* and بناه مرة ثانية *lit. built it a second
time* as *rebuilt*. This strategy is so helpful that we can even use it with full
clauses, as in the case of لا يمكن الاستغناء عنه in (33). Morphological packaging gives us *indispensable* rather than *which is not possible to do away with*.

(33) مجلة العالم الرقمي (السعودية)، ٦ أبريل ٢٠٠٣، العدد ١٥.
لقد أصبحت الإنترنت بالفعل **لا يمكن الاستغناء عنها** لاقتصادنا.
The internet has indeed become indispensable for our economy.

What makes morphological packaging such a powerful translation strategy is that it is based on patterns rather than isolated random instances. For
example, translating لا يمكن الاستغناء عنها as *indispensable* is part of a larger
pattern. Arabic-embedded clauses with يمكن *be possible* followed by an event
nominal subject—such as يمكن قبوله *lit. accepting it is possible*, يمكن تصديقه
lit. believing it is possible, and يمكن كسره *lit. breaking it is possible*—can all
be translated as adjectives ending with -able, as in *acceptable, believable
/credible*, and *breakable*. We can use the same suffix to translate open collocations with قابل لـ *lit. susceptible to*, such as قابل للاشتعال *flammable*, قابل
للذوبان *soluble*, and قابل للعلاج *curable*. If the source phrase is negated, we can
incorporate the appropriate negation prefix, as in *unbelievable* and *incur-
able*. In these examples, we package full modifying phrasal structures into
morphologically complex adjectives that are essentially modifiers. Many
patterns likes these can be generated with different affixes and other word-
formation processes.

One thing to be aware of, however, is that English morphology is not always regular. If we were to treat these patterns as rules, we would end up with inaccurate translations. For example, many Arabic prepositional phrases with بلا *without* can be translated as nouns ending with the suffix *-less*. We can translate بلا معنى ,بلا هدف, and بلا قيمة, respectively, as *aimless*, *meaningless*, and *worthless*. However, we cannot translate بلا مساعدة in (34) as *helpless* because *helpless* does not mean the same thing as *without help*. The phrase بلا مساعدة in this sentence is used as a modifier describing how victims of paralysis can stand up using the new technology—they can stand up on their own, without anyone's assistance. But if we apply the same morphological packaging pattern, we end up changing the meaning. We need to be aware of morphological exceptions such as *helpless* versus *without help* and *irresponsible* versus *not responsible* to make sure our translation is accurate.

(34) جريدة الرياض (السعودية)، ٢٧ يناير ٢٠٠٣، العدد ١٢٦٣٨.
تقنية جديدة تمكن المشلولين من الوقوف **بلا مساعدة**: نجح مهندسون في جامعة غلاسكو في تمكين ضحايا الشلل من الوقوف والمحافظة على توازنهم لفترات طويلة.

A new technology allows paraplegics to stand up unaided:
Engineers at the University of Glasgow have succeeded in
enabling victims of paralysis to stand up and maintain their
balance for long periods of time.

Morphological packaging is not limited to using derivational morphemes. It also involves lexical packaging, whereby we use one English word to translate an Arabic phrase, provided they have the same referent. This type of morphological packaging is helpful when translating modified phrases that sound redundant in English, such as عملية جراحية *lit. a surgical operation* and صورة فوتوغرافية *lit. a photographic picture*, which can be translated as *surgery* and *photograph*. Moreover, lexical packaging is perfectly suited for many compounds, because we can ignore the internal structure of the source phrase and simply find the English term that has the same referent. For example, we do not need to translate التزحلق على الجليد word for word as *slipping on ice* because there is an English term for this activity, namely, *skiing*.

The two morphological packaging strategies—derivational and lexical— are not mutually exclusive. In fact, we often use both to translate the same phrase, as in the case of لا يعرف القراءة والكتابة in (35). The phrase يعرف القراءة

والكتابة literally means *knows reading and writing*, which does not collocate in English, whereas لا adds negation. A slightly improved word-for-word translation gives us *does not know how to read or write*, which is a valid translation, but rather verbose. The most common way to describe someone who knows how to read and write is the adjective *literate* (lexical packaging), which can be negated with the prefix *il-* (morphological packaging), giving us *illiterate*. The whole phrase لا يعرف القراءة والكتابة functions as a relative clause modifying أمريكيا *an American*; thus, we end up with *an American who is illiterate*.

(35) شبكة النبأ المعلوماتية (العراق)، ٩ فبراير ٢٠٠٨.
معظم المواطنين العرب لا يتصورون أن هناك أمريكيا لا يعرف القراءة والكتابة.
Most Arabs cannot imagine that there is an American who is illiterate.

It is important to note here that reducing a phrase to a single word is not a matter of aesthetics. First, we saw that many word-for-word translations of Arabic phrases result in English phrases that do not sound natural, whereas others are simply ungrammatical. Second, Arabic sentences tend to be rather long and structurally complicated compared with English sentences. If we did not try to control for sentence length, we might end up with very long and complicated run-on sentences with multiple embedded clauses. Using English morphology to reduce some Arabic phrases to words ensures that our translation will adhere to the conventions of English writing, and consequently it can be easily comprehended, which is the ultimate goal of translation.

3.2 Phrasal Reconstruction

Phrasal reconstruction is a strategy that involves using syntactic structures in the translation that are different from those in the source text. We have already seen a few examples of how this strategy works in our discussion of structural gaps. For instance, I translated the adjectival possessive phrase محدود السلطة as a full clause, namely, *his authority is limited*. In addition to helping with structural gaps, phrasal reconstruction is particularly useful when word-for-word translation yields strings of words that do not collocate in the target language. The phrase يشعر برغبة في in (36) literally means *he feels with a desire in*, which obviously does not collocate in English. We can modify the structure slightly to get *feels a desire to*, but the problem in this sentence is that *feels a desire to* does not work with *a break* or *take a break*. We need to make sure that the output phrase collocates internally and externally. The sentence in (36) is an excerpt from a book review, in which the reviewer describes a new novel as such a page turner that readers will not want to stop reading to take a break. To express the idea of not wanting to take a break in this context, we can apply reconstruction to translate يشعر برغبة في as *feel like*, which collocates with *taking a break*.

(36) جريدة الشرق الأوسط (السعودية)، ٨ مارس ٢٠٠٦، العدد ٩٩٦٢.
رواية زينب حفني الجديدة، الصادرة عن «دار الساقي» بعنوان «ملامح»
يتجرعها القارىء دفعة واحدة، دون أن **يشعر برغبة في** استراحة.

When reading Zainab Hufny's new novel *Features*, published by Dar Al-Saqi, one goes from cover to cover without feeling like taking a break.

Many translation patterns are based on phrasal reconstruction. Let us take the family of superlative constructions as an example. The most common way of expressing superlative relations in Arabic is to use the adjectival morphological template أفعل followed by a noun, as in أكبر مشكلة *the biggest problem* and أجمل مدينة *the most beautiful city*. When we translate phrases of this kind, we simply use their structural equivalents in English. Arabic, however, allows certain variations in superlative constructions that are not permissible in English. For example, a superlative adjective can be incorporated into a possessive phrase followed by an adverbial modifier, as in أكثرها صعوبة and أكثر مهام محركات البحث أهمية in (37). This phrasal construction constitutes a gap in English, because the phrases *the most of search engine tasks difficultly/in terms of difficulty* and *the most of them importantly/in terms of importance* are outright ungrammatical. This is not a complicated problem because we can still reconstruct these phrases using the standard ways of expressing superlative relations in English and translate them as *the most difficult* and *the most important*. Reconstruction allows us to generalize the basic target language superlative pattern to complex source language superlative constructions.

(37) جريدة الغد (الأردن)، ٤ أغسطس ٢٠٠٨، العدد ٩٩٣٢.
لعل **أكثر** مهام محركات **البحث صعوبة**، لكن في نفس الوقت **أكثرها أهمية**،
ألا وهي تقييم أهمية الصفحات المنشورة على الشبكة.

Perhaps the most difficult task for search engines, yet the most important, is evaluating web pages.

The phrase الأكثر استفادة in (38) has the same grammatical structure as the superlative constructions in (37), but there is no English superlative adjective that describes someone who benefits the most from something, as in the odd phrase *most beneficiary*. Instead, we can still use *most* to maintain the superlative function while reconstructing the adjectival phrase as a verb phrase, resulting in *benefit the most*. This example does not undermine the value of the superlative translation pattern discussed above because the complexity of this particular sentence has to do with a lexical gap in English.

(38) مجلة العلم (مصر)، ١ فبراير ٢٠٠٩، العدد ٣٨٩.
وأهم نتيجة خرجت بها الدراسة كانت أن الديمقراطيين هم **الأكثر استفادة** من شبكة الإنترنت في الدعاية.

The most important conclusion of the study is that the Democrats are the ones who benefit the most from using the internet in campaigning.

Arabic constructions that express superlative relations include possessive constructions made up of two nouns derived from the same root, where the first noun is singular and the second one is plural, such as مشكلة المشاكل *lit. the problem of the problems* in (39). We can try to make our translation more natural by adding the quantifier *all*, resulting in *the problem of all problems*, which is a valid translation, but this expression is rather uncommon. Besides, it is used as a technical term in philosophical discourse and certain religious genres, which is not the case here. We can manipulate the structure by translating the first noun as a superlative adjective and deleting the preposition. This would give us *the most problematic problem*; but this translation candidate still falls short of sounding fully natural in English. Another option is to reconstruct the phrase by substituting the superlative adjective with another that fits better in this context, as in *the biggest problem*. Note that this is only a translation candidate; there might be better ways of translating this phrase, especially when we consider the sentence as a whole. For instance, we can incorporate lexical substitution with reconstruction and translate مشكلة المشاكل as *the source of all problems*. Alternatively, we can use a figurative expression that idiomatically maintains the superlative relation, such as *the mother of all problems*.

(39) جريدة الصباح (العراق)، ٩ فبراير ٢٠٠٨.
تشكل أزمة السكن في العراق **مشكلة المشاكل**، والتصدي لحلها يعني حل
العديد من المشاكل الناتجة عنها.
The housing crisis is the source of all problems in Iraq, and
dealing with it means solving a lot of resulting problems.

The reason we consider phrasal reconstruction a pattern-based strategy
rather than a rule-based strategy is that the patterns we develop do not
work all the time. For example, the pattern discussed above does not work
in the case of أستاذ الأساتذة *lit. the teacher of the teachers* in (40). A close
translation, such as *the teacher of all teachers*, is unacceptable because it
does not mean the same thing as the source phrase. Besides, the phrase *the
teacher of all teachers* is often used in religious discourse to describe faith
leaders, but this particular sentence is about an educator, not a saint or a
prophet. Reconstructing this phrase by substituting the first noun with a
related superlative adjective gives us *the most instructive teacher*; but again,
this is not what the source phrase means. If we resort to the context to
change the lexical content—say, by using *the wisest teacher*—we get close.
Perhaps a better strategy here is to use lexical packaging and translate أستاذ
الأساتذة as *master teacher*.

(40) جريدة الجزيرة (السعودية)، ٢٢ يونيو ٢٠٠٧، العدد ١٢٦٨٥.
هذا رجل قضى في مجال التعليم سبعين سنة، فهو بحق **أستاذ الأساتذة**.
This is a man who spent seventy years of his life working in
education; he is a true master teacher.

Although phrasal reconstruction is mostly pattern based, some such patterns are fairly consistent. For example, clause–initial prepositional phrases
with من *from*, followed by a definite adjective and a sentential subject with
أن *that*, can almost always be translated as *it is (adjective) that/for/to*, a
construction known as *it-cleft*. Applying this rule to the sentences below, we
can translate من الواضح أن in (41) as *it is clear that*, من النادر أن in (42) as *it is
rare to*, and من الصعب أن in (43) as *it is difficult for*. The choice among *that*,
for, and *to* depends on the selection restrictions of the embedded English
clause—that is, it is independent of the Arabic source phrases.

(41) نشرة مركز الدراسات السياسية والاقتصادية (مصر)، ١ يناير ٢٠٠١.
من الواضح أن الطبقة الوسطى هي أحد أهم القوى الممتنعة عن التصويت.

It is clear that the middle class constitutes one of the most important social forces that refrains from voting.

(42) جريدة المستقبل (لبنان)، ٨ نوفمبر ٢٠٠٧، العدد ٢٧٨٦.

الذي ساعدني هو تفكير أهلي، وأعلم أنه **من النادر** أن نجد أهلا يفكرون بهذه الطريقة.

What helped me is the way my family thinks, and I know that it is rare to find a family that thinks this way.

(43) جريدة الرياض (السعودية)، ٥ أبريل ٢٠٠٨، العدد ١٤١٦٤.

من الصعب على المؤلف أن يصنف هو روايته فهذا أمر عادة ما يترك للنقاد.

It is difficult for an author to classify his or her novel. Usually, this is left to the critics.

With phrasal reconstruction, we can delete or add a phrasal constituent or even use a grammatical structure that is completely different from the one in the source phrase, as long as the output has the same communicative function as the source phrase. However, we should not think of phrasal reconstruction rules and patterns as our only options, no matter how regular or accurate they may be. These patterns can help us generate possible translation candidates, and as translators we should consult our intuitions regarding which candidates fit best within the context.

3.3 Translation by Deletion

The translation approach we are following here is a functional one. Basically, we analyze source language phrases to identify their communicative functions, such as referring or attributing properties to entities and events. Then, we look for target language words, expressions, or phrasal constructions with the same functions that fit in the context. We can modify some of the lexical and/or structural aspects of phrases, and we can also delete them altogether, if they are deemed functionally redundant when translated. A phrase is functionally redundant if its lexical content is already encoded somewhere else in the sentence. For example, in (44) we have the reduced relative clause يمتهن الزراعة *who works in agriculture* and لا يقرأ ولا يكتب *who does not read or write*, both of which are lexically entailed by the nouns they modify. By definition, a farmer is someone who works in agriculture, and an illiterate person is someone who does not read or write.

Because these definitions are functionally redundant, we do not lose anything by deleting them.

(44) جريدة النهار (لبنان)، ١٠ فبراير ٢٠٠٩، العدد ٥١٨.
بطل القصة هو سعيد بن سليم اليطاشي وهو مزارع **يمتهن الزراعة** وصيد
الأسماك، وسعيد رجل أمي **لا يقرأ ولا يكتب** وهو إنسان عادي فقير ولم يسبق
له أن عمل عملا خارقا.

The hero in this story is Saeed Bin-Salim Al-Yatashi, an illiterate
farmer and fisherman. He is an ordinary, poor man who never did
anything extraordinary.

These phrases are not functionally redundant in Arabic, however. The
reduced relative clause يمتهن الزراعة *who works in agriculture* is structurally motivated, because it provides the grammatical structure that allows
the conjoined noun phrase وصيد الأسماك *and fishing*. This seemingly redundant phrase also allows the writer to avoid the restrictive readings of مزارع
يصيد الأسماك *a farmer who works in fishing* and مزارع يمتهن صيد الأسماك *a
farmer who fishes*, whereby Saeed could be understood to be a farmer who
does not farm anymore but instead fishes, or as a farmer whose hobby
is to go fishing. As for لا يقرأ ولا يكتب *who does not read or write*, this is a
rhetorically motivated phrase that helps maintain consistency in the length
and structure of clauses. Because these functions do not apply to English, we do not need to include these relative clauses in our translation. To
maintain the rhetorical structure of the translation, we can use *illiterate* as
an adjective modifying *farmer*, and apply morphological packaging to the
literal candidate *someone who works in catching fish* and translate it as
fisherman.

Sometimes, we can apply deletion when word-for-word translations yield
phrases that do not collocate in English. For example, in (45) we have the
collocation يختفي عن الأعين *lit. disappear from the eyes*, but this literal translation does not collocate in English. Because the English equivalent of the
semantic focus of this collocation—namely, the verb *disappear*—does not
need to be further qualified, we can safely delete the rest of the phrase. The
prepositional phrase عن الأعين *from the eyes* is relevant in the Arabic text
because it contrasts with a similar collocation—namely, يختفي عن الأسماع *lit.
disappear from the ears*—which is equivalent to *nobody hears about him*.
However, this motivation does not apply to English, and thus deleting the
prepositional phrase does not incur any loss of meaning.

(45) جريدة اليوم (السعودية)، ٢٨ يوليو ٢٠٠٣، العدد ١١٠٠٠.
أما القصة الأخيرة فهي قصة الحاج محمد عزام الذي بدأ حياته في المنطقة
كماسح أحذية ثم **اختفى عن الأعين**.

The last story is about Hajj Mohammad Azzam, who started
his life in the neighborhood as a shoeshine boy but later
disappeared.

When translating collocations, we need to make sure that the output
phrases are internally and externally coherent—that is, their constituent
words collocate together and with adjacent phrases as well. The Arabic collocation قرن من الزمان *a century of time* in (46) can be translated word for
word because its constituents collocate in English, even though it is not a
very common expression. The problem, however, is that *a century of time*
does not collocate with the adverb *ago*, as in *a century of time ago*. Because
a century is by definition a unit of time, we do not need to include the redundant prepositional phrase *of time*.

(46) جريدة الشرق الأوسط (السعودية)، ٦ نوفمبر ٢٠٠٨، العدد ١٠٩٣٦.
وكانت السيدة ماري بيكر أدي هي التي أسست «كريستيان ساينس مونيتور»
قبل **قرن من الزمان** على أساس أن «لا تجرح أحدا ولكن تبارك جميع البشر.»
It was Mary Baker Eddy who founded the *Christian Science
Monitor* a century ago, with the mission "to injure no man, but
to bless all mankind."

Like most lexical issues, there is no clear rule that tells us where to delete
phrases that would sound redundant if included in the translation. Therefore,
lexical deletion is applied on a case-by-case basis to make sure it does not
cause significant translation losses. There are, however, some structural patterns in which we can predict deletion. For example, whenever we have a singular noun modified by a prepositional phrase with من *from* followed by the
unmodified plural form of that noun, we can delete the prepositional phrase.
In (47), for instance, we have the noun phrase مشكلة من المشكلات *lit. a problem
from the problems*, in which the indefinite singular noun refers to an uniden-
tified problem, whereas the plural noun refers to the generic set of problems.
The function of the whole phrase in this context is to tell us that citizenship
was not a member of the set of problems, which is uninformative because we
do not know what kind of problems are in this set. To avoid the redundancy
and vagueness of *citizenship was not a problem from among problems*, we

can leave out the prepositional phrase altogether and end up with *citizenship was not a problem*. The sense of vagueness created by this construction is deliberate, for it emphasizes negation—that is, citizenship was not a problem of any kind. To maintain this rhetorical function, we can translate the negation marker as *never*.

(47) جريدة الراية (قطر)، ٦ نوفمبر ٢٠٠٨، العدد ٩٦٧٩.
لم تكن المواطنة **مشكلة من المشكلات** طيلة تاريخ الإسلام لأن ديار الإسلام التي كانت مؤلفة من أكثر من القارة الآسيوية والقارة الإفريقية، وبعض أجزاء أوروبا كانت على رغم تنوع شعوبها أشبه بالدولة الواحدة.

Citizenship was never a problem throughout the history of Islam, because the Muslim community, which included large parts of Asia and Africa as well as some parts of Europe, was similar to a single state, despite the diversity of its peoples.

This deletion pattern applies to most instances of this construction, but the strategies we use to compensate for deletion are always context dependent. After all, we are not translating isolated phrases. The sentence in (48) has two phrases in which we expect deletion; these are يوم من الأيام *lit. a day from the days* and مشكلة من المشاكل *lit. a problem from the problems*. If we leave out من الأيام *from the days*, we end up with *a day*, which we can change into the adverbial phrase *one day*, because the source phrase is a modifier. This strategy gives us *corporal punishment was not one day a way*, but this is not an acceptable translation, because *one day* does not co-occur with negation. Here, we need to apply substitution in addition to deletion, and to use the polarity item that fits in negative contexts—namely, *never*—yielding *corporal punishment was never*. In the case of مشكلة من المشاكل, applying deletion gives us *a way of solving a problem*. However, the indefinite noun phrase *a problem* is odd in this context because it is uninformative; we do not know which problem or what kind of problem we are talking about. To avoid the vague indefinite noun, we can delete it, along with the preposition, and end up with the bare generic plural noun, as in *a way of solving problems*. Alternatively, we can keep the indefinite singular noun and add the quantifier *any*, as in *a way of solving any problem*, where the quantified phrase has the same function as the bare plural.

(48) جريدة الفرات (سوريا)، ٢٩ يونيو ٢٠٠٦، العدد ٥٩٥.
العقوبة الجسدية لم تكن في **يوم من الأيام** أسلوبا لحل **مشكلة من المشاكل**.

Corporal punishment was never a way of solving problems.

If the prepositional phrase with من *from* is modified by an adjective or a relative clause, we need to apply phrasal reconstruction before deletion. For example, in (49), we have the complex adjectival phrase السياسية الداخلية *domestic political*, which modifies the plural noun قضايا *issues*. If we delete the prepositional phrase, we also lose the adjectival phrase because it is part of its structure. Instead, we can apply reconstruction and use the adjectival phrase to modify the singular noun, and then delete the prepositional phrase. This gives us *a domestic political issue*.

(49) جريدة الشرق الأوسط (السعودية)، ٢٣ يونيو ٢٠٠٢، العدد ٨٦٠٨.
إنها ليست قضية دولية، بل مجرد **قضية من القضايا** السياسية الداخلية.
It is not an international issue; it is just a domestic political issue.

Inserting ellipses is essentially a language–internal deletion process, but it can be useful as a translation strategy. We often use elliptical constructions to avoid repetition when the missing material can be easily retrieved from the context or previous discourse. When we say *They all went to the movie theater, but Peter did not*, we understand that the negation marker *not* is followed by the verb phrase *go to the movie theater*. If someone says *My favorite sport is football, but my wife's is basketball*, we know that there is a missing noun phrase after *my wife's*, namely, *favorite sport*. Deletion is also allowed following question words, usually in embedded clauses, in an elliptical construction known as sluicing. For example, when someone says *I left my car keys, but I cannot remember where*, we understand that *where* is followed by *I left my car keys*, which is deleted to avoid the unnecessary repetition. There are also several conjunctive ellipsis constructions, which involve using elliptical conjunctions that mark the location and syntactic nature of the elided phrase, as in *I play the guitar, and John does too*, and *I did not watch that movie, and neither did my friend*.

Elliptical constructions are not as common in Arabic as they are in English. In fact, some of the constructions I mentioned above are completely ungrammatical in Arabic. For example, if we were to translate *My favorite sport is football, but my wife's is basketball* into Arabic, we would need to spell out the elided phrase. Other elliptical constructions in contemporary Arabic are very similar to their English counterparts. We see, for instance, cases of sluicing, such as that in (50), where the clause لا أعرف لماذا can be translated directly as *I do not know why*. Because we are dealing with parallel constructions here, translating Arabic phrases with sluicing is not a problem.

(50) جريدة أخبار اليوم (مصر)، ١٣ فبراير ٢٠٠٨، العدد ١٧٤١٦.

أحب شتاء الإسكندرية لكني **لا أعرف لماذا**.

I love winter in Alexandria, but I do not know why.

We can use ellipses as a translation strategy if the source Arabic phrase includes information that is either repeated or is easily inferable from the context. The rule here is to use ellipses only when appropriate in English. For example, we can use sluicing to translate السبب الذي فعل هذا من أجله in (51) as *why* instead of the word-for-word candidate *the reason for which he did this.*

(51) جريدة أخبار الأدب (مصر)، ٢٨ يوليو ٢٠٠٧، العدد ٧٣٣.

بعد أن مات ألبيرت أينشتين بانفجار في الأورطى في ١٨ أبريل ١٩٥٥، تم الاحتفاظ بمخه لإجراء الأبحاث الطبية عليه. لكن الذي لا يعرفه الكثيرون هو أن طبيب العيون ـ هنري أبرامز ـ قد احتفظ أيضا بعيني عالم الفيزياء العظيم. ومن غير المعروف على وجه التحديد السبب **الذي فعل هذا من أجله**.

When Albert Einstein died of a heart failure on April 18, 1955,
his brain was preserved for medical research. What many do not
know is that Henry Abrams, Einstein's ophthalmologist, kept
his eyes as well, but nobody knows exactly why.

Ellipses work well in conjunction with other translation strategies. The sentence ومن غير المعروف على وجه التحديد السبب الذي فعل هذا من أجله requires various interdependent strategies. With من غير المعروف, we can follow the pattern we discussed above and translate it as *it is not known*, but we can also reconstruct it as *nobody knows*. The prepositional phrase على وجه التحديد is an open collocation that literally means *on the face of specifying*, which does not make sense in English. This collocation functions as a modifier; therefore, we need to replace it with a functionally equivalent adverb, such as *specifically* or *exactly*. This leaves us with several candidate translations, including *it is not known exactly why he did this/so, why exactly he did this—nobody knows,* and *nobody knows exactly why,* among many others.

Regardless of the strategies we use, we need to make sure that the translation candidates we choose are functionally equivalent to the Arabic source phrases. In (52) we need to do something about the clause أن تفعل غير ما فعلت *to do other than that which it had done* because this close translation is rather complicated. Ellipses can be very helpful here, because we can use *otherwise* to replace the whole prepositional phrase with the reduced relative clause. This gives us *(they) did not expect the American administration to do otherwise*. We can also apply phrasal reconstruction and lexical substitution to end up with *they did not expect the American administration to act differently*. Both strategies give us valid candidates, because the outputs describe the same idea expressed in the source phrase.

(52) جريدة القدس (المملكة المتحدة)، ٢٤ يناير ٢٠٠٨.

إن العرب وأهل غزة على رأسهم لم يتوقعوا من الإدارة الأميركية **أن تفعل غير ما فعلت**.

The Arabs, and the Gazans in particular, did not expect the
American administration to do otherwise.

Deletion is quite an effective translation strategy, but we need to use our discretion when applying it. We need to limit deletion to functionally and lexically redundant phrases that have the potential of disrupting the cohesion of the translation.

3.4 *Literalization*   *Translate the meaning and not word by word*

We saw above that idioms are figurative expressions that are conventionally associated with descriptions of specific situations. For example, when we say *She turned a deaf ear to our request*, what we really mean is that she ignored our request. We have also discussed the different kinds of relations between Arabic and English idioms. Borrowed idioms—such as العودة إلى المربع الأول *back to square one* (*lit. returning to the first square*), and those with functional equivalents, such as صفر اليدين *empty handed* (*lit. zero handed*)—are not problematic. We can simply back-translate them if they are borrowings from English, or we can use their functional equivalents, even if they use different metaphors, as long as they describe the same situations. The problem is culture-specific idioms because these have no true functional equivalents in the target language, and obviously we cannot just translate them word for word. This is where literalization is most useful, as we can simply spell out the situation description associated with the Arabic idiom by providing a nonfigurative translation, just like we did when explaining the meaning of *She turned a deaf ear to our request*.

The expression أكمل نصف دينه in (53), which literally means *completed half his religion*, is an idiom that describes getting married. This idiom is derived from a *hadith*, or a saying, of the Prophet Muhammad, in which he stresses the value of marriage. The problem is that such a strong association between marriage and religion does not transfer well to English. There are several

English idioms that mean *getting married*, such as *tie the knot*, *get hitched*, *take one's vows*, and *walk down the aisle*. We cannot use *tie the knot* or *get hitched* because they are too informal for the context of the Arabic source sentence, which is taken from a marriage announcement in a newspaper. Nor can we use *take one's vows* or *walk down the aisle*, because they have different religious and social meanings. Probably the safest way to deal with أكمل نصف دينه is to avoid metaphorical language altogether and to translate it as *he got married*. This solution makes it easier to eliminate the redundancy of the prepositional phrase بزواجه *by his marrying*, which we can delete.

(53) جريدة عكاظ (السعودية)، 19 ديسمبر 2006، العدد 2366.

في ليلة ربيعية من ليالي جازان أكمل الشاب محمد أحمد حيدري نصف دينه بزواجه من ابنة محمد صغير مغفوري.

On a fine spring evening in the city of Gazan, Muhammad
Ahmad Haydari got married to the daughter of Muhammad
Sagheer Maghfoury.

Literalization is also helpful with some compounds and other semantically noncompositional expressions. The compound عقد قران in (54) literally means *signing a marriage contract*, but if we use word-for-word translation, we mistakenly profile the wedding as an unromantic business deal. The problem is that no such connotations are available in the Arabic source sentence; the compound is simply a formal way of saying *getting married*. Nor can we use any of the English marriage idioms mentioned above, because they are not functionally equivalent to the Arabic idiom in this particular context. One solution is to say exactly what the expression means in nonfigurative language and to thus translate it as *wedding*.

(54) جريدة عكاظ (السعودية)، 9 ديسمبر 2007، العدد 2366.

أعلن القصر الملكي الأردني مساء السبت أنه تم **عقد قران** الأميرة هيا بنت الحسين على الشيخ محمد بن راشد آل مكتوم، ولي العهد ووزير الدفاع في دولة الإمارات العربية المتحدة.

The Jordanian Royal Palace announced Saturday evening the
wedding of Her Highness Princess Haya Bint Al-Hussein and
Crown Prince Sheikh Mohammad Bin Rashid Al-Maktoum,
defense minister of the United Arab Emirates.

Culture-specific figurative expressions, such as شعرة معاوية *lit. Muawiya's hair* in (55), can be rather challenging to translate because most speakers of English do not have the cultural background necessary to interpret them. For example, they might not know who Muawiya was or why his "hair" is significant. In fact, many native speakers of Arabic do not know the origin or the background of this expression either; they only know how to use it. This expression goes back to a political speech by Muawiya Bin Abi Sufyan, who founded the Umayyad Dynasty and ruled as caliph between AD 661 and 680. In this speech, he outlines his policy using the analogy of hair that binds him to people—if they pulled on it, he would loosen; and if they loosened, he would pull, but he would not let it break. Basically, this analogy has to do with compromise and diplomacy; no matter what the political differences are (i.e., how much someone pulls on that hair), he would resolve them peacefully. Attempting to use an analogy to translate this expression can be risky because similar metaphors, such as *a tug of war*, involve attempting to overpower the opponents, which is the opposite of the Muawiya's hair analogy. Literalization offers a straightforward solution, for we can translate the phrase as *diplomacy*. Note that we use another metaphor to translate قطعت بالكامل *lit. was severed completely* because this phrase is dependent on the hair metaphor.

[handwritten: The delicate give and take with the US has severed completely.]

(55) جريدة الجزيرة (السعودية)، ٢٧ يناير ٢٠٠٧، العدد ١٢٥٣٩.

إن إيران تعرف جيدا أن **شعرة معاوية** بينها وبين الولايات المتحدة قد قطعت بالكامل.

[handwritten: last straw]

Iran knows very well that diplomacy with the United States has reached a dead end.

[handwritten: The thread broke]

There are good reasons why writers use metaphors: They help establish tone, they have connotations and social meanings, and they are an integral component of style. Using literal language to translate metaphors comes at the expense of losing a potentially important part of the message. This is why we should think of literalization as a translation strategy of last resort.

3.5 Metaphorical Approximation

Metaphorical approximation involves translating idioms and frozen expressions using figurative expressions in the target language that are not true functional equivalents but are close enough. The motivation for this strategy is that sometimes we want to maintain the figurative nature of the source text because idioms invoke connotations that are not always accessible from nonfigurative language. For example, when people choose to say *He dropped the ball* instead of *He made a mistake*, they make their statement less accusatory while toning down the gravity of the mistake—probably because they are using a sports idiom. These connotations and undertones can be very important, and thus using metaphorical language can help us maintain them.

Let us take the idiom أبكي على الأطلال *lit. I cry over the ruins* in (56) as an example. This expression comes from a common prelude in Classical Arabic poetry, in which a poet reminisces about the woman he loves while contemplating the remains of her deserted home following the departure of her community. The idiom, which describes yearning for the past, has lost its association with the Bedouin lifestyle, whereby tribal groups changed location depending on the season, separating lovers in the process. Obviously, word-for-word translation is not going to help us, because most speakers of English do not know what ruins are being talked about or how they relate to the love story described in the source text. We can translate أظل أبكي على الأطلال using a nonfigurative phrase, such as *to keep lamenting the past*, but it does not carry the same undertones of the source phrase. Instead, we can use English idioms, such as *stuck in the past* or *hung up on the past*. These idioms are not true equivalents of أبكي على الأطلال because they do not have the same social meanings, but they convey the same basic idea while fitting naturally in the context.

(56) مجلة جميلة (قطر)، يونيو ٢٠٠٦، العدد ٦٨.
عشت قصة حب واحدة في حياتي لكن للأسف انتهى الأمر ولا يعقل أن أظل
أبكي على الأطلال.

I fell in love only once in my life, but unfortunately, it came to
an end, and it makes no sense to stay stuck in the past.

The frozen expression في حيص بيص in (57) presents an interesting case in which metaphorical approximation proves to be quite helpful. The archaic words حيص and بيص do not mean anything by themselves in Modern Standard Arabic. The expression is completely fixed; as a result, word-for-word translation is impossible. This expression describes a situation in which someone is surprised and very confused. Several English expressions have similar meanings, such as *a deer in the headlights, caught off guard, caught by surprise*, and *in utter confusion*. The problem is that in this particular sentence, في حيص بيص acquires additional connotations from the context, namely, the sense of embarrassment and the inability to take action. The text, which describes a government blunder, has a pervasively sarcastic tone, as indicated by the expression كوكب الحكومة *Planet Government*. The writer describes a situation in which government officials were surprised and embarrassed to find out that the new subway line goes over a water main and they had no idea what to do about it. What we need here is an expression that describes the elements of surprise and confusion (the original meaning of the frozen expression) as well as the sense of embarrassment and inability to act (the added meaning). The expression *caught with one's pants down* fits this profile, even though it is not a true equivalent of في حيص بيص. We can choose *caught with their pants down* over the other candidates because it also maintains the humorous effect intended in the source text.

(57) جريدة الأخبار (مصر)، ٦ مارس ٢٠٠٧، العدد ١٧١٢١.
من عجائب كوكب الحكومة أنها لم تتسلم خريطة مواسير مياه القاهرة من الشركة الأجنبية، ولهذا وقعوا **في حيص بيص** عندما اكتشفوا أنهم مدوا قضبان مترو هليوبوليس فوق ماسورة مياه رئيسية.

One of the amazing things about Planet Government is that they did not get the map that shows Cairo's water network from the foreign contractor. This is why they were caught with their pants down when they realized that the Heliopolis subway tracks go over a water main.

3.6 Metaphorization

This translation strategy is the reverse of literalization, in that we use common English idioms to translate semantically compositional Arabic phrases. Metaphorization is particularly helpful when we identify English metaphors that capture the connotations that we would risk losing with literal translations. For example, the phrase صرخ بأعلى صوته *He screamed in his loudest voice* in (58) can be translated as *He screamed at the top of his lungs*. Both translations are valid, but in this particular case, we have a narrative style that describes intense emotions of franticness and desperation. The close translation *He screamed in his loudest voice* does not directly express these connotations. Using an English idiom with the same communicative function as the source phrase preserves stylistic elements and connotations.

(58) جريدة الوطن (السعودية)، ٢٢ فبراير ٢٠٠٨، العدد ٢٧٠٢.
رأيته واقفا خارج المسجد يستجلي وجوه الداخلين ويتمعن فيها، وحين اقتربت منه وهممت بدخول المسجد **صرخ بأعلى صوته** وقال «إنه هو، هو.»

I saw him standing outside the mosque studying the faces of the people walking in. When I got closer, and just as I was stepping in, he screamed at the top of his lungs, "It is him. It is him."

The translation strategies we have discussed in this chapter are complementary. If we have a semantically noncompositional phrase that is problematic, we can translate it using literal language. And we can also use metaphorical expressions to translate semantically compositional phrases. If the source Arabic phrase has a structure that is not permissible in English, we can reconstruct it by adding, deleting, or substituting its constituents. All these strategies aim to make sure that the translation achieves the communicative functions of the source text. What we need to bear in mind is that the purpose of translation strategies is to generate candidate translations that we can examine and compare, so as to finally be able to choose the optimal one. The decision as to which candidate fares best has to do with the text genre, the tone, and the structure of the sentence as a whole. These are issues that we discuss at length in the following chapters.

Exercises

Exercise 1: Identifying Translation Problems

Describe the difficulties that might arise when one translates the underlined phrases. What translation strategies can you use to resolve them?

(1) جريدة الوطن (السعودية)، ٧ فبراير ٢٠٠٦، العدد ١٣٧٤٢.
وقال إنه عمل مع قبطان العبارة المنكوبة في أكثر من رحلة وإن الأمور كانت تسير **على ما يرام**، وإن ما حدث **أمر لا يمكن أن يصدقه عقل**.

(2) جريدة الأيام (اليمن)، ١٤ يونيو ٢٠٠٨، العدد ٥٤٢٨.
لقد **تم دخول** موكلي المواطن مختار حمود الشبوطي إلى إحدى المستشفيات العامة في عدن **لإجراء عملية استئصال الزائدة الدودية**.

(3) جلال أمين، ٢٠٠٢، "وصف مصر في نهاية القرن العشرين"، دار الشروق، القاهرة، ص ١٢١.
وما الخطأ في وجود **الغنى الفاحش** إلى جانب **الفقر المدقع** مادام الغني يدفع ما يطلب منه من ضرائب؟

insufficient

2 days ago

MB's, President of Kurdistan Region, talk must be taken extremely seriously.

(4) جريدة أوان (الكويت)، ١٩ نوفمبر ٢٠٠٩، العدد ٧٢٦.

الكلام الذي نقل عن رئيس إقليم كردستان مسعود بارزاني منذ يومين يتعين أن **يؤخذ على محمل الجد في** أقصاه.

on us

extreme

It must be said that the semi Judiciary satisfaction of the isolation in the social cases participated somehow

(5) جريدة الاتحاد (الإمارات)، ٢١ أبريل ٢٠٠٦، العدد ١١٩٧٨.

لابد من القول إن شبه الاكتفاء التحكيمي والقضائي والانعزال في القضايا الاجتماعية ساهم **بشكل من الأشكال في** توسيع الفجوة بين الجالية المسلمة والمجتمع المضيف العريض.

minimal

in increasing the gap between the Muslim population + the hosting society.

in one form or another

Exercise 2: Light Verbs

The underlined phrases are light verb constructions, a subcategory of collocations (for more on light verbs, see exercise 2 in the answer key; and for examples of light verbs, see appendix G). How can they be translated?

(1) جريدة المدى (العراق)، ٢٢ أبريل ٢٠٠٨، العدد ١٢٠٣.

كلما حاول أن **يلقي نكتة**، تخونه تعابير الوجه أو يكون توقيته سيئاً، فلا يضحك أحد مما يقول.

say a joke

(2) جريدة الوسط (البحرين)، ٢٤ يناير ٢٠٠٩، العدد ٢٣٣٢.

أنا عن نفسي فقد **أخذت قراراً** من فترة وجيزة، وهو أن أتعامل مع الناس المزاجيين بالضبط كما هم يتعاملون معي.

I have decided

(3) جريدة أوان (الكويت)، ٢ أكتوبر ٢٠٠٨، العدد ٣١٧.

فالزعيم الجديد للحزب الاشتراكي الديمقراطي معارض صنديد للوحدة الأوروبية، وكان قد **قطع وعداً** لناخبيه بأن يخضع الاتفاقات الأوروبية لاستفتاء شعبي.

promised this voters

(4) جريدة الرياض (السعودية)، ٢٧ يوليو ٢٠٠٦، العدد ١٣٩١٢.

أعتقد أن المبنى هو الذي يفرض ثقافته على المجتمع والمدينة والإقليم والبلد بل وحتى يمكنه أن يكون عالمي الثقافة، **وأضرب مثالاً** لذلك برج إيفل في باريس حيث إنه عندما بني قبل عدة عقود اعتبره بعض معماري ذلك الوقت كارثة معمارية.

for example

(5) جريدة الصحافة (السودان)، ١٨ مارس ٢٠٠٨، العدد ٥٢٩٧.

طرح سؤالاً آخر وهو كيف يمكن أن نتفادى مشكلة التدخل الأجنبي؟

asked another

(6) مجلة مركز الأهرام للدراسات السياسية والاستراتيجية (مصر)، ١٥ مارس ٢٠٠٩، العدد ٢٩.

أثار حكم المحكمة الإدارية العليا صدمة للفريق القانوني الذي **رفع دعوى** وقف تصدير الغاز لإسرائيل.

filed a lawsuit

bade = stop

issued

(7) جريدة البيان (الإمارات)، ٢٨ فبراير ٢٠١٠، العدد ١٠٨٤٧.
أبدى سفير مملكة الدنمارك لدى السعودية هانز كلينغنبيرغ **اعتذار** حكومة بلاده للمسلمين في العالم بشأن الرسوم المسيئة للرسول محمد التي نشرتها صحيفة دنماركية.

(8) جريدة السفير (لبنان)، ٢٨ يناير ٢٠١٠، العدد ١١٥٠٤.
يعود الشاب الذي ينهي دراسته في نيويورك إلى مصر. وعندما تكتشف لولا سفره تقرر اللحاق به، تبيع مقتنياتها كلها لتتمكن من **قطع تذكرة** الطائرة.

book, obtain, buy

(9) جريدة الاقتصادية (السعودية)، ١٣ فبراير ٢٠١٠، العدد ٥٩٦٩.
شهدت مدينة ويسلر الكندية مراسم تأبين هادئة الليلة الماضية للجورجي نودار كوماريتاشفيلي **الذي لقي مصرعه** إثر حادث فقد خلاله السيطرة على المزلقة خلال المران الأخير الذي أجري أمس الجمعة استعدادا لسباق التزلج بالمزلقة في أولمبياد فانكوفر.

passed away, kicked the bucket, pushing up daisy

(10) محمد سعيد مرسي، ١٩٩٧، "فن تربية الأولاد في الإسلام"، دار الطباعة والنشر الإسلامية، ص ٧٧.
من الخطأ تماما أن **يعقد الأب مقارنة** بين درجة التحصيل عند طفله بالنسبة لغيره من الأطفال.

compares

Exercise 3: Idioms

How would you translate the underlined idioms?

what = to sharpen

(1) محمد رجب النجار، ١٩٧٨، "جحا العربي"، سلسلة عالم المعرفة، الكويت، ص ٧٤.
ويمكن أن نقول إن الاعتصام بالدين فيما يشبه النزعة التصوفية، والاعتصام بالفكاهة والمجون **وجهان لعملة واحدة**.

2 sides of 1 coin / the same

(2) موقع قناة العربية (السعودية)، ١٢ يناير ٢٠٠٨.
الخطة الإنكليزية كانت تتضمن تقديم اللاعب إلى بليون ونصف البليون مشاهد حول العالم، ولكن الأمور لم تسر كما يجب، **وجاءت الريح بما لا تشتهي السفن** ففقد القحطاني وربما فقدت الكرة السعودية واحدة من أجمل الفرص التي كانت متاحة أمامنا.

undesirable outcome

(3) جريدة الرياض (السعودية)، ١٦ نوفمبر ٢٠٠٦، العدد ١٤٠٢٤.
جاءت أبرز أسباب تأييد النساء للقرار كالتالي: اقتحام المرأة لكافة المجالات ووقوفها **ندا لند** أمام الرجل.

on the same footing / face to face / toe to toe / manooh mano

(4) جريدة الأهرام (مصر)، ١٣ نوفمبر ٢٠٠٩، العدد ٤٤٩٠٢.
مشروع تطوير هضبة الأهرامات يسير **على قدم وساق** وذلك تنفيذا للبرنامج الزمني المطروح للمشروع والذي من المقرر أن تنتهي جميع الأعمال به قبل نهاية العام الحالي.

going all out / going uphase

ass over tea kettle

(5) جريدة الوسط (البحرين)، ٣١ يناير ٢٠١١، العدد ٣٠٦٩.

head over heel

من كان يصدق أن شابا تونسيا «حرا» يدعى محمد البوعزيزي سيقلب الدول العربية **رأسا على عقب** ويدخل الأمة العربية في قطار التغيير والحرية والكرامة؟

Exercise 4: Structural Mismatches

The underlined phrases are all used as modifiers, despite their diverse structures. Translate these phrases using English functional equivalents.

regardless, despite this

(1) جريدة الوطن (السعودية)، ٢٢ نوفمبر ٢٠٠٧، العدد ٢٦١٠.

يحق لكل مواطن ومقيم وزائر حضور تلك المهرجانات **بغض النظر** عن قبيلته وجنسيته.

accordingly based on that!

(2) مجلة المعرفة (السعودية)، ١٦ مارس ٢٠٠٦، العدد ١٥٧.

وقد أكدت البحوث أنه من الممكن الحكم على مدى فاعلية المعلم من خلال التعرف على آراء طلابه فيه، **وبناء على ذلك** فإنه يمكن تصميم استبانة تقدم للطلاب ترتبط عباراتها بسلوك المعلم اللفظي وغير اللفظي.

(3) جريدة الأهرام (مصر)، ٧ فبراير ٢٠١٠، العدد ٤٤٩٨٨.

وكان المفروض أن يبدأ في عرض أعماله وهي أرض لا تنبت الزهور على مسرحه الكبير وحي بن يقظان بالمسرح الصغير لكن **لسوء الحظ** بعد انتهاء أعمال التجديد تم اكتشاف أن إجراءات الوقاية من الحرائق لم تتم بالمسرح فكان أن استمر إغلاقه.

unfortunetly

(4) مجلة البديل (تونس)، يوليو ٢٠٠٧، العدد ٢٥٦.

sooner or later

فكل الحركات السياسية تضررت من سياسة بن علي وهو ما سيدفعها **إن آجلا وإن عاجلا** إلى ضرورة تكتيل قواها وصياغة برنامج حد أدنى للتغيير الديمقراطي يستجيب لتطلعات الشعب.

(5) جريدة الجريدة (الكويت)، ٥ نوفمبر ٢٠٠٩، العدد ٧٧٦.

مع الالتزام الواضح بالثورة الصناعية المنخفضة الكربون، سيصبح بوسع الشركات في أنحاء العالم المختلفة أن تخوض المنافسة وهي **تتحلى بالثقة**، وتستثمر أموالها في مناخ من اليقين.

full of confidence / confidently

Exercise 5: Advanced Translation

(1) أحمد بهجت، ١٩٩٩، "رحلة إلى أيرلنده"، صندوق الدنيا، الأهرام، ص ١٦.

الطريق إلى دبلن يمر بمطار هيثرو في لندن، لا أعرف لماذا؟ وصحيح أن مطار لندن منظم **بشكل لا يتوه فيه الحمار**، على الرغم من ذلك، فإن كمية المشي التي يمشيها المرء في مطار لندن تشبه مسابقات الماراثون.

(2) جريدة الرياض (السعودية)، ١٥ مايو ٢٠٠٩، العدد ١٤٩٣٥.

قال باحث في كانبرا إنه يعتقد أن فيروس أنفلونزا الخنازير ربما يكون قد **نتج بصورة غير متعمدة من جانب علماء** كانوا يعملون على بيض من أجل إنماء فيروسات جديدة واختبار أمصال جديدة.

unintentialy produced by scientists / inadvertly

(3) جريدة الرؤية (الكويت)، ٣ فبراير ٢٠١٠، العدد ٧١٣.

وتعد هذه الخطوة إحدى خطوات الجامعة نحو حوسبة العمل الأكاديمي بها، نظرا لأن استخدام التقنيات الحديثة أصبح من **الأهمية بمكان حتى** باتت الكثير من الجامعات حريصة على الأخذ بهذه التقنيات.

so important　　　technology
keen/enthusiastic

(4) جريدة الرياض (السعودية)، ٢١ فبراير ٢٠١٠، العدد ١٥٢١٧.

وانصبت اهتمامات الحضور **في المقام الأول** على مناقشة إجراءات دخول السعوديين والسعوديات إلى الولايات المتحدة والتي اتسمت بالصعوبة والحذر الشديد في السنوات الأخيرة.

in the first place / primardy / first + foremost

(5) جريدة الرياض (السعودية)، ٢٢ يناير ٢٠١٠، العدد ١٥١٨٧.

لعل **أكثر مشكلة** تواجهها الفتاة مع أهلها هي **عدم الفهم الكامل** والواعي لحقيقة المشكلة التي تعاني منها. تخيلوا أن تحاول الفتاة جاهدة شرح أن ما تعاني منه كالاكتئاب مثلا، بينما يصر الأهل على أنه مجرد دلع بنات!!

not fully understanding
bratty
most common biggest

indispensable لا يستغني عن

has made use of it الذي استقاد ه

Inside the Sentence

Functional Categories

The basic subject–predicate relation provides the essential information necessary to describe a situation, but this information is usually not enough. We need ways to locate situations in time, tell whether a subject–predicate relation is true or not, express our beliefs about these relations in terms of possibility and necessity, and even describe situations when we do not have all the necessary information. These types of information are universal across languages, but they are encoded by language-specific function words and grammatical structures. Each language expresses these categories differently, which sometimes results in interesting translation problems, as I discuss below.

1 Temporal Reference

Unlike the words and expressions that describe cultural products, practices, and belief systems, temporal reference is universal across all languages because it is based on human cognition rather than particular worldviews. In other words, though there are crosslinguistic lexical and structural gaps, there are no temporal gaps. All languages have ways of describing past, present, and future events, as well as ways of encoding temporal relations such as simultaneity and sequence. There are, of course, temporal expressions that constitute lexical and structural gaps, but these are linguistic rather than conceptual differences. For example, the preposition قبل *before* undergoes the morphological derivation process that generates diminutives, resulting in قَبِيل. There are no English diminutives for prepositions, but the concept described by قَبِيل is not alien to English, and we can easily translate it as *right before* or *shortly before*. Moreover, Arabic has active and passive participles that can have temporal interpretations, as in إِنِّي ذَاهِب إِلَى الْبَيْت *I am going home*, but these morphological categories do not have equivalents in English. Nevertheless, the situations described by these participles can be easily described using functionally equivalent English verbal constructions.

Although some languages have morphemes that encode tense, such as the English past-tense suffix *-ed*, others do not encode tense at all, but rely instead on aspectual constructions, contextual information, and adverbials. There are in fact some English verbs like this—for example, *put*, *cut*, and *shut*—in which the morphological structure of the verb does not tell us whether it is present or past, but this does not make temporal reference impossible to recognize or translate. Basically, languages can differ in how they express temporal domains and relations, but they all have ways of describing the same temporal concepts, and there are always adverbial phrases and contextual clues that can help us understand and translate temporal reference.

Arabic and English use different linguistic systems to encode temporal reference. Although English has a system that combines tense and aspect, Arabic has only an aspectual system. Tense systems relate events to the time of speaking or writing—that is, speech time. For example, when we say *Mary went home*, the sentence means that Mary's going home took place before the time this sentence was said or written. Aspect in this system provides additional information about the internal structure of events rather than their location in time. When we say *Mary was going home*, the progressive aspect is combined with the past tense to indicate that Mary's going home was in progress at a point in time that precedes speech time. Aspectual systems, such as that of Arabic, do not relate events to speech time directly. Instead, they describe events as complete or incomplete regardless of their temporal domain. For example, the sentence ذَهَبْت إِلَى الْمَكْتَبَة only tells us that my going to the library is complete, but it does not explicitly tell us the time frame of this event. Having only an aspectual system does not by any means suggest that Arabic is an impoverished language; it only means that it has different ways of expressing temporal relations, as I discuss below.

1.1 The Simple Aspects

Arabic has two main aspectual verb forms: the perfective (الْمَاضِي) and the imperfective (الْمُضَارِع). Perfective verbs denote complete event descriptions without locating them in time. To truthfully describe an event as complete, it is usually an event that ends before speech time. In other words, the Arabic perfective aspect and the English past tense share the semantic function of describing past events. This is why Arabic perfective verbs are typically translated as English past simple verbs, as in وصلت بالأمس *I arrived yesterday*. There are, however, a few notable exceptions of which we need to be aware. Some of these exceptions are motivated by the semantic properties of a particular class of verbs known as inchoatives, which are verbs that describe entering a state rather than being in a state. For example, the verb اتفق *agree* in (1) describes an instantaneous event of coming to an agreement, which is necessarily followed by a state of being in agreement. English focuses on this resultant state and uses the simple present tense to profile it, whereas Arabic focuses on the completeness of the event that brings this state about; it is still the same situation, but the two languages choose to focus on different aspects of it. When we translate such perfective verbs, we sometimes need to use the present simple tense instead of the past simple tense.

(1) جريدة الرياض (السعودية)، ٢٥ فبراير ٢٠٠٦، العدد ١٣٨١٩.
وفي حين **اتفق** علماء اليوم على توسع الكون (من خلال نظرية الانفجار الكبير) **اختلفوا** بخصوص مستقبل هذا التوسع.

Although contemporary scientists agree that the universe is expanding (within the framework of the Big Bang Theory), they disagree on the future of this expansion.

Arabic sentences with inchoative perfective verbs are inherently ambiguous. They only tell us that an event is complete, which entails the beginning of the resultant state, but they do not explicitly tell us whether this resulting state holds at speech time or not. In other words, it is not clear from the verb اتفق in (1) whether or not these scientists are still in agreement about the expansion of the universe at the time this sentence was written. If we use the present simple or the present perfect in the translation, we are committed to the continuation of this state into speech time. If we choose the past simple tense, the translation strongly suggests that these scientists are no longer in agreement. Fortunately, the context usually provides clues that help us identify the intended interpretations of perfective inchoative verbs. The subject phrase علماء اليوم *lit. today's scientists* in (1) suggests that the state of agreeing holds true at speech time, thus supporting the present-tense translation.

Time adverbs are very helpful when trying to identify the intended temporal interpretations of sentences with inchoative perfective verbs. In (2), we have the perfective verb تصدرت, which literally means *became at the forefront*. The verb phrase is only telling us that Hillary Clinton's transition to the point where she is ahead of the other Democratic Party presidential candidates is complete. This transition is in itself an instantaneous event that ends the moment it starts, but it results in a state of her being ahead of the other Democratic candidates. What the verb phrase does not tell us is whether Clinton is still ahead of the other candidates at speech time, but the sentence is not completely ambiguous. The adverbial phrase حتى الآن *until now* makes it quite clear that the state of Clinton's being ahead extends into speech time, thus suggesting that we should translate the Arabic perfective verb using the English present tense. It is important to note here that speech time should not be confused with the present time. We know that Clinton was not ahead of the other candidates for long, but this is irrelevant because we need to translate the sentence relative to the speech time of the source sentence, which is November 20, 2007.

(2) المصري اليوم (مصر)، ٢٠ نوفمبر ٢٠٠٧، العدد ١٢٥٥.
وتصدرت مرشحي الحزب الديمقراطي حتى الآن بنسبة كبيرة (هيلاري كلينتون) عضوة مجلس الشيوخ الأمريكي.

Thus far, Senator Hillary Clinton is leading all the other
Democratic Party candidates by a large margin.

Adverbials also play a major role in the decisions we make regarding the aspectual constructions we use in the translation output. Just as in the previous examples, the sentence in (3) has an inchoative perfective verb describing a past event that needs to be translated using the present tense. The difference is that this particular sentence is best translated using the present perfect rather than the present simple. The verb قلقت describes an event of becoming worried that is necessarily followed by a state of being worried. The adverbial phrase منذ الأمس *since yesterday* tells us that this state extends into speech time, which requires the present tense in the translation. The crucial issue here is that the English adverbial *since* is not allowed in sentences with present simple verbs, as in *I am worried about you since yesterday*, which is ungrammatical. This adverbial in this particular context requires the present perfect.

(3) جريدة الوطن (الكويت)، ٩ أكتوبر ٢٠٠٩، العدد ١٢١١٧.
ليا حبيبتي .. أين أنت، لقد **قلقت** عليك منذ الأمس .. أين كنت؟

Leah, sweetheart! Where are you? I have been worried about
you since yesterday. Where were you?

Sometimes, there are no temporal adverbs in the source sentence that can
help us decide whether the resultant state associated with a perfective inchoative verb holds true at speech time or not, which in turn would tell us
whether to translate it as a past simple verb or a present simple or perfect
verb. For instance, the perfective verb نص *stated* in (4) describes the event of
writing the US Constitution, but it does not tell us whether the quoted material is still valid at speech time, and there are no adverbial phrases that can
clarify the situation. However, we should still translate this perfective verb
as a present simple verb, for two reasons. First, our knowledge of American
history tells us that the quoted excerpt from the Constitution is still valid.
Second, English uses the present simple tense to describe static situations.
Therefore, in the absence of time adverbials, we can rely on our background
knowledge and the stylistic patterns of English to identify the tense that accurately conveys the information encoded in the source sentence. This would
help us rule out translating نص الدستور الأمريكي as *The American Constitution
stated* because it is factually inaccurate and stylistically unacceptable.

(4) جريدة الشرق الأوسط (السعودية)، ١٢ أكتوبر ٢٠٠٢، العدد ٨٧١٩.
ومن أجل التحرر من التوترات والمشاحنات والصراعات الدينية **نص** الدستور
الأمريكي على أنه «لن يصدر الكونجرس أي قانون بصدد ترسيخ الدين أو
منع ممارسته».

In order to avoid religious tensions and conflicts, the United
States Constitution states that "Congress shall make no law
respecting an establishment of religion, or prohibiting the free
exercise thereof."

The examples we have seen thus far have to do with cases in which inchoative perfective verbs are translated as present simple or present perfect
verbs because of their semantic properties. There are also other cases in
which we follow the same pattern, but for syntactic and pragmatic reasons.
For example, Arabic factual conditionals use the perfective aspect in the
conditional clause because the conditional relations encoded in these sentences have to do with the completion of the conditional event rather than
its location in time. English, however, uses the present simple in the conditional clause. The conditional clause in (5) has the perfective verb غاب *lit.*

became absent, but if we translate it as a past simple verb, we change the type of conditionality from a factual conditional to a hypothetical one. This sentence is a quotation from a legal text in which there are no hypothetical interpretations. To make sure the factual conditional is translated as such, we need to translate the perfective verb as a present simple one.

(5) جريدة عكاظ (السعودية)، ٢٧ أغسطس ٢٠٠٩، العدد ٢٩٩٣.
وقد نصت المادة (٥٥) من نظام المرافعات على أنه إذا **غاب** المدعى عليه عن الجلسة الأولى فيؤجل النظر في القضية إلى جلسة لاحقة.

Article 55 of the Code of Civil Procedures states that "If a defendant fails to appear in court for the first hearing, the case shall be postponed to a subsequent hearing."

We can posit a translation rule stating that any sentence with إذا *if* followed by a perfective verb in a factual conditional construction must be translated as a conditional sentence with a present simple verb in the conditional clause. This rule is valid, but it applies only to a subset of Arabic factual conditionals because we do not have to have إذا *if* in the conditional clause to express this interclausal logical relation. There are several other expressions that encode conditionality, such as the relative pronoun من *whoever*, and the subordinate conjunctions متى *whenever*, and أيا *whatever*, as in (6). These expressions require us to modify the rule so that it applies to all factual conditionals regardless of the conditional expression used. In other words, we need to first analyze the meaning of the conditional sentence to decide whether it is factual, counterfactual, or hypothetical, and then decide whether the present tense is the optimal translation. The sentence in (6) presents a legal definition including four conditional clauses, all of which have perfective verbs. Legal definitions in English are required to be factual; therefore, we cannot translate these perfective verbs as past-tense verbs because, just as we saw above, this would change the nature of the conditional relation. In order to maintain the factual interpretations of these conditional clauses, we need the present tense.

(6) جريدة الوسط (البحرين)، ١٩ يوليو ٢٠٠٩، العدد ٢٥٠٨.
جاء تعريف الصحافي في القانون: «الصحافي هو من **مارس** مهنة الصحافة بصورة منتظمة في صحيفة يومية أو دورية أو وكالة صحافية، أو **عمل** مراسلا لإحدى وكالات الأنباء أو الصحف العربية أو الأجنبية أو لأية وسيلة

إعلامية أخرى، متى **كان** عمله الكتابة فيها أو مدها بالأخبار والتحقيقات
وسائر المواد الصحافية كالصور والرسوم أيا **كان** نوعها».

The law defines a journalist as "anyone who practices
journalism on a regular basis in a daily newspaper, a periodical,
or a news agency, or works as a correspondent for a news
agency, an Arab or non-Arab newspaper, or any other media
outlet, as long as his/her work is to write or provide news,
reports, or other press related materials, such as images or
illustrations of any kind."

Imperfective verbs, as I mentioned above, denote incomplete event descriptions, but they do not locate events in relation to speech time. Although the Arabic imperfective aspect is not the same thing as the English
present tense, they can be considered functional equivalents in many contexts. For example, the imperfective aspect can describe events that are in
progress at speech time (e.g., أشاهد فيلما الآن *I am watching a movie now*),
habitual or repeated actions (e.g., أشاهد فيلما كل يوم جمعة *I watch a movie
every Friday*), and even factual statements and generalizations (e.g., يغلي
الماء عند مئة درجة مئوية *Water boils at 100 degrees Celsius*). These examples indicate that the semantic functions of the Arabic imperfective aspect
overlap with those of the English present tense, which explains why Arabic imperfective verbs in main clauses are typically translated as English
present-tense verbs. Note that when we discuss the imperfective aspect, we
should include nominal sentences with nonverbal predicates because they
also describe incomplete situations. The only difference is that these sentences describe states rather than events, and they are typically translated
using the present-tense forms of the verb *to be*.

Because the temporal reference of sentences with imperfective verbs or
nonverbal predicates is not tied to speech time, they can be used to describe
incomplete past and future situations, as well as present ones. The text in
(7), for instance, describes a past experience, as indicated by the perfective
verbs كان *was* and أحسست *I felt* in the first two sentences. However, once the
narrative moves to the details of that experience (the events that made the
author feel as though she was missing something), she opts for the imperfective aspect, which stops the progress of the narrative to provide static descriptions. The imperfective verbs in the last three clauses do not change the
temporal reference of the text; it is only a rhetorical technique that makes

writing more effective. English uses the historical present in the same way, providing us with a functional equivalent that we can use to translate this particular text.

(7) نوال السعداوي، ١٩٨٩، "تعلمت الحب"، دار الآداب، بيروت، ط ٣، ص ١٦.
وكان يوما قاسيا علي .. أحسست في كل لحظة من لحظاته أنني أفتقد شيئا
ضخما .. المرضى يدخلون بلا نظام .. وحجرة الغيار لا تصلح لشيء ..
والتمورجية على كثرتهم **يروحون ويجيئون** بغباء شديد وبلا نتيجة.

It was a hard day for me. Every moment, I felt as though I was missing something big: The patients enter the clinic in no order, the exam room is good for nothing, and the many nurses keep going back and forth stupidly without getting anything done.

We also have the option of translating these verbs using the past tense. After all, these are events that took place in the past. The past tense adds another complication, however, which is giving the impression that these events took place sequentially in the order of the clauses: First, the patients entered in no order, then the examination room became good for nothing, and finally the nurses went back and forth. The order of conjoined clauses with imperfective verbs does not reflect the order of events—that is, these events are overlapping, incomplete situations that together add up to a complex situation. This is why the historical present is more functionally accurate in this sentence.

Imperfective verbs can also be used to describe future events, provided that they are scheduled or expected with high probability. This use of the imperfective aspect is easy to detect because it requires the use of adverbs with future time reference. The adverb غدا *tomorrow* in (8), for instance, clearly indicates that the pope's visit to Jordan starts the day following speech time, even though this event is referred to with the imperfective verb يبدأ *he starts*. Using the imperfective aspect to describe future events adds a sense of certainty and relevance to the current situation. The present tense in English has the exact same function; therefore, we can translate the sentence in (8) using the present tense. Note that الفاتيكان *the Vatican* is left out in the translation because it is rather redundant. It is included in the source sentence to help the Arabic reader identify Pope Benedict XVI as the pope of the Catholic Church, as opposed to the pope of the Eastern Orthodox Coptic Church.

(8) وكالة الأنباء الكويتية (كونا)، الكويت، ٧ مايو ٢٠٠٧.

يبدأ بابا الفاتيكان بنديكت ال ١٦ غدا زيارة إلى الأردن تستمر أربعة أيام.

Pope Benedict XVI starts a four-day visit to Jordan tomorrow.

The event descriptions denoted by imperfective verbs include situations that cross temporal domains because their semantics only tell us that these events are incomplete, with no specific time reference. For example, the adverbial phrase منذ أكثر من سنتين *lit. for more than two years* in (9) makes it unambiguously clear that the verb نسمع *we hear* describes an event that started in the past and continues into speech time. In this case, we cannot use the present simple tense in the translation because English does not allow the adverbial *for* in present simple sentences. We cannot use the past tense either, because the event is still in progress at speech time. Instead, we can use the present perfect continuous tense, which describes events that start in the past and continue into the present, and thus we translate سمع as *we have been hearing*.

(9) جريدة النور (سوريا)، ٢٩ نوفمبر ٢٠٠٦، العدد ٣٨٥.

منذ أكثر من سنتين ونحن **نسمع** عن مشروع استبدال شبكة الصرف الصحي، ولكن أحدا لم يحرك ساكنا.

We have been hearing about the project to replace the waste-water network for over two years, but thus far, nothing has happened.

Although English uses morphology and grammar to distinguish the present progressive tense from the present simple tense, Standard Arabic does not. Arabic imperfective verbs are inherently ambiguous between habitual /simple and progressive interpretations. A simple sentence, such as منى تستمع إلى الأخبار, can be translated as *Mona is listening to the news (now)* or *Mona (usually/often) listens to the news*. This means that every time we encounter an Arabic imperfective verb in a main clause, we need to make a decision regarding the aspect we would use in the translation. Adverbial phrases, as we have seen above, are the best kinds of evidence when it comes to resolving temporal and aspectual ambiguity. The adverbial phrase في وقت الإجازات *lit. in the time of vacations* in (10) tells us that the spread of allergies is seasonal because it is a recurrent phenomenon, as indicated by the plural noun الإجازات *vacations*, which we understand from the context

to be summer vacations. In this particular sentence, the imperfective verb
ينتشر is best translated as *spreads* rather than *is spreading* because the
source sentence describes a recurrent situation.

(10) جريدة الأهرام (مصر)، ٥ مايو ٢٠٠٠، العدد ٤١٤٢٣.
هناك نوع من الحساسية **ينتشر** بصورة واضحة في وقت الإجازات خاصة
للمترددين على حمامات السباحة.

There is a certain type of allergy that spreads widely during the
summer vacations, especially among those who use swimming
pools.

In (11), conversely, the imperfective verb ينتشر *spread/is spreading* only
describes the spreading of the computer virus in question as an incomplete event, but it does not locate this event in time—and the morphological
structure of the verb does not tell us whether this spreading is a recurring
event or a one-time event that is in progress at speech time. The adverb الآن
now makes it clear that the spreading of the new computer virus was in
progress at the time when this sentence was written; therefore, this verb is
best translated using the present progressive tense.

(11) مجلة الإنترنت التربوي (الكويت)، أكتوبر ٢٠٠٤، العدد ٥.
ينتشر الآن فيروس جديد عبر الإنترنت، غير أن الفيروس الجديد على عكس
الفيروس الذي انتشر الأسبوع الماضي فهو يصلح الأجهزة ويحصنها ضد
هجمات الفيروسات.

A new computer virus is now spreading through the internet,
but unlike the one that spread last week, the new virus actually
fixes computers and protects them against virus attacks.

In the absence of time adverbs, we need to rely on the context to decide
whether an imperfective verb should be translated as a present simple verb
or a present progressive one. In (12), there are no adverbs that can tell us
whether the verb ينتشر *spread/is spreading* is intended to describe an event
in progress or a habitual/recurrent event. The decision depends on our understanding of the context and the rhetorical functions of the imperfective
aspect. The source sentence is taken from an expository text describing
scientific facts. Because English uses the present simple tense to describe
facts, we need to translate ينتشر in this particular sentence using the present simple.

(12) مجلة العلوم (الكويت)، ١٩٩٨، المجلد ١٤، العدد ١١.

ينتشر الصوت في الجو على طول منحنيات خاصة تدعى الأشعة الصوتية.

Sound spreads through the air in the form of curves known as "sonic waves."

1.2 *Complex Aspects*

In addition to the basic perfective and imperfective aspects, Arabic has a myriad of complex aspectual constructions that provide a wide range of event descriptions. These constructions are formed by combining perfective and imperfective verbs with aspectual verbs or particles to provide more detailed event descriptions. For example, the prospective aspect is formed by using the particle سوف, or its prefix form ـس, preceding an imperfective verb. In most cases, the prospective aspect describes future events. In other words, it is functionally similar to the English future tense, as in سوف أراك غدا *I will see you tomorrow*. We should not, however, assume that the prospective aspect can always be translated as the future tense because the future tense describes events that are expected to happen at a point subsequent to speech time, whereas aspect does not. For example, translating the phrase سوف يعيق in (13) as *will hinder/restrict* is inaccurate because this embedded clause describes a past event that is subsequent to another past event. In this sentence, سوف is more accurately translated as *would*, which maintains the future in the past temporal reference.

(13) إملي نصر الله، ٢٠٠١، "نساء رائدات من الغرب"، الدار المصرية اللبنانية، ص ٦٣.

واستقالت من الصحافة، بعد ممارسة سنوات، لأنها شعرت بأن بقاءها **سوف يعيقها** عن كتابة ما تريد.

She quit journalism after years of practice because she felt that staying in the profession would restrict her ability to write freely.

The auxiliary verb كان *to be* is used with perfective and imperfective verbs to describe various kinds of aspectual relations. When the perfective form of كان is used with an imperfective verb, the resulting construction can be translated using the past habitual or the past progressive because it inherits the aspectual ambiguity of the imperfective aspect, as in كان يقرأ الشعر, which can be translated as *He used to read poetry* or *He was reading poetry*. The combination of the perfective form of كان and a perfective verb yields a construction with past perfect interpretations in embedded clauses, as in عندما وصلت كان قد رحل بالفعل *When I arrived, he had already left*. When the perfective form of كان is used with a prospective verb, the combination results in future in the past readings, as in كان سوف يفوز *He was going to win*. The prospective form of كان also combines with perfective verbs in a construction that is similar to the future perfect, as in عندما أصل سيكون قد رحل *When I arrive, he will have left*. The aspectual constructions that involve كان help establish temporal relations between events across clauses.

What we need to remember is that the verb combinations I mentioned above are all aspectual constructions rather than tense constructions. Although they share many of their semantic functions with English semi-equivalent tense constructions, there are many cases in which we do not have one-to-one correspondences. For example, the perfective form of كان, when combined with an imperfective verb or a nonverbal predicate, semantically functions to describe the beginning and middle parts of an event, without giving any information regarding its termination or its location in time. This is why this construction can describe situations that start and end in the past—in which case it is translated as the past simple, habitual, or progressive tense—or to describe situations that start in the past and continue into the present, as in (14). In this sentence, the last clause has the perfective form of the verb كان, followed by the nonverbal predicate رئيسا *president*; but in this particular context, we cannot translate it as *He used to be the president* or *He was the president* because the adverbial phrase حتى الآن *until now* makes it clear that the state of Amr Salama's being president persists into speech time. Obviously, if we use the past tense, as in *He was /used to be the President of Hilwan University until now*, our translation would be both inaccurate and ungrammatical. This is why we are better off using the present perfect or the present simple tense.

(14) جريدة المستقبل (لبنان)، ١٣ يوليو ٢٠٠٤، العدد ١٦٤٣.
وستسند حقيبة التعليم إلى عمرو سلامة (٥٣ سنة)، وهو أستاذ متخصص في الهندسة الإنشائية **وكان حتى الآن رئيسا** لجامعة حلوان في القاهرة.
Amr Salama (fifty-three years of age) will be the minister of education. He is a professor of structural engineering and is currently president of Hilwan University in Cairo.

Another example of how the Arabic aspectual system does not align perfectly with the English tense system has to do with the aspectual construction in which the perfective form of كان *to be* combines with a perfective verb, a construction that is usually translated as the past perfect tense. The problem here is that this construction can be used in independent main clauses, as in (15), but English does not allow the past perfect in these contexts. Using the past perfect to translate the main clause of this sentence is simply ungrammatical. Moreover, the past perfect locates an event at a point in the past that precedes the temporal reference of another past event—that is, it encodes the past in the past. There are two events in the source sentence: one in April, and the other in May. If we translate كان قد ارتفع as *had gone up*, we would be describing the event that took place in May as preceding the one that took place in April. Only the event that takes place first can be translated using the past perfect, namely, the event described in the source sentence using the perfective aspect without كان *to be*, resulting in the literal translation: *The volume of loans given to nonnational residents went up by 0.4 percent in May making up for the decrease it had witnessed in April*. To avoid ungrammaticality and confusion, we can translate both كان قد ارتفع and شهده using the past simple tense, which can be further improved, as shown below.

(15) جريدة القبس (الكويت)، ٢٧ سبتمبر ٢٠٠٩، العدد ١٣٠٥٠.
وكان حجم القروض الممنوحة إلى المقيمين قد **ارتفع** في مايو بواقع ٠,٤%،
معوضًا الانخفاض الذي شهده في أبريل.
The volume of loans granted to nonnational residents went up in May by 0.4 percent, making up for its fall earlier in April.

Although كان *to be* is the most commonly used aspectual verb, there are many others that form aspectual constructions, with finer and even more specific event descriptions. In fact, Arabic has more than a hundred aspectual constructions that provide a comprehensive and detailed inventory of event descriptions. For instance, the perfective forms of the "verbs of becoming"—such as أصبح, أمسى, and صار, all of which mean *to become*—combine with imperfective verbs to encode the inceptive aspect, which profiles only the initial parts of events. These verb combinations are usually translated using functionally equivalent constructions, such as *started to*, as in أصبح يتكلم *He started talking*. Other aspectual verb combinations emphasize the developmental stages of events—such as ظل *to remain*—which, when used with imperfective verbs, give a continuous interpretation, as in ظل يحاول *He kept trying*. Aspectual constructions can be further combined to provide even more detailed descriptions, as in كان سوف يظل يحاول *He was going to keep trying* or *He would have kept trying*. Despite the complexity of the Arabic aspectual system, all its aspectual constructions are translatable because English has ways of describing similar kinds of situations and temporal relations.

1.3 Adverbial Ambiguity

Although time adverbials provide the best clues to help us interpret the meanings of aspectual constructions, they are not without their own problems. Many of these problems, however, can be dealt with using the word- and phrase-level strategies I discussed above. For example, some time adverbs are lexically ambiguous, such as منذ, which can be translated as *since, for*, or *ago*, depending on the grammatical context. If منذ is followed by a phrase that describes a point in time in a construction that describes an incomplete situation, we can translate it as *since*, as in نائم منذ منتصف الليل *He has been asleep since midnight*. But if منذ is followed by a phrase that describes a period of time, we can translate it as *for*, as in أسكن هنا منذ أربع سنوات *I have been living here for four years*. However, if منذ is used with a perfective verb and followed by a phrase describing a time period, we can translate as *ago*, as in توفي منذ أربع سنوات *He died four years ago*.

Time adverbials can also be structurally ambiguous, as in قبل ثلاث سنوات من الانتخابات الرئاسية in (16). This adverbial phrase could mean *before three years of presidential elections* or *three years before the presidential elections*. The issue here is whether the prepositional phrase من الانتخابات الرئاسية *lit. from the presidential elections* is a complement of the quantifier phrase ثلاث سنوات *three years* or an adjunct that only modifies it. It is our background knowledge about French presidential elections that can help us resolve this ambiguity. We know that these elections do not last for three years; therefore, we can rule out the complement reading, and can translate the ambiguous phrase as *three years before the presidential elections*, which can be rephrased as *three years ahead of the presidential elections*.

(16) جريدة الأهرام (مصر)، ٢٢ يوليو ٢٠٠٤، العدد ٤٢٦٩٢.
وهكذا أصبحت نوايا ساركوزي معروفة **قبل ثلاث سنوات من الانتخابات الرئاسية**.
Thus, Sarkozy's intentions were known three years ahead of the presidential elections.

Other adverbial phrases are structurally complex, such as فيما بين يونيو
١٩٥٦ ومارس ١٩٥٨ in (17), which literally means *in that which is between
June 1956 and March 1958*. This structurally complex phrase, which also
involves redundancy, can be translated by leaving out the main prepositional phrase along with the relative pronoun, to end up with just *between
June 1956 and March 1958*.

(17) محمد الجوادي، ١٩٩٩، "سيد مرعي: شريك وشاهد على عصور
الليبرالية"، مكتبة مدبولي، القاهرة، ص ٢١.
وفيما **بين يونيو ١٩٥٦ ومارس ١٩٥٨** ظل سيد مرعي يشغل منصب وزير
الدولة للإصلاح الزراعي.

Between June 1956 and March 1958, Sayyid Marei continued to
hold the position of minister of agricultural reform.

The sentence in (18) poses a different kind of ambiguity; there are three
adverbial phrases—حوالي في سنة ١٩٢٧ *in 1927,* سنة ١٩٢٦ *in 1926,* and
أربعة عشر عاما *about fourteen years*—as well as two perfective verbs—تولى
took over and أسسها *founded it*. It is clear that the first adverbial phrase,
في سنة ١٩٢٧ *in 1927,* modifies the verb تولى *took over* because it precedes
the verb in the same clause. The second adverbial phrase, سنة ١٩٢٦ *in 1926,*
modifies the verb أسسها *founded it* in the relative clause. The problem is that
it is not clear which verb is modified by the adverbial phrase حوالي أربعة عشر
عاما *about fourteen years*.

(18) سيد صديق عبد الفتاح، ٢٠٠٢، "سير ونوادر ظرفاء وعظماء القرن
العشرين"، دار غريب، القاهرة، ص ٢٧٧.
وفي سنة ١٩٢٧ تولى رئاسة تحرير مجلة ((الفكاهة)) التي أسسها ((آل زيدان))
سنة ١٩٢٦ **حوالي أربعة عشر عاما**.

In 1927, he became editor-in-chief of *Al-Fukaaha magazine,*
which was founded by the Zeidan family a year earlier, and he
held this position for about fourteen years.

The phrase حوالي أربعة عشر عاما *about fourteen years* cannot modify the
verb أسس *founded* in the embedded relative clause because these two elements are semantically and structurally incompatible; we know that the
magazine was founded in 1926, which means it is impossible that it was
founded over fourteen years. This leaves only one option: This adverbial
phrase modifies the verb in the main clause, but they are separated by a

relative clause. This is fine in Arabic, but English does not allow this structure. As a result, we need to move this adverbial phrase to the main clause
in our translation. This gives us two adverbial phrases modifying the same
verb: *In 1927 he took over the position of editor-in-chief of Al-Fukaaha magazine for about fourteen years*. This translation conveys the same information
as the source sentence, but it sounds inconsistent. Moreover, the new site of
the adverbial phrase in this candidate translation makes it difficult to include
the relative clause, which cannot be separated from the noun it modifies. One
way to resolve this issue is to apply phrasal reconstruction and translate the
adverbial phrase as a separate clause to be conjoined with the main clause.

Just as adverbials can help us accurately interpret temporal relations, aspectual constructions can help us resolve the translation problems related
to adverbials. For instance, the first clause in (19) includes the nominative
subject ثلاثون عاما *thirty years*, the perfective verb مرت *passed*, and the time
adverb بالأمس *yesterday*. Obviously, it is impossible for thirty years to pass
within the twenty-four-hour period referred to by أمس *yesterday*—that is,
there seems to be a conflict between the subject and the adverbial time reference. The key to translating this sentence has to do with the semantics of
the perfective aspect rather than the adverb. Because the verb مرت *passed*
marks the perfective aspect rather than the past tense, it does not profile the
internal structure of the event—that is, it does not describe the passing of
thirty years as a durative situation, but only its termination. Therefore, we
can use lexical substitution while reconstructing the sentence to avoid the
contradictory phrase *thirty years passed yesterday*.

(19) جريدة الأهرام (مصر)، ٢٧ مارس ٢٠٠٩، العدد ٤٤٦٧١.
ثلاثون عاما مرت بالأمس على اتفاقية السلام بين مصر وإسرائيل، ومازال
«السلام باردا».

Yesterday marked the thirtieth anniversary of the Peace Accord
between Egypt and Israel, but this peace is still "cold."

The examples discussed above clearly demonstrate that Arabic and English use different linguistic systems to encode temporal domains and relations. Regardless of these differences, the aspectual system of Arabic and
the tense system of English overlap quite a bit in terms of their functions,
and the translation challenges we have seen come up only in particular
areas where the two systems work differently. The good news is that we
can always translate Arabic temporal expressions because they are based

on universal concepts, and we can still use the same translation strategies I discussed in the previous chapters to resolve these issues.

2 Negation

Negation is a semantic function that expresses denial by changing the truth values of sentences. If I say *John is in his office*, and he is indeed in his office, then this sentence is true. When negation is applied to this sentence, we get *John is not in his office*, which denies its affirmative counterpart and is therefore false in this context. The reverse is also true; if an affirmative sentence is false in a particular context, its negated counterpart is true. This logical function of negation is universal across all languages. In other words, we do not expect conceptual mismatches when translating negated sentences. In fact, most of the negation-related translation problems we might encounter are syntactic in nature and result from the interaction between negation and other functional categories.

Although negation has only one semantic function, it appears in various grammatical configurations or strategies. The main such strategy is sentential negation, which applies to a complete sentence to deny the relation between the subject and the predicate. This type of negation is expressed in English by using *not* following an auxiliary verb, as in *John does not work in this office*. Arabic, conversely, employs various sentential negation markers, depending on the structure of the sentence and its temporal interpretation. For instance, the negation markers لا, لم, and لن are used in sentences with imperfective verbs, in which لا marks negation in the present, لم expresses negation in the past, and لن encodes negation in the future. The negation marker ما co-occurs with both imperfective and perfective verbs regardless of temporal interpretations, whereas ليس is most commonly found in nominal sentences with nonverbal predicates that describe present situations. The distribution of Arabic sentential negation markers reflects a close connection between negation and temporal reference, an issue that I discuss in detail in this section.

In addition to sentential negation, we need to distinguish two other negation strategies: phrasal negation and lexical negation. Phrasal negation targets only a phrase rather than a whole sentence, and it is common in elliptical constructions, as in *I am usually free, but not now* and *I met John but not Mary*, as well as in quantified phrases, such as *not every student* and *for no reason.* Arabic can express the same kind of negation directly using ليس and لا—as in ليس الآن *not now,* ليس كل *not every,* and لا أمل *no hope*—or indirectly through the expressions of exception, such as دون *other than,* as in منى دون نادية *Mona but not Nadia.* Lexical negation, conversely, is encoded morphologically using prefixes, such as *un-, non-,* and *dis-,* among others. Because lexical negation is a constituent of a word rather than a phrase or a sentence, it does not change the truth value of the whole sentence; a sentence such as *Mary is unhappy* is still affirmative. Although Arabic does not typically incorporate negation morphologically, we are seeing more and more instances of prefixed لا, as in اللاإرادي *involuntary* and اللانهائي *infinite.* It is very important to determine the type and function of negation when translating because misinterpreting negation strategies can result in misleading translations; a sentence such as ليس كل ما يلمع ذهبا *Not all that glitters is gold* means something very different from كل ما يلمع ليس ذهبا *All that glitters is not gold.*

2.1   *Reversing Polarity*

Intuitively, translating negation is a straightforward matter. If the source sentence is negated, we use negation in the translation; otherwise, the translation output should be affirmative. However, in certain contexts we might consider translating a negative sentence as an affirmative one, and vice versa. Adding negation can be a useful translation strategy when dealing with lexical gaps. If an Arabic word does not have an equivalent in English, but its antonym (or opposite) does, we might consider using lexical negation with the English equivalent of the antonym. For example, the adjective عاجز in (20) constitutes a lexical gap; it means *lacking the ability.* English does not have a common adjective that refers to this property in an affirmative way that would fit in this context. We can consider morphological unpacking to generate translation candidates, but phrases like *someone who lacks the ability to work* add new aspects of meaning that are not intended in the source sentence. As an alternative, we can use lexical negation with the equivalent of the antonym قادر *capable.* This gives us several translation candidates, including *incapable, unable, cannot,* and *not able to,* among others. Of course the optimality of the translation depends on what we do with the rest of the sentence.

(20) جريدة الرأي العام (السودان)، ١٠ سبتمبر ٢٠٠٩، العدد ٤٢٠٩٦.
فأنت تتحول بسبب ضياع بطاقتك إلى شخص مجهول الهوية **عاجز** عن العمل، والتعامل الرسمي، والعلاج.

When you lose your identification card, you become a living John Doe; you cannot get a job, do official business, or get medical treatment.

The phrase مجهول الهوية in the sentence above poses a similar problem. It is an adjectival possessive phrase that is equivalent to *whose identity is not known*. The issue here is that we do not want to add a new negated clause, which we can avoid by using lexical negation, as in *whose identity is unknown*. However, this candidate is rather redundant after *when you lose you identification card*, and it fails to maintain the connotation of being unrecognized by the state, which motivates the use of this phrase in the source sentence. We could apply lexical substitution and use other lexically negated adjectives—such as *incognito, invisible*, and *unknown*—or a noun phrase such as *a nobody*. Still, these candidates have different connotations; *incognito* suggests choosing to be unknown, whereas *invisible* suggests being unrecognized by everyone, not just the state. Both *unknown* and *a nobody* have to do with being not famous or significant. Perhaps using a figurative expression, such as *a living John Doe*, offers a better alternative, because it maintains the connotations of the source phrase and it is not negated.

There is a group of Arabic words that lexically entail the meaning of negation, such as عدم *lack/nonexistence* and انعدم *ceased to exist* in (21). The problem is that there are contexts in which we cannot use the equivalents of these words because they would not collocate with the other words in the text. For example, we cannot translate في حالة عدم استطاعتهم تصريفها, as *in the case of their lack of/nonexistence of ability to sell* or يكون الطلب قد انعدم عليها as *demand for it (the cotton) had already ceased to exist*. One solution is to make negation explicit while reconstructing the translation accordingly. This strategy gives us *they cannot sell* and *there is no more demand for cotton*, which sound more natural while maintaining the overall meaning of the source sentence.

(21) جريدة الأهرام (مصر)، ١٦ فبراير ٢٠٠٣، العدد ٤٢٤٥٠.
يستمر هؤلاء التجار في حجب هذه الأقطان عن السوق على أمل ارتفاع الأسعار وفي حالة **عدم** استطاعتهم تصريفها يطالبون الدولة باستلامها في نهاية أغسطس في الوقت الذي يكون الطلب قد انعدم عليها.

These dealers withhold cotton from the market hoping for prices to go up, but if they get to a point where they cannot sell it, they demand that the government take it at the end of August when there is no more demand for cotton.

Just as we sometimes resort to adding negation as a translation strategy, there are contexts in which we might want to delete it, provided that we do not change the overall meaning of the source sentence. Deleting negation is a translation strategy that can help us resolve lexical gaps, including those that involve ambiguity. Some Arabic verbs are aspectually ambiguous, in that they have more than one sense with different situational descriptions. For example, the verb يقل has an event reading that means *decrease/fall*, as in يتم تجميد حساب الادخار الخاص بك عندما يقل الرصيد عن مئة دولار *Your savings account will be frozen when the balance falls below a hundred dollars*. Under this reading, the verb describes a situation in which the subject, the account balance, undergoes change. The same verb has a stative sense that does not involve change at all, as in (22). In this sentence, لا تقل does not mean *does not fall below* because a time span (residence in Saudi Arabia) cannot decrease. In other words, the function of negation in this context is to fix a static lower bound on the eligibility requirement for Saudi citizenship. The problem here is that English does not have a stative verb that means *less than*; therefore, we need to apply reconstruction. We can use negation with the stative verb *to be*, as in *for a period that is not less than ten consecutive years*, but this translation candidate is rather cumbersome. Alternatively, we can delete negation and use an affirmative sentence with an adverbial phrase that expresses the *not less than* relation, as in *at least ten consecutive years*.

(22) جريدة الوطن (عمان)، ٢٠ أكتوبر ٢٠٠٤، العدد ٧٧٦٤.
يجوز منح الجنسية العربية السعودية للأجنبي شرط أن يكون عند تقديم طلب الجنسية العربية السعودية قد بلغ سن الرشد واكتسب صفة الإقامة لمدة **لا تقل** عن عشر سنوات متتالية.

Saudi citizenship can be granted to a foreign national if, at the time of application, he or she is an adult who has been a legal resident of Saudi Arabia for at least ten consecutive years.

2.2 Double Negation انكار / رفض / نفي

Another context that calls for deleting negation has to do with constructions that look like double negation. Arabic does not allow having two sentential negation markers in the same clause, but sometimes we encounter grammatical structures that might result in double negation in the translation, which is not grammatical in English. Suppose we have an Arabic sentence made up of a main clause and a subordinate clause, with negation in both. If we cannot keep the two clauses separate in the translation—say, by starting the embedded clause with *that*—we end up with double negation. For example, the sentence in (23) includes two negated clauses: the main clause لا أستطيع *I cannot/I am not able to*, and the embedded complement clause أن لا أحب *that I do not like*. The problem here is that the modal *can* and the adjective *able to* require infinitive verbs without *that*, resulting in *I cannot not love* and *I am not able not to love*, both of which are obviously ungrammatical. One way of avoiding double negation is to apply substitution and reconstruction together to incorporate one negation marker morphologically, as in *I am incapable of not loving*. Perhaps a better option in this particular context is to leave out one of the negation markers and use an expression that conveys the idea of having only one option or possibility, such as *cannot help but*.

(23) جريدة الصباح (السعودية)، ٢٥ مايو ٢٠٠٦، العدد ١١١٣٦.
لا أستطيع أن لا أحب قصائدي القديمة، لأن حياتي القديمة هي حياتي سواء أحببتها أم لا.

I cannot help but love my old poems because my old life is still part of my life, whether I like it or not.

Double negation also comes up when translating sentences with language-specific combinations of negation strategies. For example, Arabic allows having sentential negation in addition to phrasal negation in the same clause, as in (24). The phrasal negation particle لا is repeated in combination with the conjunction و *and* to form a construction that is equivalent to *neither . . . nor*. Because phrasal negation is limited in scope to the subject noun phrase, nothing rules out using the sentential negation marker لم to deny the relation between the subject لا أهلي ولا أهل زوجتي *neither my family nor my wife's family* and the predicate كانوا يملكون هذا المبلغ *lit. had that sum of money*. Maintaining both types of negation in the translation would give us ungrammatical structures, such as *neither my family nor my wife's family did not have that kind of money*, which is clearly ungrammatical because of double negation. One solution to this problem is to leave out sentential negation because *neither . . . nor* by itself expresses this kind of negation in English.

(24) مجلة المعرفة (السعودية)، ٢٥ يونيو ٢٠٠٦، العدد ٩٢.
كنت أتمنى قبل ذلك وأنا في بلدي أن يكون معي خمسة آلاف دولار حتى أسافر وأشق طريق الدراسة في الولايات المتحدة، ولكن **لم يكن لا أهلي ولا أهل زوجتي يملكون** هذا المبلغ.

Back in my home country, I wished I had five thousand dollars
to study in the United States, but neither my family nor my
wife's family had that kind of money.

2.3 Contrastive Negation

Although negation is essentially a clause internal feature, it sometimes interacts with other features across clause boundaries. One such interaction
has to do with contrastive coordination, when the particle بل conjoins two
contrasting clauses, one that is in some way inaccurate and another that
provides the correction. The clause لا يوجد عندي آخر لحن *I do not have a latest composition* in (25) is in contrast to the conjoined clause عندي ألحان *lit.
I have (latest) compositions*. Even though the first clause is negated, the
conjunction does not result in a contradiction because what the first clause
denies is the assumption that the speaker has only one recent composition. Note that in this particular sentence, the second clause entails the
first one because having many compositions necessarily means having at
least one. The first clause is semantically redundant, and we can simply
delete it, but this comes at the expense of the rhetorical function of contrast, which we need to maintain. Translating this type of conjunction is
not very complicated because it has several functional equivalents in English. Among other possibilities, we can use (1) the contrastive conjunction
but, as in *I do not have one latest composition, but many*; (2) the reverse
contrast construction, as in *I have many latest compositions, not just one*;
or (3) a semicolon, as in *I do not have just one latest composition; I have
many*. Adding adverbs such as *just* and *only* helps us make the contrast
easier to recognize. What matters most is maintaining the contrast in the
translation.

(25) جريدة ١٤ أكتوبر (اليمن)، ٢٤ أكتوبر ٢٠٠٩، العدد ١٤٦٢٥.
أما عن آخر لحن فيقول الفنان فيصل: لا يوجد عندي آخر لحن، **بل عندي**
ألحان.

As for his latest work, the composer Faisal says "I do not have
just one latest composition; I have many."

The contrast in this type of conjunction is expressed by the particle بل,
not negation. Consequently, we can have contrastive conjunction without
negation at all. Using negation is only a way of making it easy for readers

to recognize the focus of contrast. When we have contrastive conjunction without negation, we might consider adding it in the translation. For example, in (26) بل conjoins the two affirmative clauses: يتوقع المزيد من المواجهات وإراقة الدماء *he predicts more confrontations and bloodshed,* and يتوقع قيام حرب عالمية ثالثة *he predicts a third world war.* The contrast is achieved in Arabic by using the particle بل, whereas the focus of contrast is indicated by the repetition of the verb يتوقع *expect/predict,* which makes it clear that the direct objects are in contrast. More specifically, the contrast here has to do with degree, assuming that a third world war would be worse than just confrontations and bloodshed. In this case, literal translation yields redundancy, as in *he predicts more confrontations and bloodshed, and he predicts a third world war.* If we combine the two clauses in the translation while conjoining the direct objects—as in *he predicts more confrontations, bloodshed, and a third world war* or *he predicts more confrontations and bloodshed as well as a third world war*—we avoid the redundancy while accurately conveying the information encoded in the source sentence. However, we completely lose the rhetorical effects of contrast. To maintain this contrast, we can combine the two clauses while adding negation in the appropriate contrastive construction. Because we are dealing with contrast in degree, we can use the *not only . . . but also/even* construction.

(26) جريدة الأهرام (مصر)، ١٣ مايو ٢٠٠٤، العدد ٤٢٨٩٢.
أما هنتجتون، أستاذ هارفارد، فإنه يتوقع المزيد من المواجهات وإراقة الدماء،
بل يتوقع قيام حرب عالمية ثالثة.

As for the Harvard professor Samuel Huntington, he predicts
not only more confrontations and bloodshed, but even a third
world war.

Because Arabic has a specialized particle for contrastive conjunction, it is possible to have negation in both clauses. This is a potential problem for translation because English allows negation only in the main clause. For example, if we use *but* to maintain contrast when translating the sentence in (27), we end up with *it is not true that the Bastille Prison . . . was full of prisoners, . . . but there was not a single prisoner in it,* or *the Bastille Prison . . . was not full of prisoners, . . . but there was not a single prisoner in it.* Neither translation candidate is valid because they fail to maintain the contrast while adding unnecessary redundancy and confusion. In a case like this, we need to reconstruct the sentence in a way that maintains

the contrast without using a conjunction. One possible solution is to reconstruct the second clause as a new sentence starting with the contrastive
adverbial *in fact*.

(27) جريدة الأهرام (مصر)، ١٢ أغسطس ١٩٩٩، العدد ٤١١٥٦.
وليس صحيحا أن سجن الباستيل الذي حوله الرئيس ميتران إلى أوبرا كان
مملوءا بالمعتقلين يوم قيام الثورة، **بل لم يكن** به سجين واحد!

The Bastille Prison, which President François Mitterrand
turned into an opera house, was not "full of prisoners" when
the Revolution broke out. In fact, there was not a single
prisoner in it.

2.4   Negation and Temporal Reference

Negation also interacts with different kinds of linguistic forms within the
same clause or across clause boundaries to delimit temporal reference. We
already saw that some sentential negation markers, such as لم *did not* and
لن *will not*, encode both negation and temporal reference. Aspectual verbs,
such as عاد *return*, have their own lexical meanings, but when they combine
with negation, they can form new semantically noncompositional constructions with specific temporal interpretations. For example, the combination of
negation and the aspectual verb عاد, as in لم يعد, can mean *He did not return*
but it can also function as a way of indicating that the situation described
by the complement used to be true in the past but is not anymore. This is
why this aspectual construction can be translated via reconstruction using
the adverbials *anymore* or *no longer*; a sentence such as لم يعد مريضا can be
translated as *He is not sick anymore* or *He is no longer sick*. This negated
aspectual construction can also take clausal complements, as in (28), but
this is not a problem, because we can use the combination of negation and
adverbs to translate لم يعد يشكل as *no longer constitutes*, which we can optionally be rephrased as *is no longer*.

(28) جريدة الوطن (البحرين)، ١١ نوفمبر ٢٠٠٩، العدد ١٤٣١.
ورغم أن النفط **لم يعد** يشكل العمود الفقري للاقتصاد، إلا أنه لا يزال يلعب
دورا رئيسيا.

Although oil is no longer the backbone of the economy, it still
plays a major role.

A few other verbs also form semantically noncompositional aspectual constructions with negation, including ما زال, ما انفك, ما فتئ, ما برح, and ما. What is special about these verbs is that when combined with negation, which is usually encoded with ما, they form constructions in which the situation described by the complement is understood to have started in the past and to continue into the present. As a result, these constructions can all be translated via reconstruction as *still*. For example, ما زال يحاول is better translated as *He is still trying* rather than the more literal candidate *He has not ceased trying*. Note that these constructions have clausal structures of their own while their complements are different clauses, which allows the use of negation in both clauses, as in (29). The thing to remember here is that negation in these aspectual constructions does not interact with the complement clause. In other words, we do not have double negation, whereby the two negation markers would cancel each other out. In other words, لا يزال لا يعرف in (29) should be translated as *still does not know* rather than *still knows*.

(29) جريدة الشرق الأوسط (السعودية)، ١٢ سبتمبر ٢٠٠٢، العدد ٨٦٨٩.
قال الرئيس الأميركي جورج بوش إنه **لا يزال لا يعرف** ما إذا كان أسامة بن لادن حيا أو ميتا.

President George W. Bush said that he still does not know whether Osama Bin Laden is alive or dead.

When I introduced translation by substitution above, I mentioned the verb كاد, which means *to be very close to doing something but not doing it*. This verb constitutes a lexical gap, and it is usually translated via substitution as the adverb *almost*, as in كاد يفوز *He almost won*. What is interesting about this verb is that it functions like negation; an affirmative sentence with كاد tells us that the situation described by the complement clause did not happen, even though there are no negation markers. When كاد is preceded by a negation marker, the sentence is interpreted as if there are two negation markers that cancel each other out. As a result, the event described in the complement clause is understood to have indeed taken place, but only to a very small extent, as in (30). If we keep *almost* in the translation of لم يكد يتغير, we get *the place did not almost change*, which is not acceptable. We can reverse the order of negation and the adverb to get *the place almost did not change*, which is a better candidate. Alternatively, we can leave out negation and use another adverb that fits better in this context, such as

hardly, which means that the place did change but only very little, just like
the source sentence.

(30) جريدة المستقبل (لبنان)، ١ مارس ٢٠٠٩، العدد ٣٢٣٤.
عشت هناك قبل ٣٥ عاما عندما كنت في نهاية سني مراهقتي، لكن المكان **لم
يكد يتغير** عما كان عليه.

I used to live there thirty-five years ago when I was in my late
teens, but the place hardly changed.

The negated aspectual construction لم يكد interacts with the subordinated
conjunction حتى *until* to establish temporal relations between clauses, as
in (31). In this sentence, لم يكد and its complement clause ينتهي من حديثه
مع والدته *finish his conversation with his mother* describe a situation in
which he barely finishes his conversation with his mother. The subordinate clause حتى قام رجال الأمن بانتزاعه *lit. until the security men pulled him*
describes a situation that starts immediately after the first one is complete.
Therefore, we can translate this sentence using any construction that expresses the temporal relation of immediate sequence, including *as soon as*,
no sooner . . . than, and *immediately after*, among others. Another option is
to apply substitution and translate لم يكد as *hardly*, as I did in the previous
example, and حتى as *when*. No matter what construction we use, we cannot
translate حتى as *until* because it is part of a new construction with لم يكد.

(31) جريدة الرياض (السعودية)، ٢٦ يناير ٢٠٠٧، العدد ١٤٠٩٥.
لم يكد ينتهي من حديثه مع والدته **حتى** قام رجال الأمن بانتزاعه من وسط
الطابور.

He hardly finished his conversation with his mother when the
security agents pulled him out of the line.

We find the same pattern of negation and subordinate conjunctions combining to establish temporal relations between clauses, even without aspectual verbs. The sentence in (32) has two clauses انطلقت صفارة الإنذار *the
siren went off*, which is preceded by أن *that* and the negation marker ما, and
تراكض الناس *people rushed*, which is preceded by the subordinate conjunction حتى *until*. This complex structure indicates that the event described in
the first clause happened first, and it was immediately followed by the event
described in the embedded clause. In other words, the negation marker ما is
outside the clause structure, and it does not deny the first event—that is, the

siren did go off. What negation does in this construction is deny the existence of a temporal gap between the two events. This is why we cannot have ما preceding a clause initial أن *that* unless we have an embedded clause. Despite the complexity of this construction, it is not difficult to translate. All we need is an English construction or adverbial that encodes the immediate sequencing of events, hence the use of *as soon as* in the translation below.

(32) جريدة الوقت (البحرين)، ٩ فبراير ٢٠٠٩، العدد ١٠٨٥.
ما أن انطلقت صفارة الإنذار **حتى** تراكض الناس إلى الأسطح ليروا صواريخ باتريوت تطارد صواريخ سكود وتفجرها في الهواء.

As soon as the sirens went off, people rushed to the roofs to
watch the Patriot missiles chase and destroy the Scud missiles
in midair.

Even though negation has a unique semantic function that is manifested in diverse strategies and constructions, we can still apply the same translation strategies we saw in the previous chapters. We can add negation or delete it, and we can reconstruct the translation in ways that are structurally different from the source sentences. These strategies are acceptable as long as the translation output has the same overall meaning of the source text. We need to be careful, however, because mistranslating negation affects the truthfulness of the message.

3 Modality

Modality is an umbrella category for expressions that reveal speakers' beliefs about propositions that connote possibility and necessity. When we say *John might come to the party*, we communicate our belief that the proposition *John comes to the party* is possible; but when we say *John has to attend the meeting*, we express our belief that John's attending the meeting is necessary. From a pragmatic perspective, necessity and possibility are gradient attributes rather than absolute values; the sentence *Mona may arrive on time* conveys a higher degree of probability than *Mona might arrive on time*, whereas *I should read this book* expresses a lower degree of necessity than *I have to read this book*. In addition to encoding possibility and necessity, modal expressions lend themselves to various contextual interpretations, such as expressing obligation, certainty, imposition, probability, and ability,

صيغ (شكلن)

neccerity

among others. When it comes to translating modal expressions, we need to pay attention not only to their meaning that connotes necessity and possibility but also to their contextual interpretations.

Although English modal expressions are mostly auxiliary verbs (e.g., *must, can, may,* and *should*) and adverbs (e.g., *perhaps, likely,* and *maybe*), Arabic has a much wider range of modal expressions. These include lexical modal verbs—such as يجب ,ينبغي ,يتحتم ,يضطر ,يتعين, and يلزم, all of which express necessity—and يحتمل, and يجوز ,يمكن, which encode possibility. In terms of grammatical structure, these verbs take either nominal subjects, as in يجب الرحيل الآن *lit. Leaving now is necessary*, or sentential subjects, as in يجب أن أرحل الآن *lit. That I leave now is necessary*, which can be rephrased as *I have to leave now*. Moreover, Arabic uses prepositional phrases that function as modal adverbials (e.g., من الواجب ,من اللازم ,من المفروض ,عليه, بوسعه ,من المحتمل ,من الممكن) that express necessity, and من الضروري) and يامكانه ,بمقدوره, and في المستطاع that express possibility. Finally, modality is also encoded by some frozen expressions and particles, such as the negative phrases لا بد and لا مفر, which encode necessity, and the adverbial particles قد and ربما, which encode possibility. The diversity of Arabic modal expressions does not necessarily lead to translation problems, even though some such expressions constitute lexical and structural gaps. That is because the translation approach I adopt here focuses on communicative functions rather than grammatical structures.

Each of the above-mentioned modal expressions has its own semantic and pragmatic properties. On the scale of necessity, يتحتم encodes the highest degree of obligation, followed by يتعين and then يجب, but يتحتم and يتعين suggest external sources of obligation, whereas يجب is neutral in this regard. The verb ينبغي, which is lower than يجب on the scale of necessity, indicates moral obligation, whereas يضطر expresses yielding to a high degree of external obligation. These pragmatic properties help us identify the English modal expressions that can be considered functional equivalents to Arabic modals. For example, the notion of moral obligation suggests that ينبغي is best translated as *should*, because both have the same semantic and pragmatic functions. The modals of necessity that invoke external obligation—namely, يضطر ,يتعين ,يتحتم—are best translated as *have to*, because this expression also indicates external obligation. The verb يجب, conversely, can be translated as *should, must,* or *have to*, depending on our interpretation of the source and type of obligation indicated in the Arabic sentence. On the scale of possibility, يمكن encodes a higher degree of probability than يحتمل,

therefore, they can be considered functional equivalents to *may* and *might*, respectively. The verbs يستطيع and يقدر encode ability, which is the function of the modal auxiliary *can*. The particles قد and ربما are the lowest on the possibility scale, and they describe low probability rather than ability. Although it is possible to identify crosslinguistic functional equivalencies between individual Arabic and English modal expressions, translating modality is always dependent on the context. In other words, these equivalencies are helpful suggestions, but we cannot treat them as translation rules.

The pragmatic functions of modal expressions are traditionally classified into three categories that cut across the possibility/necessity dichotomy: deontic modality, epistemic modality, and dynamic modality. Deontic modality includes all uses of modal expressions that involve controlling other people's actions, including deontic possibility (e.g., يمكنك الذهاب الآن *You may go now*), and deontic necessity (e.g., عليك الذهاب الآن *You have to go now*). In other words, we find deontic modality in sentences that are used to issue directives, make promises, or give permissions. The idea of controlling actions extends to include subjective and gradient assessments of moral and social obligations, as in ينبغي أن نشكرها على الهدية *We should thank her for the gift*. Epistemic modality conveys logical inferences and judgments regarding the truthfulness of propositions. For example, when we say *John left an hour ago. He must be home by now*, we are communicating our inference that the proposition *John is at home now* is true based on the information in the first sentence. The only Arabic modal expression that encodes epistemic modality is لا بد, as in لا بد أنك جوعان *You must be hungry*. Dynamic modality has to do with objective descriptions of abilities and needs; therefore, it includes most uses of يستطيع *can* and يقدر *can* as well as modal expressions of necessity if they describe needs, such as يلزم. This classification is very helpful when one analyzes the communicative functions of Arabic modal expressions, which is necessary to evaluate translation candidates.

3.1 Double Modality

As we saw with temporal reference and negation, the semantic properties of functional categories are universal, yet their grammatical properties are language-specific, which can lead to structural gaps and possible translation problems. For example, قد and ربما are modal expressions of possibility that encode low probability; therefore, they are equivalent to the modal auxiliary verbs *may* and *might*. Unlike modal verbs, ربما and قد do not affect the internal grammatical structure of the clause, and as a result, they can be used together in the same sentence, as in (33). English does not allow more than one modal auxiliary verb in the same clause, which rules out the possibility of translating قد ربما using two adjacent modal verbs. Substituting one of the modal expressions in the source sentence with a modal adverb saves the grammaticality of the translation but it yields redundancy, as in *Perhaps he may be there*. The double modality in this sentence calls for a functional approach; we need to identify the communicative function of the source construction and translate it using a functional equivalent in the target language. The Arabic expression قد ربما is not functionally redundant; it expresses a degree of probability lower than what we would get if we used either modal by itself. The lowest level of probability is expressed in English by the modal verb *might*; therefore, we can apply deletion and translate ربما قد as *might*. This way we can avoid both ungrammaticality and redundancy.

(33) جريدة المصري اليوم (مصر)، ١٤ مارس ٢٠٠٩، العدد ١٧٣٥.
ووصلت معلومات إلى إدارة تنفيذ الأحكام تؤكد أن نبيل لديه شقة في
الإسكندرية **ربما قد** يكون متواجدا بها.

The Sentence Enforcement Agency received a tip that Nabil has
an apartment in Alexandria, where he might be.

The syntactic properties of قد and ربما allow them to appear in sentences with lexical modal verbs of possibility and necessity. When قد or ربما is followed by a modal verb of possibility, as in ربما/قد يمكن and ربما/قد يحتمل, we get constructions that encode very low levels of probability that we can translate by applying deletion, as we did in (33) above. If the modal verb encodes ability, as in ربما/قد يستطيع, we can apply substitution to translate the resulting construction as *might be able to* or *perhaps . . . can*. When these modals co-occur with modal verbs of necessity, as in ربما/قد يجب and قد يتحتم/, we do not need any special strategies to translate them, because we can simply use the permissible equivalent structures in English, such as *might have to* and *may be necessary to*, among others, depending on the context. When translating sentences with ربما or قد followed by a modal verb, we need to pay special attention to their rhetorical functions because these constructions are often used as discourse hedges to indicate that the speaker is not the source of obligation or as a way of undermining obligation or probability.

Because many modal expressions in Arabic are lexical verbs that can take sentential subjects, we sometimes find complex structures in which the sentential subject itself has a modal expression of its own. Although no grammatical rules limit such combinations, they are highly restricted for semantic reasons. For example, we can have a modal verb of necessity with an embedded modal verb of possibility, provided that the embedded modal describes ability rather than probability, as in يجب أن يستطيع and يجب أن يمكنه, both of which can be translated as *has to be able to*. When we say that a situation is necessarily true, we automatically commit ourselves to its possibility. This is why we do not find structures such as يتحتم أن يحتمل *it is necessary that it is possible*, in which the embedded verb can only describe probability. The combinations of modal verbs of possibility with embedded modal verbs of necessity are even more restricted because of the potential inconsistency in describing a situation both as necessarily true and merely possible at the same time. The only permissible combinations are those that describe the possibility of external obligation, such as يمكن أن يضطر and يحتمل أن يضطر, both of which can be translated as *he may/might have to*. The least common modal combinations are those in which we have modals of the same type (necessity or possibility) both in the main and embedded clauses, as in يمكن أن يحتمل *it is possible that it is possible* and يجب أن ينبغي *it is necessary that it is necessary* because these are semantically redundant. If we encounter such a combination, we can simply apply deletion to avoid phrases such as *can be able to* and *must have to*, which are not acceptable in English.

3.2 Modality and Negation

The biclausal structure associated with Arabic lexical modal verbs provides two positions for negation, because it can be in the main clause preceding the modal verb (external negation), as in لا يجب أن ترحل *lit. It is not necessary that you leave*, or in the subject clause following أن (internal negation), as in يجب أن لا ترحل *lit. It is necessary that you do not leave*. The difference in meaning between these two examples is clear; negation in the main clause of a modal of necessity denies obligation, whereas negation in the subject clause expresses prohibition. We see the same semantic distinction in the negation of *have to* and *must*, in which *do(es) not have to* denies obligation, whereas *must not* expresses prohibition. This functional parallel allows us to translate لا يجب أن ترحل as *You do not have to leave* and يجب أن لا ترحل as *You must not leave*. Although this solution works well in many cases, we should not treat it as a translation rule because when negation precedes a modal verb in Arabic, it is functionally ambiguous because it can encode prohibition as well, as in (34). This ambiguity can only be resolved by analyzing the context to figure out the intended function of negation in the source sentence. One way of doing this is to look at the affirmative embedded clause and determine the writer's attitude toward it, which is the motivation for using negation in the first place. If the situation described in the embedded clause is something that the writer would not like to see at all, we have a case of prohibition, and we can translate it using *must not*. If it is a situation that the writer would not mind seeing sometimes, we are dealing with lack of obligation, which can be translated using *do(es) not have to*. In this particular example, we need to choose between *criminal evidence does not have to be obtained illegally* and *criminal evidence must not be obtained illegally*. The paraphrase in the second sentence in (34) makes it clear that the intended function of negation is prohibition.

(34) جريدة الوطن (الكويت)، ٧ يونيو ٢٠١٠، العدد ١٢٣٦٦.

إن دليل الجريمة **لا يجب** أن يجيء عن طريق غير مشروع، فقد ضبط الرجل وهو يشرب الخمر وبعض موبقات أخرى ولكن ينبغي هنا أن يكون ضبطه وفقا لإجراءات مشروعة.

Criminal evidence must not be obtained illegally. The man was arrested while consuming alcohol and other illegal substances, but his arrest should have followed legal procedures.

Although the negation patterns we just saw with يجب apply to all other Arabic lexical modal verbs of necessity, we cannot generalize the translation strategies that work with يجب to other such verbs because each one has its own unique semantic properties that interact differently with negation. For example, we saw earlier that يضطر is a modal verb of necessity that expresses yielding to external obligations. In other words, it is functionally equivalent to *have to*. When negation precedes يضطر, we get a construction that denies obligation, and, accordingly, it can be translated as *does not have to*. The problem is that when يضطر takes an embedded negative clause, as in اضطررت ألا أشارك in (35), we get a construction that encodes the obligation of a negative situation. We cannot translate اضطررت ألا أشارك as *I had to not participate/attend* because, though it captures the meaning of the source phrase, its grammaticality is questionable at best. Of course, if we translate it as *I did not have to participate/attend*, we completely change the meaning. Here, we need to apply some of the word- and phrase-level translation strategies we discussed earlier to come up with a translation candidate that preserves the meaning of the source sentence. We can, for example, apply substitution to get *I could not participate/attend*, in which we translate a modal of necessity using a modal of possibility because being forced to not do something is equivalent to not being able to do it. Alternatively, we can maintain the modal of obligation *had to* while substituting the verb in the complement clause in a way that entails the meaning of negation without expressing it overtly, as in *I had to miss*.

(35) جريدة النهار (لبنان)، ١٤ أبريل ٢٠٠٧، العدد ٢٢٩٧٣.

أشعر بضياع كامل يوم الأحد إذا **اضطررت ألا** أشارك في القداس الإلهي.

I feel completely lost on Sunday if I have to miss the Holy Mass.

Arabic modal verbs of possibility have the same grammatical patterns as modal verbs of necessity; we can have negation in the main clause preceding the modal verb, as in لا يمكن أن ترحل *It is not possible that you leave*, or in the subject clause, as in يمكن أن لا ترحل *It is possible that you do not leave*. However, there is one critical semantic difference: Externally negated modal verbs of possibility do not display the kind of ambiguity we saw with يجب. In other words, when negation precedes a modal verb of possibility, we have a structure that can only deny possibility, meaning *it is not possible that*. The whole phrase لا يمكن أن can be directly translated using *cannot*, as in (36), in which possibility is interpreted as probability. We can use a different negated modal of possibility, such as *may not* and *might not*, if the negated possibility is interpreted as denying permission.

(36) جريدة الوسط (البحرين)، ٣ يناير ٢٠٠٨، العدد ١٩٤٥.

يعتقد على نطاق واسع أن الأمهات المرضعات **لا يمكن** أن يصبحن حوامل لكن أطباء النساء يحذرون من أن هذا قد لا يكون صحيحا تماما.

It is widely believed that mothers who are breastfeeding cannot become pregnant, but ob/gyns warn that this might not be completely true.

In (37), conversely, we have negation in the subject clause. As a result, the sentence expresses possibility rather than the lack thereof, even though it is a possibility of a negated state of affairs. This is a structural gap because English does not have a construction that would be equivalent in this context. The relative clause يمكن أن لا تتجاوز العام encodes dynamic modality, and it is interpreted as *it is possible that it (the period) does not exceed a year*. Because the source sentence is describing possibility, we can consider *may* and *can* as equivalents of يمكن, as in *a period that cannot/may not exceed a year*. The problem here is that using either modal would result in a functional mismatch because these candidates would either deny that probability or add an unwarranted ambiguity by triggering a deontic interpretation—namely, that the duration of the project is not allowed to exceed a year. The solution lies somewhere else in the source sentence. The modal clause itself is embedded within the adverbial clause headed by آملين *hoping*, which implicitly expresses probability; when we hope for something, we imply that we believe it is possible. In other words, the modal expression is rather redundant, and we can leave it out without causing translation losses or ambiguities. We can also leave out negation if we reconstruct the interim translation *does not exceed a year* in a way that implicitly expresses negation. We can do this by reconstructing the subject clause as a temporal adverbial phrase using prepositions, as in *hoping to complete it (the project) within a year/in less than a year*.

(37) جريدة السفير (لبنان)، ٣٠ أكتوبر ٢٠٠٩، العدد ١١٣٤٣.
وقد اختارت البلدية مكانا آخرا لإقامة هذا المشروع حدد في جبل الضهر
غربي حاصبيا، آملين إنجازه خلال فترة **يمكن أن لا** تتجاوز العام.

The municipality has chosen a different site for this project on
Jabal Al-Dahr, west of Hasbia, hoping to complete it within
a year.

Having two possible positions for negation means that it is possible to have negation in both. For example, the sentence in (38) has two instances of negation: One is in the main clause preceding the modal verb يمكن and the other is in the modal's subject clause preceding the predicate يستشير *consult*. In semantic terms, this sentence means *it is not possible for Al-Khidr not to consult the authorities* or *Al-Khidr cannot not consult the authorities*, which is not permissible. As we saw in our previous discussion of double negation, this is not the kind of construction in which two negations would cancel each other out. Neutralizing negation here would give us *Al-Khidr can consult the authorities*, which is not what the source sentence means at all. The combination of two negations with a modal of possibility gives us a construction that describes necessity. In this particular sentence, necessity does not describe obligation, but rather probabilistic necessity and the lack of volition. In other words, in every possible situation in which Al-Khidr makes a decision, he is certain to consult the authorities. To maintain this interpretation, we need to keep the negation that denies the modal verb, while rephrasing the subject clause in a way that does not require negation. We can do this by using the preposition *without*, as in *Al-Khidr cannot make such decisions without consulting the authorities*. This solution takes care of the structural problem, but there is still the unresolved issue of volition, which can be reflected in the translation if we use a negated modal of volition, such as *would*.

(38) جريدة الصحافة (السودان)، ١٨ مارس ٢٠٠٨، العدد ٥٢٩٧.
كما أن عبد الرحمن الخضر – الذي أعرفه جيدا – **لا يمكن أن لا يستشير**
السلطات في مثل هذه القرارات.

Besides, Abdel-Rahman Al-Khidr, whom I know very well, would never make such decisions without consulting the authorities.

Double negation works differently with modal verbs of necessity because the negation in the subject clause is blocked. The sentence in (39) has a very similar structure to the one in the previous example; we have a negated modal verb in the main clause, and a subject clause that also includes negation. The subject clause describes the following state of affairs: *This is at the expense of our environment*, which is negated, resulting in *This is not at the expense of our environment*. This negated clause is within the scope of the modal verb of necessity يجب, which can be translated as *should*, because the sentence describes deontic moral obligation, yielding *It is necessary that this not be at the expense of our environment*, which can be paraphrased as *This should not be at the expense of our environment*. Obviously, the problem is that the main modal verb is negated in a construction that would literally mean *It is not necessary that this should not be at the expense of our environment* or *This should not not be at the expense of our environment*, neither of which can be considered a valid translation. The two negations do not cancel each other out; otherwise, the sentence would mean *This should be at the expense of our environment*. What is unique about negated modal verbs of necessity is that they block the semantic function of negation in their subject clauses. Because negation in the subject clause is semantically irrelevant, we can simply ignore it and translate the sentence as if there were only one negative operator.

(39) جريدة الرؤية الاقتصادية (الإمارات)، ٢ نوفمبر ٢٠٠٩، العدد ٢٣٢.
إننا مطالبون دائما بالعمل على تحسين قدراتنا التقنية، في وقت **لا يجب أن لا**
يكون ذلك على حساب بيئتنا.

We are always required to work on improving our technological capabilities, but at the same time, this should not be at the expense of our environment.

3.3 Modality and Temporal Interpretations

Finally, we turn to the temporal interpretations of sentences with modal expressions. Because many Arabic modal expressions are lexical verbs, we expect them to have perfective, imperfective, and prospective forms that describe modality in different temporal domains, just like other verbs. This is true for most modal verbs, but some, particularly ينبغي *should* and يحتمل *may*, are strictly stative predicates that describe static situations of possibility and necessity. Consequently, the perfective forms of these verbs—namely, انبغى and احتمل—do not occur in main clauses. If these verbs are to describe past modalities, their imperfective forms combine with كان, as in كان ينبغي *should have* and كان يحتمل *might have*.

Other modal verbs, such as يجب, يستطيع, and يمكن, are ambiguous between inchoative and stative readings, and as a result, their perfective forms can only have inchoative interpretations in which they describe the transition of situations into being necessary or possible. For example, the perfective verb استطاع literally means *became able to* rather than *was able to*, whereas the perfective verb وجب means *became necessary* rather than *was necessary*. Just like other perfective inchoative verbs, these perfective modal verbs are temporally ambiguous, as they tell us that a situation became necessary or possible, but we do not know whether this possibility or necessity holds at speech time. As a result, these perfective modal verbs can be translated using the past simple, the present perfect, or the present simple tense, depending on the context. For example, the verb phrase with وجب in (40) tells us that the situation of indebted countries accumulating foreign currencies became necessary, but it does not tell us whether this necessity holds at speech time. However, we have the adverbial phrase خلال سنوات ١٩٧٠ *during the '70s*, which specifies the past as the temporal domain of this modality, thus indicating that the modal verb in this particular sentence is best translated as *had to*.

(40) الأهرام الاقتصادي (مصر)، ٢٩ سبتمبر ٢٠٠٨، العدد ٢٠٧٣.
وكانت الغالبية العظمى من القروض مسعرة بعملات قوية كالدولار هكذا **وجب**
خلال سنوات ١٩٧٠ على البلدان المستدينة التزود بكميات متزايدة من العملة
الصعبة لأجل السداد.

The vast majority of loans were in strong currencies, such as
the US dollar. Thus, during the 1970s, indebted countries had to
accumulate increasing amounts of foreign currencies to pay back.

The second clause in (41) also has the perfective form of the inchoative
modal verb وجب, which is modified by the present adverb الآن *now*. The
modal verb describes acting quickly as a situation that became necessary
in the past, whereas the adverb indicates that the resultant state of being
necessary holds at speech time. The best way to describe this temporal
structure in English is the present perfect tense, but it does not work well
with modal expressions, as in *have had to*. Besides, the present perfect
would not collocate with the adverbial *now* in this context. Alternatively,
we can use the present simple, because the focus is on the present resultant
state.

(41) المصري اليوم، (مصر)، ٨ يوليو ٢٠٠٩، العدد ١٨٥١.
لم تتخذ وزارة الخارجية إجراء حتى الآن لإنقاذ الصيادين، لذلك **وجب** علينا
الآن التحرك السريع.

Thus far, the Ministry of Foreign Affairs has not taken any
action to rescue the fishermen. Therefore, we must act quickly.

In the absence of temporal adverbs, we need to rely on the context to
identify the clues that would help us determine the intended temporal reference of perfective modal verbs and, in effect, their appropriate translations. In (42), for instance, we have the modal phrase وجب تواجد هذه
المغذيات *lit. the presence of these nutrients became necessary*, but it does
not tell us whether the resultant state of being necessary is true at speech
time or not. In this case, we can rely on the discourse type of the source
sentence to determine how to translate it. The source sentence is a factual
statement serving as a logical conclusion in an expository text. Therefore,
we can assume that the resultant state holds at speech time, and translate
the perfective modal verb وجب as *have to* (present simple tense), as we
usually do with statements that describe scientific facts. Note that translating وجب using past constructions—such as *had to* and *should have*,
which is how we usually translate perfective verbs—is inaccurate in this
case because these translation candidates would change the meaning, as
they would strongly suggest that the availability of these nutrients is no
longer necessary.

(42) جريدة الصباح (العراق)، ١٧ نوفمبر ٢٠٠٩، العدد ١٨٢٥.
ويعد النتروجين والفسفور والبوتاسيوم من مغذيات التربة الأساسية، لذلك
وجب تواجد هذه المغذيات للحفاظ على التربة من التصحر.

Nitrogen, phosphorus, and potassium are essential soil
nutrients. Therefore, they must be available to protect
against desertification.

The temporal structure expressed by كان, followed by the imperfective
form of an inchoative modal verb (e.g., كان يمكن, كان يستطيع, and كان يجب), is
semantically equivalent to the temporal structure of the perfective forms of
these verbs when used alone (e.g., أمكن, استطاع, and وجب). The former structure tells us that the resultant state of being possible or necessary started
in the past, whereas the latter tells us that the transition into being possible
or necessary is complete, thus entailing the beginning of the resultant state.
Neither construction tells us whether or not the resultant state persists into
the present. The real difference between these two temporal modal constructions has to do with the realization of modality. The temporal construction
made up of كان and the imperfective form of a modal verb of possibility (e.g.,
كان يمكن and كان يستطيع) indicates that the modal situation never took place;
it was only a possibility. The perfective forms of inchoative modal verbs of
possibility, conversely, tell us not only that the modal situation was possible but also that it did take place. For example, both كان أمكن أن يفوز and
كان يمكن أن يفوز tell us that it was possible for him to win, but
means that he did not win, whereas أمكن أن يفوز means that he won. This
difference does not come up with modal verbs of necessity; perfective modal
verbs of necessity are ambiguous in this regard, whereas their imperfective
forms with كان strongly suggest that the modal situation did not take place.
For example, وجب عليه أن يسافر *He had to travel* does not tell us whether he
traveled or not, whereas كان يجب أن يسافر *He should have traveled* indicates
that he did not travel.

The expression of future modality in Arabic is straightforward; lexical
modal verbs take the future prefix ـس or they are preceded by the future
marker سوف, yielding prospective modal constructions, such as سوف يجب
It will be necessary and سوف يمكن *It will be possible*. The future markers ـس
and سوف are functionally equivalent to the auxiliary modal verb *will*, which
disallows the use of other modal verbs, as in the ungrammatical sequences
will must and *will can*. The solution here is to find a nonauxiliary modal

expression to translate the lexical modal verb, hence translating سوف يجب as *will have to* and سوف يمكن as *will be able to*, *will be possible*, *will likely*, or *perhaps will*, depending on the contextual interpretation of modality and the grammatical structure of the translation.

Modal particles and frozen expressions, such as قد, ربما, and لا بد, do not determine temporal reference by themselves; temporal interpretations are dependent on the clausal structures that follow them. For example, لا بد can be followed by a clause with an imperfective verb (or a nominal clause) to describe present epistemic modality, as in لابد أنك جوعان *You must be hungry*, or a clause with a perfective verb to describe past epistemic modality, as in لابد أنك كنت بالبيت *You must have been at home* and لا بد أنه رحل مبكرا *He must have left early*. The same modal expression can be followed by a clause with an imperfective verb to encode deontic modality, as in لا بد أن نرحل الآن *We have to leave now*, but the aspectual verb كان must precede it to describe past deontic modality, as in كان لا بد أن نرحل, which can be translated as *We should have left* or *We had to leave* depending on the context. When لا بد is followed by a clause with a prospective verb, it can only have an epistemic interpretation making an inference about a future state of affairs, as in (43). The problem, of course, is that English rarely allows future epistemic modality, leaving us with substitution as the only option. In this particular sentence, we cannot use *have to* because it would express future obligations, as in *will have to be published*. Instead, we can use *will* to maintain the future reference, and translate لا بد using the adverbial phrase *most likely*, which describes the same degree of probability as the source sentence.

(43) جريدة عكاظ (السعودية)، ٨ يوليو ٢٠٠٦، العدد ١٨٤٧.
ومن حسن الحظ أن مندوبي صحيفة النيويورك تايمز كانا يسجلان نفس الحديث الذي **لا بد أنه سينشر** فيها قريبا.

Fortunately, the two *New York Times* reporters were recording the same interview, which will most likely be published soon.

The temporal interpretations of lexical modal verbs are the same as those of other verbs of the same semantic classes—for example, stative and inchoative verbs. The only thing that distinguishes modal verbs from others is that the former describe attitudes toward propositions rather than just propositions. Therefore, they cannot have progressive or iterative interpretations, just like English auxiliary modal verbs.

4   Voice

The basic function of an active voice sentence, such as *The company hired Hanna*, is to provide a basic, yet complete, description of a situation; the verb denotes some type of action (an event of hiring), whereas the subject (the company) and the direct object (Hanna) refer to the participants in this situation, with the subject position reserved for the most prominent participant. This sentence can be augmented with adverbial phrases to provide information about time, place, and manner, and so on, but the basic description of this situation is complete without these additions. The passive voice, as in *Hanna was hired*, allows us to describe the same situation differently, as it profiles the participant who undergoes the action (Hanna) as the most prominent one by placing it in the subject position, while the original subject, also called the logical subject, is deleted. Of course, we can add a prepositional phrase to represent the logical subject, as in *Hanna was hired by the company*, but the passive sentence is still about Hanna, not the company, which is secondary in importance. There are many reasons to use the passive voice; it helps avoid first-person pronouns, conceals the identity of the logical subject, and describes situations in which we do not know the logical subject. Still, the main rhetorical function of the passive voice is to put the participant affected by the situation in the prominence position.

4.1   The Passive Voice

Voice in Arabic is essentially a word-level construction because it is expressed by changing the internal vocalic melody of the verb. The basic rule for deriving a perfective passive verb involves replacing the penultimate stem vowel with /i/ and changing all other stem vowels to /u/, as in كتب (*katab-a*) *wrote* versus كتب (*kutib-a*) *was written*, and استقبل (*istaqbal-a*) *received* versus استقبل (*ustuqbil-a*) *was received*. Note that the final vowel is the indicative mood marker, which is not part of the stem or the vocalic melody. For imperfective verbs, the passive form is derived by replacing the first vowel with /u/ and changing the stem final or penultimate vowel to /a/, as in يكتب (*yaktub-u*) *writes* versus يكتب (*yuktab-u*) *is written* and يستقبل (*yastaqbil-u*) *receives* versus يستقبل (*yustaqbal-u*) *is received*. The final output of the passive derivation rules is subject to the general phonological constraints of the language. For instance, Arabic does not allow words with two vowels in a row. As a result, if a perfective stem has a long vowel in the penultimate position, it becomes a long /i:/ to avoid the sequence of the passive /i/ and a long vowel, as in قال *said* versus قيل *was said* and استعار *borrowed* versus استعير *was borrowed*. Moreover, if the penultimate vowel of an imperfective verb is long, it is replaced with a long /a:/, as in يقول *says* versus يقال *is said* and يبيع *sells* versus يباع *is sold*. Using the passive voice affects the grammatical structure of the whole sentence, as the object is moved to the subject position, where it is marked with the nominative case instead of the accusative case associated with the object position, and the logical subject is deleted or represented in a prepositional phrase—such as على يد, بواسطة, or من قبل (pronounced *min qibal*)—all of which can be translated as *by*. In terms of function, the passive voice in Arabic has the same rhetorical functions as the English passive I mentioned earlier. Therefore, the Arabic and English passive constructions can be considered functionally equivalent.

Whether we are dealing with a translation problem that involves voice in the source sentence or changing voice as a translation strategy, there are consequences for the structure of the entire sentence. For example, the active voice verb يخضع in (44) means *to submit to, be subject to*, or *undergo*, but none of these candidates collocates with *exhibit* in the sense described in the source sentence. The source sentence is about an art exhibit where artists present their work, and a panel of experts evaluates them. The verb *submit to* requires a sentient agent willing to give up power, whereas *subject to* suggests that the panel evaluates the artworks only sometimes. Perhaps, *undergoes* is the most successful of these candidates, but its optimality depends on how we translate the rest of the sentence. We have another collocation problem with عملية تحكيم *lit. a process of judging/jurying*, which does not collocate with *an exhibit*, even if we use *jury* as a verb. In order to avoid awkward translations, such as *the exhibit undergoes a process of jurying*, we can apply lexical substitution and reconstruction to translate يخضع لعملية تحكيم as the passive form *is juried*, which is a common English expression used to describe this type of situation. In addition to resolving the collocations issue, the passive voice helps keep the exhibit as the topic of the sentence by keeping it in the subject position.

(44) جريدة اليوم (السعودية)، ٢١ أبريل ٢٠٠٤، العدد ١٠٩٠٢.
المعرض **يخضع** لعملية تحكيم **اعتيد** اختيار أعضائها من خارج السلطنة وتمثلت هذه السنة في الفنان العراقي شوكت الربيعي والفنان الأردني محمد العامري والفنان السعودي د. حمزة باجودة.

The exhibit is juried by a committee whose members are usually
selected from abroad. This year, the committee is made up of
three artists: Shawkat Al-Rabi'i from Iraq, Mohamed Al-Amiry
from Jordan, and Dr. Hamza Bajouda from Saudi Arabia.

Another voice-related issue in this sentence is the passive verb اعتيد,
which is the perfective form of يعتاد *get/be used to*. This is a functional
gap because the English equivalents, *was used to* and *was accustomed to*,
are not used the same way. The subject we have in the source passive sentence is اختيار أعضائها *the selection of its members*, but we cannot translate
اعتيد اختيار أعضائها as *the selection of its members was used to being from
abroad*. Usually, when we encounter a problematic passive sentence in Arabic, we consider translating it using its active voice counterpart, but this
is not an option in this particular case because we do not know the logical
subject, the person(s) or agency who selects the committee members. To
resolve this problem, we need to analyze the context to identify the function
of the source construction. The passive verb اعتيد is an inchoative perfective predicate that describes a situation as having become recurrent enough
to be considered a habit. Just as we saw with other inchoative verbs, this
situation can end in the past or extend into speech time. The latter is the
case here, as indicated by the adverbial phrase هذه السنة *this year*. Thus, we
need an English construction that describes a recurrent or habitual present situation. We can rephrase *the selection of its members is used to being
from abroad* as *a committee whose members are used to being selected from
abroad* or *a committee whose members used to be selected from abroad*,
but these translations do not mean the same thing as the source sentence.
Another alternative is to apply reconstruction and use the adverb *usually*,
which is functionally equivalent to *is used to* in this context. The problem
now is that we have lost the main verb of the source sentence; therefore,
further reconstruction is in order. To make up for the loss induced by substituting *is used to* with *usually*, we can keep the translation of اختيار *selecting* as a passive verb, resulting in *a committee whose members are usually
selected from abroad*. These strategies give us a translation that maintains
the temporal interpretation of the source sentence (the habitual present), the
passive voice (thus keeping the committee members in the prominence position), and the syntactic structure of the embedded relative clause.

The sentence in (45) is similar to the one I just discussed in that it has a
clause with an active verb that can be translated as a passive verb—namely,

صدر *lit. came out*—and a clause with a passive verb that constitutes a functional gap—namely, جِيء به *lit. was come with*. The verb صدر is used in this context because it is an intransitive verb whose subject refers to the entity that undergoes change. This way the decree is used in the subject position, which reflects its prominence without mentioning the logical subject or the source of the decree. The problem is that English equivalents of صدر, such as *came out* and *emerged*, do not collocate well in this context, as in *a decree came out/emerged to build a memorial*, which are awkward at best. The discourse function of these types of verbs is the same as the passive construction, in which the entity that undergoes change is expressed in the subject position with no mention of the logical subject. Therefore, we can translate this active voice verb using the passive via lexical substitution and reconstruction to end up with *a decree was issued to build a memorial*.

(٤٥) جريدة الشرق الأوسط (السعودية)، ٧ يناير ٢٠٠٩، العدد ١٠٩٩٨.
في يناير(كانون الثاني) عام ١٩٢٤ تاريخ وفاة لينين **صدر** قرار إقامة ضريح تاريخي يليق بقدر زعيم الثورة البلشفية. وفي زمن قياسي وخلال ثلاثة أيام فقط صمم المعماري شوسيف هذا الضريح الذي أعيد بناؤه لاحقا من أحجار الغرانيت وأفخر أنواع الرخام الذي **جيء** به خصيصا من أرمينيا.

When Lenin died in January 1924, a decree was issued to build
a historical memorial worthy of the Bolshevik Revolution leader.
In a record time of three days, the architect Shchusev designed
this memorial, which was later rebuilt with granite and marble
of the highest quality, specially imported from Armenia.

Intransitive verbs, such as جاء *came*, do not normally have passive forms because there is no object that would function as the subject of the passive sentence. However, if the verb is followed by a preposition, the complement of that preposition can be used as the subject of the passive verb, as in جِيء به *lit. it was come with* in (46). English allows the use of prepositional complements as subjects in passive sentences only if the verb and the preposition function as a phrasal verb, as in *The president was looked up to* and *My house was put up for sale*. This means that جِيء به cannot be translated as *was come with* because *come with* is not a phrasal verb. Translating this sentence using the active voice is not possible because we do not know who came with the marble from Armenia. This leaves us with only one option: To look for a transitive verb that can describe the same situation, and to apply lexical substitution. For example, the verb *bring* means more or less the same thing as *come with*; therefore, we can translate جيء به as *was brought* or *imported*, because the granite was brought from abroad.

Just as noun phrase objects can be used as subjects in passive sentences, clausal objects can also be subjects in these sentences. The only issue is that neither Arabic nor English allows sentence–initial clausal subjects in passive sentences. In English, we can start the sentence with *it*, as in *It is rumored that John will be the next president*, or we can start with the subject of an embedded infinitive clause, as in *John is believed to be a spy*. These syntactic strategies are not necessary in Arabic because we can resolve this issue by starting the passive sentence with the verb, as in أذيع أن كريم هو الرئيس الجديد *It was announced that Karim is the new president*. The only problems we might encounter when translating Arabic passive sentences with sentential subjects are lexical in nature. For example, the verb خيل is rather unique in that it profiles a mental event of imagining with the imagined material described in the subject clause, whereas the logical subject is expressed in a prepositional phrase, as in (46). Of course, we cannot translate خيل لي أن الطبق الطائر يقف في الميدان as *It was imagined to me that the UFO was standing in the square*. We can slightly improve this candidate translation by leaving out the prepositional phrase, to end up with *It was imagined that the UFO was standing in the square*, which is grammatical, but this change comes at the expense of losing the logical subject; now there is nothing in the sentence to tell us who imagined this scene. To avoid the complications of trying to include the clausal subject and the logical subject in a passive sentence, we can reconstruct the whole sentence in the active voice.

(46) جريدة الاتحاد (الإمارات)، ٤ يناير ٢٠٠٩، العدد ١٢٢٣٦.
هذه المرة فاض بي فأغلقت الكمبيوتر وغادرت المكان متسللا. في طريقي
للبيت **خيل** لي أن الطبق الطائر يقف في الميدان فعلا، وكائنات خضراء اللون
لها هوائيان على الرأس تخرج منه لتخاطب الناس.

This time, I got fed up, so I turned off the computer and slipped
away. On my way home, I imagined that the UFO actually
landed in the city square and green aliens with antennas
sticking out of their heads were walking out to address people.

4.2 Lexical Passive

Although the passive voice has the same discourse functions in Arabic and English, there is one significant difference: Arabic uses passive verbs less frequently, perhaps because many of them look exactly like their active counterparts in the absence of vowel marking. In fact, the most common way to partially describe a situation without expressing the logical subject in Arabic involves lexically passive verbs, passive participles, and the aspectual verb تمّ *completed*. Many Form V and Form VII verbs are intransitive predicates that are similar to passive verbs in that they describe situations with the participant that undergoes change as a subject, as in انفتح الباب *The door opened* and تحطم الزجاج *The glass shattered*. Many English verbs called unaccusatives work the same way, as in *The vase broke*; *The chicken is cooking*; and *The car drives well*. If there is an unaccusative English verb that profiles the situation described in the Arabic source sentence in the same way, we do not have a problem; but if there is no functional equivalent, we can consider translating these lexically passive verbs using the passive voice, as in انهزم *was defeated* and تقرر *was decided*. The problem with Form V and Form VII verbs is that we cannot make any generalizations about them because they do not all function like the passive voice. For example, some Form V and Form VII verbs are reflexive—that is, the entity that is affected is itself the one that initiates the action, such as تقدم *advance* and اندمج *merge*—whereas some Form V verbs are transitive, such as تصور *imagine* and تعلم *learn*. Therefore, decisions regarding how to translate these verbs have to be made on a case-by-case basis.

Passive participles are adjectives that function like the passive voice in that they describe the affected participant(s). As adjectives, they can be used as noun phrase modifiers (e.g., الباب المفتوح *the open door*), or as predicates (e.g., الباب مفتوح *the door is open*). The derivation of passive participles follows two morphological rules: (1) They take the template مفعول if derived from a basic root—for example, معروف *known*, مسروق *stolen*, and مملوء *filled*—but if the root has a semivowel, it is copied in the same position, as in مدعو *invitee* and موعود *promised*; and (2) if the root has more than three consonants, we add the prefix *mu-* and a short vowel /a/ in the penultimate position—for example, مستعمل *used* and محترم *respected/respectable*—but if the corresponding verb has a vowel, it remains in the same position, as in مختار *chosen/selected*. The most common way to translate passive participles is to use adjectives—for example, مشهور *famous* and مقبول *acceptable*—as well as adjectival passives—for example, مكسور *broken* and منسي *forgotten*. When we run into an Arabic passive participle that does not have a functionally equivalent adjective or adjectival passive in English, we can apply substitution and reconstruction to translate it using the passive voice, as in the case of معثور in (47), where we cannot use *found* as a modifier.

(47) جريدة المصري اليوم (مصر)، ٢٧ يوليو ٢٠٠٩، العدد ١٨٧٠.

كما تناول الدفاع البصمات **المعثور** عليها بغرفة إقامة المتهم الأول بفندق شاطىء الواحة ولم يرد ذكرها فى تقرير البصمات.

The defense brought up the fingerprints that were found in the first defendant's room at the Oasis Beach Hotel, which were not mentioned in the forensics report.

Passive participles are typically derived from transitive verbs, but if an intransitive verb takes a prepositional complement, we can derive a passive participle. For example, the verb سكت *become quiet* is intransitive, but when it is followed by the preposition عن *about*, we can derive the passive participle phrase مسكوت عنه *lit. the thing that is being silent about*, as in (48). Because we cannot translate this phrase literally, we might consider using adjectival passives or the passive voice, such as *muted topics* and *silenced topics*, but these candidates suggest that someone intentionally disallows discussions of these topics, which is not what the source sentence suggests. Alternatively, we can use lexical substitution and translate موضوعات مسكوت عنها as *taboo topics*.

(48) جريدة الأهرام (مصر)، ١٩ يناير ٢٠٠٥، العدد ٤٣١٤٣.

قدمت المخرجة إيناس الدغيدي ١٢ فيلما على مدى ٢٥ سنة، وحصدت عدة جوائز ولكنها مازالت تواجه هجوما شديدا على اعتبار أنها تقدم أفكارا جريئة وتناقش موضوعات **مسكوت عنها**.

The film director Inas Al-Degheidy made twelve feature films over twenty-five years and received several awards. Yet she is still subject to much criticism because she presents daring ideas and discusses taboo issues.

One negative side effect of using the passive voice as a translation strategy is the possibility of shifting discourse perspectives. For example, in (49) the author is stating the position of the Party for Justice and Development on religion as a school subject, while contrasting it to what he sees as a less favorable position, namely, taking religion out of the school curriculum. To make his message more effective, the author chooses to use the passive participle المطلوب *lit. what is wanted/desired* in order to avoid identifying those who support the opposing position by name. In this way, the author makes his statement less confrontational while attempting to establish agreement with the reader. If we use the passive voice to translate the passive participle—as in *The Party for Justice and Development continues to strive to keep religion as an obligatory school subject, while canceling it is desirable/what is wanted/desired*—we get a contradiction, and we change the discourse perspective. The first clause suggests that the author supports the position of the Party for Justice and Development, but in the second clause he adopts a contradictory position. In order to maintain the rhetorical structure of the source text, we can translate the passive participle using the active voice while adding a vague third-person subject, such as *others*, which would preserve the original perspective.

(49) جريدة السفير (لبنان)، ٨ نوفمبر ٢٠١١، العدد ١١٧٣٨.
إن حزب العدالة والتنمية يواصل السعي لإبقاء درس الدين الإجباري في المدارس، في حين **المطلوب** إلغاؤه.

The Party for Justice and Development continues to strive to keep religion as an obligatory school subject, while others want to get rid of it.

The last passive-like construction to discuss is made up of the aspectual verb تم *completed* or جرى *happened*, followed by an event nominal subject, which refers to a type of action, with the affected entity represented by a noun or a pronoun following the event nominal in a possessive construction. If we want to include the logical subject, we can add it in a prepositional phrase, such as من قبل, على يد, or بواسطة, just as we do in passive sentences. Because these constructions are functionally equivalent to the passive voice, we can usually translate them as such—for example, تم بناء السد *The dam was built by Russian engineers* and جرى تحديث جميع البرامج *All programs were upgraded*. However, if the passive voice yields unsuccessful translation candidates, we can resort to other strategies, as in the case of (50). In this sentence, the clause تم انتظار مندوب الإعلام ساعة واحدة cannot be translated word for word using the active voice, as in *The waiting for the media representative for an hour was complete*. We cannot translate it using the passive voice either, because *The media representative was waited for for an hour* is odd at best. Instead, we can apply lexical substitution and reconstruction to get *The media representative was an hour late*, which describes the situation in a slightly different way but keeps the media representative as the focus of the clause.

(50) جريدة الوسط (البحرين)، ٧ يونيو ٢٠٠٣، العدد ٢٧٤.
تم انتظار مندوب الإعلام ساعة واحدة اضطر بعدها رئيس الجلسة إلى افتتاح الاجتماع.

The media representative was an hour late when the session
chair had to call the meeting to order.

What the passive voice, passive participles, lexically passive verbs, and
the aspectual constructions with تم and جرى have in common is that they all
provide incomplete descriptions of situations. They specify the type of action as well as the entity affected by that action, whereas the logical subject
is optional. From a rhetorical perspective, these constructions allow us to
talk about situations for which we do not have all the relevant information,
or, in other contexts, to describe situations without sharing all the relevant
information. More important, they allow us to present the affected entity
as the focus of the sentence. Although these constructions have functional
equivalents in English and we can establish translation patterns, as we have
seen, we cannot posit any translation rules because of cross-linguistic lexical variation. Whenever we encounter voice-related translation problems, we
can use the strategies we discussed as long as the translation is functionally
equivalent to the source text.

Exercises

How would you translate the underlined phrases? What translation candidates
would you consider? Discuss your reasons for selecting a successful candidate.

Exercise 1: Temporal Reference

(١) جريدة الشرق الأوسط (السعودية)، ٢٩ ديسمبر ٢٠٠٨، العدد ١٠٩٨٩.
ولكن طه حسين قال إنه **سوف** يعقد اجتماعا آخرا يجيب عن كل تساؤلاتنا.

(٢) جريدة الأهرام (مصر)، ١ يناير ٢٠١١، العدد ٤٥٣١٦.
من خلال الموجات الكهرومغناطيسية أو إرسال رسائل صوتية معينة يمكن تحديد مكان
الهاتف سواء **كان** مفتوحا أو مغلقا، حيث يحدث تواصل بين الجهاز ومحطات التقوية
والإرسال للشركة مقدمة الخدمة.

(٣) جريدة الرياض (السعودية)، ١٤ نوفمبر ٢٠٠٦، العدد ١٤٠٢٢.
وتحتوي التونة الخفيفة المعلبة على ٠,١٢ جزء من المليون من الزئبق وتحتوي بعض
الأنواع الأخرى على ٠,٣٥ جزء من المليون من الزئبق وذلك يعد ذا خطورة على صحة
الحامل وكلما **كانت** سمكة التونة كبيرة في الحجم كلما **كان** محتواها من الزئبق أعلى.

(4) مجلة روز اليوسف (مصر)، ٧ أغسطس ٢٠٠٤، العدد ٤٢٨٧.

كشف نبيل زكي الأمين العام المساعد للشؤون السياسية والمتحدث الرسمي باسم التجمع أن قائمة التجمع **ضمت** حتى الآن ٦٨ مرشحا في ١٧ محافظة منهم ٩ سيدات على مقاعد الكوتة و ٤ أقباط.

(5) جريدة المستقبل (لبنان)، ١٠ يناير ٢٠٠٥، العدد ١٨١٦.

فيما كان لافتا الغياب ''القسري'' للرئيس الفرنسي جاك شيراك والذي فرضه سوء الأحوال الجوية ـ علما أنه **كان سيكون** أول رئيس فرنسي يشارك في الاجتماع.

Exercise 2: Negation

(1) جريدة الأيام (البحرين)، ٢٢ يونيو ٢٠١٠، العدد ٧٧٤٣.

هذه المباراة **لم تستمر سوى** ١٥ دقيقة بعدما لعب فريق بنا غاز بـ ٧ لاعبين فقط وغياب بقية اللاعبين لأسباب مختلفة ومع إصابة حارس المرمى **وعدم استطاعته إكمال** المباراة اضطر حكم الساحة لإنهاء اللقاء باعتبار أن القانون لا يسمح باستمرار المباراة بوجود ٦ لاعبين فقط على أرضية الميدان.

(2) جريدة الدستور (العراق)، ٢٣ ديسمبر ٢٠١٠، العدد ٢١١٥.

إن زيارته التفتيشية التي يقوم بها هي مفاجئة بنفس الدرجة، **وليس من غير المعروف عنه** في ساعات الصبح أن يأمر بإعداد سيارة ويقطع مسافة ٧٥ ميلا أو أكثر وينزل بصورة مفاجئة على قوات نائية فيثور ويصخب ساعة أو ساعتين ثم يختفي فجأة أيضا بنفس الطريقة التي جاء بها.

(3) جريدة الأيام (البحرين)، ١٣ أغسطس ٢٠١٠، العدد ٧٧٩٥.

تتحدث الرواية، التي وضع مقدمتها الكاتب اللبناني المعروف إلياس خوري وتقع في ٢٦٣ صفحة من القطع الوسط، عن عودة بطلها إلى بلاده بعد عشرين سنة من المنفى عاش خلالها رحلة **تنتفي** فيها الفروق أحيانا بين الحقيقة والخيال.

(4) جريدة الدستور (الأردن)، ٣ يناير ٢٠١١، العدد ١٥١١٤٣.

لا يخفى على أحد أن نظام فرانكو الديكتاتوري في أسبانيا قتل ما يربو على ١٠٠ ألف من خصومه بعد فترة وجيزة من انتهاء الحرب الأهلية في البلاد (١٩٣٦–١٩٣٩).

(5) جريدة الشروق (مصر)، ٣١ ديسمبر ٢٠١٠، العدد ٦٩٩.

فالرجل نشأ في أسرة بسيطة للغاية، ولكنه أصبح من ألمع رجال مصر ومن أكثرهم تأثيرا في الحياة الثقافية المصرية والعربية. **لم يكن هناك أي شيء لا في** أسرة بهاء، **ولا في** البيئة المحيطة به، **ولا في** مصر كلها، **ولا** في ذلك الوقت بالذات، **أي شيء** ينبئ بأن هذا الطفل سوف يكون له شأن كبير.

Exercise 3: Modals

(1) جريدة الأهرام (مصر)، ١٢ سبتمبر ٢٠٠٠، العدد ٤١٥٥٣.
أكد كوفي عنان السكرتير العام للأمم المتحدة في تقريره الأخير المقدم لمجلس الأمن أن المخطط يواجه عدة صعوبات وأنه في نظره **ربما يجب** البحث عن حل آخر.

(2) جريدة السفير (لبنان)، ٣٠ سبتمبر ٢٠٠٨، العدد ١١١١٣.
لا تزال أسمهان لغزا بحسب شريفة زهور كاتبة سيرتها المكتوبة بالإنكليزية والمترجمة إلى العربية عن دار المدى. **لا بد أننا لا نعرف** بدقة سر هجرة الأسرة إلى مصر وابتعادها عن الأب والزوج.

(٣) جريدة الجمهورية (اليمن)، ١٠ مارس ٢٠٠٧، العدد ١٣٦٥٤.
وكل شاب مشارك في هذه الاجتماعات وورش العمل التي ينظمها المجلس **يمكن أن يستطيع** جمع العديد من الرؤى المختلفة لشباب دول العالم الذين التقى بهم ويستفيد من تجاربهم.

(4) جريدة البعث (سوريا)، ١٨ مايو ٢٠١٠، العدد ١٣٩٤٦.
وعلينا أن نعي أن العروبة في خطر حقيقي، والأمة العربية في خطر حقيقي، فإما أن نعمل من أجلها أو نستقيل من الحياة، العروبة مستقبل، ولكنها في خطر حقيقي، ومواجهة هذا الخطر **ضرورة لا بد منها** للدفاع عن العروبة.

(5) جريدة ٢٦ سبتمبر (اليمن)، ٤ مارس ٢٠٠٣، العدد ١٠٥٩.
ونحن في اللجنة العليا للانتخابات والاستفتاء راعينا ثلاثة قوانين: أولا النص الوارد في قانون الانتخابات الذي جعل التزكية مسألة نصية وليست مسألة اجتهادية تخضع للاجتهادات والتقدير وكذلك النص الآخر الموجود في قانون التوثيق، والذي **ألزم** التزكية أن تكون خطية **كي يجب** أن يصادق أمين المحل على التزكية.

Exercise 4: Voice

(1) جريدة السفير (لبنان)، ١٦ ديسمبر ٢٠١٠، العدد ١١٧٦٧.
أهي حقيقة أم شائعة؟ لا نعرف، لكن العلاقة **المزعومة** مادة ممتعة **للقيل والقال**، رغم أن بوتين نفى ما **قيل** بأنه انفصل عن زوجته لودميلا، أم طفليه، ليكون مع عشيقته كاباييفا!

(2) فاروق أحمد مصطفى، ٢٠٠٦، "التراث والتغير الاجتماعي"، مركز البحوث والدراسات الاجتماعية، ص ٢٠٨.
الحياة في الإسلام مقدمة على الدين، ولهذا أجاز الإسلام للمؤمنين ترك الصيام إذا **خيف** منه المرض.

(3) جريدة الأهرام (مصر)، ٤ ديسمبر ٢٠٠٩، العدد ٤٤٩٢٣.
تم الانتهاء من استكمال ٥١٧ مركز شباب في جميع المحافظات، أي لدينا ٦٦٠ مركز شباب أقمناها من الألف إلى الياء وجاري حاليا إنشاء ٢٥٠ مركزا بمحافظات الصعيد.

(4) جريدة الرياض (السعودية)، ٥ مايو ٢٠٠٦، العدد ١٣٨٢٩.
٢٥٠٠٠٠ دولار هي القيمة التي فاز بها حسين، بعد أن تراوحت المبالغ **التي تم الفوز بها** في حلقات سابقة بين ٥٥,٠٠٠ دولار كحد أقصى وبين نظارات شمسية كحد أدنى.

(5) جريدة الوطن (الكويت)، ٢٨ سبتمبر ٢٠١٠، العدد ١٢٤٧٩.
وبهذه المناسبة عبر عدد من مديري المناطق التعليمية عن سعادتهم البالغة بتكريم سمو الأمير للمعلمين المميزين مشيرين إلى أن وزارة التربية عملت **مشكورة** على دعم المعلمين وتطوير أدائهم العلمي والمهني.

Exercise 5: Advanced Translation

(1) جريدة الصباح (العراق)، ٢٤ أكتوبر ٢٠٠٩، العدد ١٨٠٤.
وقد نشرت الكثير من الدراسات والبحوث حول أزمة السكن في العراق وتضمنت حسابات دقيقة لعدد الوحدات السكنية **المطلوب إنشاؤها** لإنهاء الأزمة.

(2) مجلة الشباب (مصر)، ١ مارس ٢٠٠٣، العدد ٣٠٧.
أصيب بالتهاب بسيط في عينيه، **كان يمكن أن يشفى منه** بسهولة، لكن الطبيب أخطأ في علاجه ففقد بصره.

(3) جريدة الأهرام (مصر)، ١٧ يوليو ٢٠٠٣، العدد ٤٢٥٩١.
استهل الاستقالة بالإعراب عن أسفه لنقل الدكتور طه حسين ''لأن هذا الأستاذ **لا يستطاع أن يعوض**''.

(4) جريدة القبس (الكويت)، ١٠ سبتمبر ٢٠٠٩، العدد ١٣٠٣٥.
رحب مكتب حقوق الإنسان التابع للأمم المتحدة بالإفراج عن لبنى الحسين، لكنه قال إن الإفراج لم يغير رأي المكتب في أنه **لم يكن يجب إلقاء القبض عليها أو إدانتها**.

(5) جريدة الأهرام (مصر)، ٢٦ يناير ٢٠٠٧، العدد ٤٣٨٨٠.
لأن الصحفي **لا يملك إلا أن يسأل**.. ولا يحلم **إلا** بأن يلقى إجابات محددة.. مقنعة وصادقة لكل ما يسأل فيه ويفتش عنه.. ولأنني لم أعد أملك رفاهية الوقت والمساحة لكل المفردات ومعانيها.. فإنني الآن أكتفي بهذه الأسئلة.

The Sentence and Beyond

Discourse and Genre Features

Throughout my discussions of translation problems and strategies in the preceding chapters, I have repeatedly emphasized the role of context. When analyzing a text for translation, we use contextual clues to determine the intended referents of pronouns and other referential expressions, resolve lexical and grammatical ambiguities, and recognize metaphorical expressions and their functions. At the same time, we try to make our translations as clear as possible by providing sufficient contextual clues that will, in turn, help our readers analyze and understand the text. For example, we can reconstruct sentences, use transparent referential chains, paraphrase expressions with which we suspect readers might not be familiar, and even provide additional information that can facilitate comprehension. Context is by no means limited to linguistic forms; "context" is an umbrella term that includes all sorts of information that are relevant to a text—including nonlinguistic information, such as the purpose for writing the text, its layout, and its genre, in addition to the text's cultural background and subject matter.

In order to appreciate the value of contextual information, let us imagine three translators working independently on the paragraph in (1); each translator is assigned one section without knowing its source or seeing the rest of the text. The translator working on the first section is likely to assume that there is an individual whose job is to call on people during Ramadan to wake them up for their predawn meal, and that this person was a target. The second translator is most likely to assume that the middle section is about military operations against some regions known as Al-Ahly, where an intense resistance has foiled some attacks. The third translator will have a very difficult time making sense of the first portion of the last section. Only the last clause has a chance of actually rendering a meaningful translation about a sports event, ending with one team winning with one goal. If we put together these translations, which were generated with no access to the larger context of the text, we could end up with something like the translation in (1a).

(1) شبكة ووكالة بال سبورت (فلسطين)، ٨ أكتوبر ٢٠٠٦.
كان هذا الهدف "مسحراتي" رمضان الذي أيقظ لاعبي طارق، فشنوا هجمات ضارية على مناطق الأهلي، الذي رص صفوفه الخلفية، في مقاومة تستحق الإشادة، فأبطل الدفاع الأهلاوي كل محاولات طارق، فيما خرجت عالية تسديدة خلدون الجاهزة من البديل عمار شبانة، وخرجت تسديدة أخرى من رشاد جانبية، لتنهي المباراة بفوز ثمين للأهلي على طارق بالهدف اليتيم.

(1a) This target was a *misaharaty*, a man whose job is to go around the streets at night during the holy month of Ramadan to call on people to wake them up for their predawn meal. He woke up the players of Tariq. They launched vicious attacks on the districts of Al-Ahly, where the rear defense lines put up a remarkable resistance, thwarting all of Tariq's attempts. Meanwhile, Khaldoun's shot, which he got ready from Ammar Shabana, an alternate, came out high; and another shot by Rashad went sideways, to end the game with a precious victory for Al-Ahly over Tariq with a single goal.

The translation in (1a) is obviously unacceptable, but not much can be done in the absence of sufficient contextual clues. There are a few critical ambiguities that cannot be immediately resolved, such as الهدف, which can mean *goal* or *target*, and لاعبي طارق, which can mean *my player whose name is Tariq* or *the players of the Tariq team*. Some parts of this paragraph are quite vague. For example, because there are no capital letters in Arabic, we can only guess that Tariq and Al-Ahly are proper nouns, but there is no way of telling whether they refer to individuals, places, or something else. More important, we do not know which phrases are being used metaphorically and which ones are being used literally. Perhaps the biggest problem is that we cannot determine the logical connections between the clauses that make up the paragraph; we have no way of telling which events were the causes or results of which other events, or how they relate to each other in the temporal sequence. In short, this translation does not make sense. The problem here is that to make sense of the text, we tend to fill in the gaps in our understanding with additional information, but this raises the risk of ending up with a translation that hardly means the same thing as the source text. To avoid this problem, we need to analyze the context of the text to make sure that the information we add to resolve ambiguities is related to the author's original intentions.

Once we know that this text is an excerpt from a sports news article reporting on a soccer game, everything makes sense. On the basis of our knowledge of soccer, we know that there are two teams trying to score points by kicking the ball into the opponent's goal net. This seemingly banal piece of information helps us recognize Al-Ahly and Tariq as the names of soccer teams, which resolves the ambiguities of لاعبي طارق *Tariq players* and مناطق الأهلي *Al-Ahly positions*. We also realize that Khaldoun and Rashad are soccer players, not militia members, and that their shots involved kicking a ball, not launching missiles. Moreover, our experience with sports writing helps us recognize metaphors and their functions; we know that this genre of writing tries to recreate the excitement of watching a game by adopting certain rhetorical strategies. For example, sports writing often profiles games as battles; hence the military metaphors and expressions. It tries to keep the reading tempo fast and exciting by using shorter clauses separated by commas, rather than periods that would signal longer pauses. Finally, this genre has a clear preference for verb-initial sentences that help heighten the tension and keep the readers engaged. Using these kinds of contextual information leads to a very different translation, as in (1b).

> (1b) Al-Ahly's goal came as a wakeup call for the Tariq
> players, who went on the offensive, attacking Al-Ahly's defense
> positions, but Al-Ahly's backline put up a remarkable defense
> and foiled all attempts by the Tariq players to score. Substitute
> Ammar Shabana slipped a perfect pass to Khaldoun, who took
> a shot, but the ball went flying over the bar. Another shot, this
> time by Rashad, went off target to end the game with a precious
> 1–0 victory for Al-Ahly.

This example clearly demonstrates that word-, phrase-, and sentence-level translation strategies do not function in a vacuum; it is almost impossible to accurately translate a text without making full use of the context. However, contextual clues are not without their own problems, because some genre features may exist in the source language but not in the target language, or they might be used to achieve different communicative objectives. In this chapter I discuss six major discourse features that are crucial to translation: sentence structure, rhetorical structure, punctuation, text cohesion, tone, and genre.

1 Sentence Structure

A sentence is made up of two essential constituent phrases: the subject and the predicate. But we can augment this basic structure with optional modifiers, such as prepositional phrases, adverbial phrases, and embedded clauses. The rules that determine the order of these phrases vary across languages, resulting in sentence-level structural gaps. For example, Arabic allows a sentence to start with the verb rather than the subject, but English does not. This kind of structural mismatch is not problematic for translation because we can easily switch the order of the subject and the verb in the same way we switch the order of nouns and their modifying adjectives. However, there are many cases in which a simple switch is not an option because the result is either ungrammatical or functionally inadequate, as in (2). The subject of this sentence is the clause starting with أن يحل *that they arrive*, whereas the predicate is the sentence-initial prepositional phrase من المنتظر *lit. from what is expected*. Obviously, we cannot start the translation with a clausal subject because this is ungrammatical in English, and we cannot maintain the structure of the source sentence either. We have seen in earlier discussions that a prepositional phrase of this type can be translated using an *it*-cleft construction followed by an adjectival passive or an adjective. Applying this translation strategy yields *it is expected that*, as in the close translation in (2a), which is still a work in progress.

(2) جريدة الصباح (تونس)، ٩ يونيو ٢٠٠٨، العدد ١٩٠٦٧.
من المنتظر أن يحل بيننا في الأيام القليلة القادمة ٧٥٠٠ سائح ألماني
ونمساوي من بين الشباب الذين لا يتجاوز سنهم العشرين سنة ممن اجتازوا
منذ أيام في بلدانهم مناظرة البكالوريا.

(2a) It is expected that 7,500 German and Austrian tourists
among the youths whose age does not exceed twenty years
among those who passed a few days ago the high school
examinations in their home countries will arrive among us in
the next few days.

Let us turn now to the subject clause, which starts with أن يحل *that they arrive* and extends to the end of the sentence. The subject of this clause is the noun phrase ٧,٥٠٠ سائح ألماني ونمساوي *7,500 German and Austrian tourists* with its modifiers, whereas the predicate is the verb phrase starting with يحل *arrive*. The complementizer أن *that/to* requires the verb–first word order, which we can switch, but the problem is that the subject is modified by the prepositional phrase من بين الشباب *from among the youth*, which is in turn modified by the relative clause الذين لا يتجاوز سنهم العشرين سنة *whose age does not exceed twenty years* and yet another modifier, namely, ممن اجتازوا منذ أيام في بلدانهم مناظرة البكالوريا *lit. from among those who passed a few days ago in their home countries the high school exams*. Although reversing the order of the subject and the predicate is grammatical, the translation is still far from sounding natural because of the stacked modifiers that separate the subject and the predicate. Besides, English does not allow modifier phrases to intervene between verbs and their direct objects, as in *who passed a few days ago in their home countries the high school exams*. We need to further reconstruct the translation in ways that help avoid these problems. One way of doing so is to split the sentence into two, while using the relative clause *whose age does not exceed twenty years* as a modifier for the main noun *tourists* in the first sentence. In order to maintain the cohesion of the text, we can add a demonstrative phrase, such as *those tourists*, at the beginning of the second sentence, in which we include the rest of the modifiers in the revised order, as in (2b).

(2b) It is expected that 7,500 German and Austrian tourists, whose age does not exceed twenty years, will arrive among us in the next few days. These tourists are among the youths who passed the high school exams in their home countries a few days ago.

The translation in (2b) is grammatical, but it still needs work. For one thing, we used the *it*-cleft in the first sentence to avoid a sentence initial clausal subject, but this solution creates a new problem. The discourse function of the *it*-cleft conflicts with the discourse function of the source text. An *it*-cleft construction selects the constituent that represents the most salient information item, whereas the rest of the sentence presents presupposed information—that is, information that our readers are assumed to already know. Accordingly, the translation in (2b) assumes that the readers already know about the German and Austrian tourists, whereas the fact that their visit is expected is particularly informative or new. The source text is about these tourists who are the focus of attention. Therefore, we need to reconstruct our translation yet again to avoid the *it*-cleft while profiling the tourists as the topic of the sentence. One way to do this is to use the passive voice, as in (2c).

> (2c) A total of 7,500 German and Austrian tourists, whose age does not exceed twenty years, are expected to arrive among us in the next few days. These tourists are among the youths who passed the high school exams in their home countries a few days ago.

Having resolved the main structural issues in this sentence, we can now use some word- and phrase-level strategies to improve the quality of the final translation. For example, it is not clear who is meant by *us* in the first sentence. Because this sentence is taken from a Tunisian newspaper, in which a Tunisian writer is addressing a Tunisian audience, we can safely conclude that these youths are traveling to Tunisia and can rephrase the sentence accordingly, as in (2d). We can also substitute *arrive* with *visit* and *a few days ago* with *just* or *recently*. Other changes are possible, but they are optional, and it is up to the individual translator to decide what the final translation will look like, as long as it accurately transfers all the information encoded in the source text.

> (2d) A total of 7,500 German and Austrian tourists are expected to visit Tunisia in the next few days. They are all under the age of twenty, as they just finished high school in their home countries.

Although our goal is to convey the information encoded in the source text, we need to maintain its discourse functions as well. For example, the main problem in (3) is that the sentence-initial topic noun phrase, starting with رواية *novel*, corresponds to a pronoun embedded in a possessive noun phrase. In other words, the original position of the entire topic noun phrase, along with its modifier and the embedded relative clause, is that of the pronoun ها in قراءتها *reading it*. This is fine in Arabic, but not in English. Because the problem is the topic noun phrase, we can consider restoring the original structure by representing that phrase in its nontopicalized position while making the necessary changes to make the translation grammatical, as in (3a).

(3) جريدة الأهرام (مصر)، ١٩ أكتوبر ٢٠٠٦، العدد ٤٣٧٨١.
رواية "القلعة البيضاء"، للكاتب التركي أورهان باموك الحاصل على جائزة
نوبل للآداب أصبح من المتاح لقراء العربية قراءتها مترجمة حيث انتهت
الهيئة المصرية العامة للكتاب من إصدار ترجمة الرواية ضمن سلسلة
الجوائز التي استحدثها د. ناصر الأنصاري رئيس الهيئة.

(3a) It has become possible for readers of Arabic to read the
novel *The White Castle* by the Turkish writer Orhan Pamuk, who
received the Nobel Prize in Literature in translation, because the
General Egyptian Book Organization has finished publishing a
translation of the novel in the Awards Series that was introduced
by Nasser Al-Ansary, chairman of the organization.

We can improve this first candidate by splitting the sentence into two: one
about the availability of the novel in Arabic, and one about how the translation became available. There are a few candidate topics with which to start
the first sentence; we can choose a phrase referring to the novel, the author,
or the publisher, as in (3b) and (3c). Word- and phrase-level translation
strategies will help improve the quality of the translation. For example, we
can substitute *who received the Nobel Prize* with *Nobel Prize laureate*, delete
the phrase *the novel* and use italics to represent the title, and rephrase *it has
become possible for readers of Arabic to read it in translation* as *the Arabic
translation is now available*.

(3b) The Nobel Prize laureate Turkish writer Orhan Pamuk's
novel *The White Castle* has become available in Arabic
translation. The General Egyptian Book Organization has just
published its translation in the Awards Series, introduced by
Nasser Al-Ansary, chairman of the organization.

(3c) The General Egyptian Book Organization has just published
the Arabic translation of *The White Castle* by the Turkish writer
Orhan Pamuk, who was recently awarded the Nobel Prize in
Literature. The translation is published in the Awards Series,
introduced by Nasser Al-Ansary, chairman of the organization.

Both candidates are grammatical, and they convey the same information
as the original sentence. The problem, however, is that they fail to maintain
the discourse functions of the source sentence, in which topicalization is

intentionally used to emphasize the novel, not its author or publisher. We need to discard these candidates and use a translation that starts with the novel, as in (3d).

(3d) *The White Castle*, by the Turkish Nobel laureate Orhan Pamuk, is now available in an Arabic translation. It is published by the General Egyptian Book Organization in its Awards Series, introduced by Chairman Nasser Al-Ansary.

Reconstruction is by no means restricted to cases in which a close translation of an Arabic sentence yields an ungrammatical structure. In fact, reconstruction is most commonly used when a close translation is grammatical but does not comply with the standards of English rhetoric. Arabic discourse patterns can sometimes be so different from English writing conventions that reconstruction is necessary, especially when the source sentence has several clauses. For example, if we take a close look at the text in (4), we will find that this whole paragraph is actually one sentence comprising several conjoined and embedded clauses, which is common in Arabic. Needless to say, the close translation in (4a) is unacceptable, but it is a good place to start.

(4) جريدة الأخبار (مصر)، ٢٦ أكتوبر ٢٠٠٦، ص ٣.
قرأت في صحيفة "الوفد" خبرا يقول إن الجالية الألمانية بالغردقة وأعضاءها
المبهورين بسحر الطبيعة هناك حيث يعملون بالمشروعات والأنشطة
السياحية المختلفة قرروا البقاء حتى نهاية العمر في هذه المدينة المصرية
وأن يتم دفنهم هناك بعد الوفاة ولذلك تقدموا بطلب إلى المجلس المحلي
للمدينة يطالبون فيه بتخصيص مدافن لهم هناك، ولكن مجلس محلي
المدينة قرر رفض هذا الطلب وأكد السيد عبد السلام حمزة عضو المجلس أن
الأراضي المخصصة للمقابر لا تكفي المصريين وأنه لو حصل الألمان على
أراض خاصة بمقابرهم فسوف يلجأ الإنجليز والروس إلى تقليدهم!

(4a) I read in *Al-Wafd* newspaper a news article saying that the German community in Hurgada and its members, who are infatuated with nature there, where they work in various tourism projects and activities, decided to stay in this Egyptian town until the end of their lives, and to be buried there after death, and this is why they submitted a request to City Hall asking for designating a cemetery for them there, but City Hall decided to reject this request, and Abd Al-Salaam Hamza, City Hall member, stressed that the land designated for cemeteries is not enough for Egyptians, and that if the Germans got a piece of land

that is designated as their cemetery, the British and the Russians
will resort to imitating them.

We can try to improve the translation by applying various word- and
phrase-level strategies. For example, the reduced relative clause in خبرا يقول
a news article that says and the prepositional phrase بعد الوفاة *after death*
can be deleted because they would sound redundant if incorporated into
the translation. We can also reduce the translation of الجالية الألمانية بالغردقة
وأعضاءها *lit. the German community in Hurgada and its members* to *the
Germans living in Hurgada*. There is some room for phrasal reconstruction,
such as translating the participial phrase المبهورين *who are infatuated* as a
predicate rather than an embedded structure. Adding background information, such as *the resort town*, makes the context easier to understand. These
strategies give us the translation candidate in (4b).

(4b) I read in *Al-Wafd* newspaper that the Germans living
in Hurgada, where they work in the tourism industry, are so
infatuated with nature in this Egyptian resort town that they
decided to spend the rest of their lives there, and for this reason
they applied for a permit to build a German cemetery, but
surprisingly, City Hall turned down their request, and City Hall
official Abd Al-Salaam Hamza stressed that the land designated
for cemeteries in Hurgada is not enough for Egyptians, and that
City Hall is concerned that if the German community got this
permit, the British and Russian communities might follow suit.

However, the improved translation in (4b) falls short of the standards of
English writing because it is still a run-on sentence. We need to reconstruct
this sentence by splitting it into shorter sentences, provided that the translation constitutes a cohesive text, as in (4c). Splitting sentences is sometimes
done by incorporating relative clauses as adjectival phrases or simply by
ending sentences and starting new ones.

(4c) I read in *Al-Wafd* newspaper that the Germans living in
Hurgada, where they work in the tourism industry, are so
much in love with nature in this Egyptian resort town that they
decided to spend the rest of their lives there. They even applied
for a permit to build a German cemetery, but surprisingly, City
Hall denied their application. City Hall official Abd Al-Salaam

> Hamza explained that the land designated for cemeteries in
> Hurgada is not enough for Egyptians. He added that City Hall
> is concerned that if the German community got this permit, the
> British and Russian communities might follow suit.

These reconstruction attempts do not give us a final translation; the candidate in (4c) can be further improved by applying additional word- and phrase-level strategies. The purpose of reconstructing sentences is to avoid ungrammatical and stylistically unacceptable structures in the translation output, thus helping readers reconstruct the context.

البنية / ترتيب

2 Rhetorical Structure

Writing is a purposeful act of communication, as writers are always attempting to change the way we view the world in some way or another. A writer might compose a text with the intention of making us adhere to a particular ideology, feel better about the economy, learn about a sports event, or buy a certain brand of soap. To help achieve these goals, writers have myriad tools at their disposal, including analogies, examples, and metaphors. However, having the ideas and the tools is not enough to achieve successful communication. Writers need a plan, or a strategy, that breaks down their main communicative goal into smaller goals that can be achieved in successive steps. This plan is reflected in the structure of the text, specifically in the ordering of sentences and paragraphs. When translating a text, we rarely alter its structure by deleting or reordering full sentences and paragraphs, but there are times when we need to intervene and reconstruct the text to make sure the author's intentions are communicated accurately.

For example, the first three sentences in (5) say the same thing, more or less. This is not superfluous repetition, because each sentence has a distinct rhetorical function. The first sentence makes a clear thesis statement that serves as the focus of the entire text. The second sentence supports this thesis by refuting a possible counterargument or antithesis. The third sentence functions as a transition, in which the main idea is reiterated to maintain the text's cohesion while providing new information (e.g., the stages of the revolution process). This kind of repetition is acceptable in Arabic rhetoric as a good writing technique that strengthens arguments and maintains the text's cohesion. The problem is that when this technique is used in English, it becomes confusing, if not redundant. It even has the potential to weaken the argument, as in the translation candidate in (5a).

(5) زكي نجيب محمود، ١٩٨٧، ''مجتمع جديد أو الكارثة''، دار الشروق، القاهرة، ص ١٨.

إن طريق الثورة في الحياة الفكرية هو نفسه طريق الثورة في أي مجال آخر: في السياسة، أو الاقتصاد، أو بناء المجتمع، وليست الحياة الفكرية شذوذا وحدها، تحتاج إلى طريق ثوري مختلف في طبيعته عما تحتاج إليه الحياة السياسية أو الاقتصادية أو الاجتماعية، فطريق الثورة في كل هذه الميادين على حد سواء هو أن يضيق النمط القائم عن مواجهة ما استحدث من مشكلات، فتتأزم صدور الناس، ويشتد التأزم بها كلما اتسعت الهوة بين المعايير القائمة من جهة، وما يراد إخضاعه لتلك المعايير من جهة أخرى، فلا يجد الناس عندئذ سبيلا إلى الخروج من أزمتهم تلك إلا بالبحث عن نمط جديد، يمدهم بمعايير جديدة، تتكافأ مع المشكلات التي استحدثتها حياتهم الجديدة.

(5a) The process leading to an intellectual revolution is the same process that leads to a political, economic, social, or any other revolution. Intellectual life is not an exception that requires a revolution process different in nature from what political, economic, or social revolutions require. The process of revolution in all these areas is the same: The status quo fails to deal with new problems, and people get frustrated. This frustration grows as the current standards continue to fall short of achieving their objectives. Finally, people realize that there is no way out of their crisis but to search for new standards that are compatible with their new problems.

We can further revise the translation by deleting the repeated elements to make the author's message clear and straightforward, as in (5b). In this particular case, we do not need to do anything to compensate for the deleted clauses because their rhetorical functions are already incorporated in the translation. For example, the polarity item *any other* in the first sentence implicitly blocks against the counterargument, whereas the demonstrative phrase *this process* maintains the cohesion of the text. The adverbial phrases *as a result* and *finally* explicitly describe the temporal sequence of events. The result is a text that adheres closely to the standards of English discourse while achieving the same goals as the source text.

(5b) The process leading to an intellectual revolution is the same process that leads to a political, economic, social, or any other

kind of revolution. This process starts when the status quo fails
to handle new problems, and as a result, people get frustrated.
This frustration grows as the current standards continue to fall
short of achieving their objectives. Finally, people realize that
the only way out of their crisis is to search for new standards
that are compatible with their new problems.

Arabic argumentative writing is sometimes designed to resemble formal spoken discourse in a communicative strategy that effectively engages
readers and helps achieve the author's goals. As a result, we often find some
conversational features embedded in written texts, even though they might
not seem to be immediately related to the main argument, as in the case of
(6). This text starts with a sentence that reiterates a previous conclusion
while serving as the premise for a new deductive argument. The next two
clauses present the logic of the argument along with the conclusion. Note
that this conclusion is rather weak, but this is part of the author's strategy;
he intentionally presents this weak conclusion before making his strongest
claim in the subsequent sentence. This technique maximizes the effect of
the strong claim, especially when combined with the example at the end.
This technique is not uncommon in English, and translating this text is not
complicated. The only problem has to do with the two sentences that separate the strong claim from the example. The first one is a statement in which
the author reveals his discourse plan to support his claim with an example,
whereas the second is an aside in which the author calls for further research
on the topic. These two sentences constitute a digression from the main argument, as indicated by the shift in viewpoint from the first-person plural
to the first-person singular. The translation candidate in (6a) is a first step
in developing a rhetorically equivalent translation.

(6) محمود حمدي زقزوق، ١٩٨٨، "قضايا فكرية واجتماعية في ضوء
الإسلام"، دار المنار، ص ١١٦.
لقد اتضح لنا مما تقدم أن الفلسفة الإسلامية كان لها تأثيرها العظيم في
الفلسفة الأوروبية في القرون الوسطى، وإذا كانت هذه الفلسفة قد أثرت بدورها
في الفلسفة الأوروبية الحديثة فإننا نستطيع أن نقول بوجود تأثير غير مباشر
للفلسفة الإسلامية على الفلسفة الحديثة. ولكن هذا لا يعني عدم وجود تأثير
مباشر أيضا. ونريد هنا أن نشير إلى بعض جوانب هذا التأثير، وآمل أن يجد
هذا الموضوع حقه من الاهتمام من جانب الباحثين المعنيين. وأول جوانب
التأثير في العصر الحديث يتمثل في تأثير الغزالي على ديكارت.

(6a) It has become clear to us from the previous discussion that
Islamic philosophy had a significant influence on European
philosophy during the Middle Ages. If this philosophy, in turn,
influenced modern European philosophy, we can say that Islamic
philosophy had an indirect influence on modern philosophy.
This does not mean that there was no direct influence as well.
Here, we want to point to some aspects of this influence, and I
hope concerned researchers will give this issue the attention it
deserves. The first aspect of this influence in modern times is
represented in the influence of Al-Ghazaly on Descartes.

Digressing from the main argument is quite acceptable in the Arabic
source text, which has the structure and style of a lecture. The English
reader, however, might find it distracting, if not confusing, because it disrupts the flow of the main argument, as in (6b), which is a revised translation based on (6a).

(6b) We established earlier that Islamic philosophy had a
significant influence on medieval European philosophy. If the
latter, in turn, influenced modern European philosophy, we
can conclude that Islamic philosophy had an indirect influence
on modern philosophy. In fact, Islamic philosophy had a direct
impact on modern European philosophy as well. Here, we want
to highlight some aspects of this impact, hoping that scholars
will give this issue the attention it deserves. Perhaps the most
obvious example of this direct impact is Al-Ghazaly's influence
on Descartes's work.

One possible solution is to reconstruct the text by deleting the two sentences that are not directly related to the main argument, as in (6c). Deleting the metastatement does not affect the argument, especially when it is
clear that the last sentence presents an example. If we delete the sentence
in which the author calls for further research on the issue, this message
is completely lost. We can potentially move it to the end of the paragraph,
but then the example would lose its function as a transition to the next
paragraph, in which the author would elaborate on the influence of Al-
Ghazaly's philosophy on Descartes's work. Besides, the sentence might
be misunderstood as a call for further research on how Descartes's work

was influenced by Al-Ghazaly's philosophy rather than the general issue of how Islamic philosophy contributed to modern European philosophy. We cannot move it to the first sentence either, because the author is calling for further research on the direct impact of Islamic philosophy on modern European philosophy, not the indirect impact. Note that if we reconstruct this sentence as an appositive phrase, as in *an issue that needs further research*, we undermine the author's argument because that would make it sound as if he is not certain of his conclusion. Our only option, then, is to move this sentence to a subsequent paragraph after the author is done discussing the influence of Islamic philosophy on modern European philosophy.

> (6c) We established earlier that Islamic philosophy had a
> significant influence on medieval European philosophy. Because
> the latter influenced modern European philosophy, we can
> conclude that Islamic philosophy had an indirect influence on
> modern philosophy. In fact, Islamic philosophy also had a direct
> impact on modern European philosophy, such as Al-Ghazaly's
> influence on Descartes's work.

Although text reconstruction is a translation strategy of last resort, radical text reconstruction is sometimes necessary, especially when the overall structure of the source text is problematic, as in (7). This is the first part of an article published in a religious magazine, which explains why it has the style and structure of a sermon. The article starts out with an anecdote to which readers can easily relate (the broken television story). The next step is to do a bit of reflection to come up with an analysis of the anecdote, or the moral of the story (i.e., a TV set does not work unless all its parts are functioning properly). This analysis is followed by hypothetical parallel examples that can be explained along the same lines (tanks, factories, and other complex systems do not function properly unless all their parts are functioning properly). These examples lead to a generalization that applies to all possible similar situations (any system with malfunctioning or missing components does not work properly). Knowing that there are possible counterexamples to this generalization, the author plugs the holes in the argument by making a complementary assertion (even if a system works despite missing components, it does not really function properly). This elaborate rhetorical strategy culminates with a thesis statement, namely, that the teachings of Islam constitute a fully integrated system that cannot function properly if any of its components is ignored.

Starting out with anecdotes and building generalizations on basic examples are common rhetorical strategies in Arabic argumentative discourse, and their combination can be quite convincing despite the indirect approach. The argument is structured in well-defined steps, each represented as a separate, short paragraph. The author does not state the thesis first and then defend it. Instead, he walks the readers through the process of building the argument as if they are participating in making the case for it; hence, the second-person reference in the paragraph refuting the expected counterargument. After three specific examples and two complementary generalizations, there is little room, if any, for disagreeing. The thesis is presented at the very end as a conclusion that seems to be directly deduced from the generalizations. The problem, again, is that a translation that maintains the source text's structure, such as that in (7a), might not be as effective with English-speaking readers who might not be used to this writing style.

(7) عبد الحميد حسانين حسن، ٢٠٠٥، 'من مقالات الشيخ الغزالي''، ج ١، نهضة مصر للطباعة والنشر، ص ٤١.

أصاب جهاز «التليفزيون» عندي عطل مبهم فلم تظهر الصورة المرتقبة، ونظرت إلى الجهاز الجاثم في مكانه لا يؤدي عمله نظرة استغراب! وتحسسته بيدي فخيل لي أنه لا ينقص شيئا من آلاته الجلية والخفية.

وأخيرا جاء العامل المختص في إصلاحه، واستبدل بجزء تالف منه جزءا صالحا، واستأنف الجهاز عمله، وشرع يحقق الفائدة المرجوة منه!!

وقلت في نفسي: إن الجهاز كله توقف عن أداء رسالته حتى تعاونت أجزاؤه الصغار والكبار على تحقيق وظائفها المنوطة بها!!

ولا عجب فقد تتوقف الدبابة عن السير والقتال لقطعة تنقصها في مقدمتها أو مؤخرتها.

وقد يتعطل مصنع عن الإنتاج تكلف إنشاؤه الألوف المؤلفة من الجنيهات؛ لأنه يفتقر إلى تكملة لا تساوي مائة جنيه.

وهكذا شؤون الحياة المادية والأدبية، قد يصيبها عطب فادح؛ لأن شطرها أو أغلبها موجود، وبقيتها الأخرى مفقودة عن خطأ أو تعمد.

ومن ثم قد ترى أمامك أشياء صالحة، ولكنها قليلة الجدوى، لأنها مبتورة، وما تتم قيمتها وتبرز ثمرتها إلا إذا دارت الحياة فيها وفيما يكملها، وعندئذ ينطلق التيار في دائرته المغلقة فيسطع النور.

إن تعاليم الإسلام كذلك لا تصلح الحياة وتقيم المجتمعات إلا على النحو الذي شرحنا.

(7a) My TV set mysteriously stopped working, and I could no
longer see the picture. I stared at it sitting there doing nothing.
I even felt it with my hands, but it looked to me as if it was not
missing anything.

Finally, a technician came and replaced a malfunctioning
part, and the TV set was working again.

I thought to myself: The TV set would not work unless all of
its parts, large and small, functioned properly.

There is nothing new here. A tank would not run or fight if it
was missing a piece somewhere.

Production at a factory that costs millions of pounds might
come to a standstill because of a missing piece of equipment
that is not worth a hundred pounds.

The same applies to all aspects of life, material and spiritual.
They can be fatally disabled if they are mostly intact but some
parts are missing or left out on purpose.

It is true that you might find things that work despite missing
parts, but they never flourish or achieve their full potential. Only
when an electric circuit is complete can there be light.

The teachings of Islam can establish and sustain
communities only if they are applied all together as one system,
just like any other system.

There are several reconstruction techniques that we can use to make the
author's message easily accessible to English readers. For example, we can
combine all eight short paragraphs into a single paragraph presenting the
argument as a whole. We can also incorporate the thesis statement in the
first sentence, so that our readers will know where the argument is going.
Reiterating the thesis statement at the end provides the conclusion while
transitioning into the rest of the text, in which the author would discuss this
statement in more detail. Some parts of the text can be deleted, and others
can be merged to make the sentences concise and well connected and to
avoid digressions. Despite all these changes, the revised translation in (7b)
maintains the author's tone while securing a more accurate understanding
of his message.

(7b) The other day, my TV set mysteriously stopped working,
and while waiting for a technician to come and fix it, I was

thinking how any system, whether it is a TV set or the
teachings of Islam, cannot function properly unless all its
components are working. I stared at the TV set, sitting there
with no picture on its screen. I even felt around it with my
hands, but it looked to me as though it should work; it was
not missing anything. Finally, when the technician came and
replaced a malfunctioning part, the TV set worked again. I
thought to myself: The TV set would not work unless all of
its parts, large and small, function properly. There is nothing
new here: A tank or a factory would not function if a piece of
equipment, no matter how small or insignificant, was missing or
malfunctioning. In fact, all aspects of life, material or spiritual,
can be rendered ineffective or fatally disabled if they are mostly
intact, but some parts are missing or left out. The same applies
to the teachings of Islam; they cannot establish and sustain
communities unless they are applied all together as one system.

Text reconstruction is an invasive translation strategy that involves
changing the way the message is delivered; hence the risk of misrepresent-
ing the original work and consequently failing to achieve its objectives.
There needs to be a good rationale for every instance of text reconstruction.
Basically, we need to limit it to cases in which, after applying word- and
phrase-level translation strategies, we realize that we can understand what
the author is saying, but not what he or she is trying to do. These will be
instances in which the source text involves writing techniques or rhetorical strategies that have clear communicative objectives in Arabic but fail to
achieve them when applied to English.

3 Punctuation

Punctuation is a system of nonlinguistic symbols that guide readers through
the structure of a written discourse. Unlike linguistic units, such as morphemes, punctuation marks do not have meaning in their own right. Rather,
they have discourse functions, such as marking the endings of sentences,
signaling pauses between clauses or phrases, and indicating whether a sentence is a statement, a question, or an exclamation. Punctuation marks also
help reduce grammatical and rhetorical ambiguities. Commas, for instance,

tell us whether a relative clause is meant to be restrictive or nonrestrictive, whereas quotation marks distinguish our own words from those of others. When it comes to translation, punctuation plays a dual role; it helps us understand the structure of the source text, and it can be used as a translation strategy, especially when the structure of the Arabic source text cannot be transferred directly to English.

Arabic has developed two separate punctuation systems. The first emerged during the evolution of the Qur'anic script, and was fully standardized by the end of the ninth century. This detailed punctuation system is mainly concerned with regulating Qur'anic recitation and pronunciation rules. It includes, for example, symbols that mark the endings of verses and the positions in which pauses within verses are obligatory, optional, or disallowed. This punctuation system is still widely used, but only in relation to the scripture. The other system, which is the focus of our discussion, developed toward the end of the nineteenth century for nonreligious texts. It was mostly adopted from English and French, which explains why the symbols are very similar to their counterparts in these languages, albeit with some minor differences. In terms of form, some punctuation marks were slightly modified to accommodate the direction of the Arabic script and to keep them distinct from the letters, such as the right-facing question mark (؟), the upside down comma (،), and the upside down semicolon (؛). In terms of function, Arabic punctuation marks are very similar to English ones, with a few notable differences. For example, in English, we distinguish a parenthetical phrase from the rest of the sentence by placing it between commas. Arabic, conversely, uses dashes or parentheses. The lack of capital letters in Arabic is sometimes compensated for by using double quotation marks, double parentheses, or chevrons («») to distinguish foreign and proper names and titles.

The challenges that the Arabic punctuation system poses stem from the fact that it is not fully standardized; it is more of a style than a set of strict rules. For example, some authors use Arabic punctuation in a fashion that is very similar to what we see in English texts, as in (8). The way the commas and periods are used in this paragraph is not problematic at all, as most of them can be carried over into the translation. The only change is that we need to add commas in the last clause to separate the countries on the list: مصر والمغرب وتونس *Egypt, Morocco, and Tunisia*, in which the final comma before *and* (i.e., the Oxford, or serial, comma) is optional in some cases.

(٨) سعد الدين إبراهيم، ١٩٩٦، مقدمة "المجتمع المدني والتحول الديموقراطي
في السودان"، حيدر إبراهيم علي، دار الأمين للنشر والتوزيع، ص ٢٥.
لعل النقابات المهنية أن تكون أنشط التنظيمات المدنية في الوطن العربي في
الوقت الراهن. ويرجع ذلك في جزء منه إلى أنها تتيح لأعضائها مكاسب فئوية
مادية، وفي جزء آخر إلى المستوى العالي من التعليم والوعي السياسي. ونظرا
لما تتمتع به هذه النقابات المهنية العربية من استقلالية نسبية في مواردها
المالية، فقد أصبحت لها الريادة في حركة المجتمع المدني في بلادها. ففي
بلد كالسودان، تمكنت هذه النقابات من خلع النظام العسكري الحاكم مرتين
(١٩٦٤ و ١٩٨٥). وفي كل من مصر والمغرب وتونس، تحولت إلى جماعات
ضغط قوية إبان السبعينيات والثمانينيات.

Labor unions are probably the most active civil society
organizations in the Arab world today. This is partly due to
the financial benefits these organizations offer their members,
and partly due to their higher levels of education and political
awareness. Thanks to the relative financial independence of
these unions, they led the mobilization of civil society in their
respective countries. In Sudan, these trade unions brought down
two military regimes (in 1964 and 1985). In Egypt, Morocco,
and Tunisia, trade unions developed into powerful pressure
groups in the 1970s and the 1980s.

As we saw above, some Arabic argumentative writing styles have discourse patterns that resemble spoken discourse, as if the written text were
a transcript of a formal speech. Consequently, the punctuation marks that
indicate pauses, the commas and periods, play a more significant role than
they do in a punctuation system that is closely associated with grammar,
such as that of English. The difference between the comma and the period
in Arabic is that the period marks a long pause at the end of a "complete
thought," defined in rhetorical rather than grammatical terms, whereas a
comma indicates a shorter pause anywhere. This is why we often see commas between sentences that are not conjoined (comma splices), and whole
paragraphs that are made up of one sentence. These differences suggest that
we should not take punctuation for granted when translating Arabic texts,
and that we might need to change punctuation because the translation output needs to follow the writing rules of English.

Sometimes punctuation marks seem inconsistent within the same text,
but this is expected when the punctuation system is not fully standardized.
For example, we might initially think that the double parentheses in (9) are

used to distinguish names in lieu of capital letters, but this is not done in
a systematic way. The name Yussef Rashad is in parentheses, but not the
names Sheriff Pasha, the Iron Guard, or Alexandria. Double parentheses are
also used with the borrowing الكابتن *the captain*, but غير مرتاح *uncomfortable* is neither a borrowing nor a name. These nonstandard uses are not
erratic mistakes; they achieve different rhetorical functions using the same
punctuation mark. For example, most of the names in this text are not in
parentheses, but because Yussef Rashad is the most important individual
in this narrative, his name is singled out with these parentheses to signal emphasis. The double parentheses used with غير مرتاح *uncomfortable*
and الكابتن *the captain* are in fact functionally equivalent to scare quotation
marks. If الكابتن was in parentheses because it is a foreign title, it would have
been followed by the name Sheriff Pasha, as in الكابتن شريف باشا زوج ابنته
Captain Sheriff Pasha, his son-in-law, but the word order tells us that we
have an appositive phrase rather than a simple noun phrase. The issue is, of
course, how to maintain these functions in the translation. This inconsistency means that whenever we translate an Arabic text, we need to identify
the features of the author's idiosyncratic punctuation style.

(9) سيد جاد، ١٩٩٣، ''الحرس الحديدي''، الدار المصرية اللبنانية، ص ٤٠.
بعد أيام .. طلبني الدكتور ((يوسف رشاد)) لحضور اجتماع للحرس الحديدي
في بيته .. وسألني الدكتور ـ وهو يضحك ـ عن تلك الرحلة التي يقال أنني
قمت بها .. وعندما كان يضحك ((يوسف رشاد)) نعرف أنه في حالة ضيق ..
وفهمت أنه ((غير مرتاح)) لهذه العلاقة الجديدة .. وطلب مني أن أسافر معه
في طائرة ((الكابتن)) زوج ابنته شريف باشا إلى الإسكندرية لأنه سيحتاجني
في بعض الأمور.. ولم أتراجع رغم أني شعرت بأنهم بدأوا ينظرون إلي بعين لم
أعهدها منهم!

A few days later, Yussef Rashad summoned me to an Iron Guard
meeting in his house. He laughed when he asked me about
the trip I allegedly took, and we knew that he laughed when
he was stressed, so I understood that he was "uncomfortable"
with this new relationship. Then, he asked me to fly with him to
Alexandria on the plane owned by "the Captain," his son-in-law
Sheriff Pasha, because he would need me there. I did not hesitate
to go, even though I felt that they started to see me differently.

A punctuation system that is not fully standardized gives writers some
leeway for innovative use, as in the case of (10). The writer of this text uses

several instances of double periods and commas, which indicates that they have different functions, unlike the text in (9), in which double periods are used in all the positions in which commas are expected. When a text includes both double periods and commas, the double periods signal pauses that are somewhere between those associated with periods and commas. They are meant to give the reader a chance to respond to what the author is "saying," just as in a public speech. The text starts with the topic noun phrase مشكلتنا *our problem*, followed by a pause for the readers to guess what the problem is. Then, the author states the problem in أننا ننسى بسرعة *that we forget quickly*, but gives his readers a moment to wonder what they forgot before elaborating. This strategy is repeated throughout the text to keep the readers engaged. Note that the double periods are not related to the grammatical structure of the text. For example, the first instance of double periods separates a subject from its predicate, whereas the second separates conjoined sentences, and the third separates a dependent clause from a main clause. Changing these double periods to English punctuation points that fit in the grammatical context is not a complicated task, as we can see in (10a).

(10) سمير رجب، ١٩٩٩، "خطوط فاصلة"، الهيئة العامة المصرية
للكتاب، ص ١٤.
مشكلتنا.. أننا ننسى بسرعة.. فنحن مثلا نرفض أن نرجع بذاكرتنا إلى الوراء..
عندما كنا نقف في طوابير طويلة.. للحصول على كيلو سكر، أو باكو شاي،
أو كيس دقيق، أو زجاجة زيت، أو عشرة أرغفة خبز.. من الفرن!

(10a) Our problem is that we forget quickly. For example, we
refuse to go back in memory to the days when we had to stand
in long lines to get a kilogram of sugar, a packet of tea, a bag of
flour, a bottle of cooking oil, or bread from the bakery.

The main challenge in translating this text is to make sure that the rhetorical functions of the double periods are reflected in the translation without conflating them with the commas. Note that the rate of reading starts slowly with the double periods, but then it speeds up with the commas, and finally it slows down again with the double periods at the end in a rhetorical structure that is similar to that of jokes. The first four instances of double periods engage the readers by giving them time to think along (the premise), the four periods build up the suspense (the setup), and finally double periods deliver the punchline: Unlike the other items on the list (sugar, tea, etc.), bread is actually produced at the bakery, and there is still a line. If we provide a translation that focuses only on the information content of the text, as in (10a), we lose these rhetorical strategies and their effects. If we want to maintain them, we need to manipulate the text and the punctuation because we cannot replace all these double periods with commas or single periods. We can rephrase parts of the text and reconstruct others to create similar rhetorical effects, as in (10b).

> (10b) Our problem is that we forget quickly. We refuse, for
> example, to go back in memory to those days when we had to
> stand in long lines to get anything: a line for a kilogram of sugar,
> a line for a packet of tea, a line for a bag of flour, and yet another
> line for a bottle of cooking oil. Even bread, we had to stand in
> line to get it . . . from the bakery!

Although the Arabic punctuation system is a source of innovation for writers, it is a source of problems for translators; it is not fully standardized, it is not fully restricted by grammar, and it involves ambiguities. Identifying the intended functions of punctuation marks depends entirely on our ability to analyze the source text and the context. Once we recognize the discourse relations signaled by punctuation, we can apply the strategies we discussed above to preserve them in the translation. In the end, the punctuation in the translation needs to comply with the target language conventions.

4   Text Cohesion

Cohesion is what makes a text a meaningful unit of written discourse rather than a series of unrelated sentences randomly strung together. A text is considered cohesive when readers can easily identify the logical, temporal, and referential relations that connect its sentences and clauses. For example, when we read a cohesive text, we can tell whether a situation is the result or the cause of another, and whether a statement is a conclusion based on other statements or a premise that leads to a conclusion. These relations are signaled by cohesive devices, or linking words, such as coordination conjunctions (e.g., *and*, *but*, and *so*), subordination conjunctions (e.g., *because*, *however*, and *while*), and sentential adverbs (e.g., *accordingly*, *consequently*, and *finally*), among others. In addition to establishing links between sentences and clauses, cohesion involves the unity of discourse topics. Synonyms and related words are used in different clauses and sentences to establish referential chains that hold the text together. For example, in a text about a car, we can introduce it as *my car* in one sentence; but later in the text we can refer to it as *the vehicle, the gas guzzler*, or *the jeep*. There are, of course, many deictic and anaphoric expressions, including demonstratives and pronouns, which establish referential chains. Basically, cohesion pertains to every technique that helps maintain the internal structure of a text.

Text cohesion in Arabic is established by techniques that are very similar to those used in English. Arabic uses coordination conjunctions, such as لكن *but* and و *and*; subordination conjunctions, such as بينما *while* and إذا *if*; and sentential adverbs, such as أخيرا *finally* and ثالثا *thirdly*. Some Arabic cohesive devices are suffixes, such as ف- *as/then* and ل- *in order to*, whereas others are full phrases, such as بالرغم من *despite* and إلا أن *however/nevertheless*. The diversity of Arabic cohesive devices is morphological in nature, and it does not pose major translation problems because most of them have functional equivalents in English. Lexical chains in Arabic are established in the same ways as in English, but Arabic tends to use lexical repetition more frequently, as we discussed above. The most obvious differences between Arabic and English cohesion strategies is that Arabic uses clausal conjunctions far more frequently, and it allows coordination conjunctions at the beginning of paragraphs. Discourse relations—whether temporal, logical, or referential—are universal; therefore, we expect only linguistic issues rather than cultural or conceptual translation problems.

Cohesive devices sometimes allow context-dependent interpretations in addition to their basic functions. For instance, the basic function of *and* is to encode logical conjunction—that is, two statements are true at the same time, but we often find contexts in which *and* indicates temporal sequencing, as in *I took a shower and went to bed* compared with *I went to bed and took a shower*. Semantically, these two sentences are equivalent, but pragmatically we interpret the order of the conjuncts as a reflection of the sequence of events; hence the awkwardness of the second sentence. Arabic cohesive devices also allow this kind of pragmatic extension and functional ambiguity. For example, the semantic function of the preposition حتّى *until* is to profile the persistence of a situation in time or space preceding a change, but it can extend pragmatically to indicate causal relations, as in (11). In

this sentence, حتى does not profile publishing a book abroad as a continuous or repeated action that ends when the book covers it expenses. Rather,
it encodes a direct causal relation between two situations: Publishing a book
abroad causes it to cover its expenses. Because the English counterpart *until*
does not allow this functional extension, we can apply lexical substitution
and use the cohesive device *in order to*, which is a true functional equivalent
in this particular context.

(11) جريدة الوطن (عمان)، ١٩ يوليو ٢٠٠٤، العدد ٧٦٧١.
وهل يعني هذا أنني لو أردت إصدار كتاب آخر فالأفضل أن يكون ذلك خارج
السلطنة **حتى** أتمكن من تغطية تكاليف الطباعة والتوزيع؟ وللأسف الشديد
وجدت الإجابة (نعم).

> Does this mean that if I wanted to publish another book, I would
> be better off publishing it abroad in order to cover the production
> and distribution expenses? Unfortunately, I found out that the
> answer is "yes."

Note that in translating this sentence, some of the source text's cohesive
devices had to be left out because they are used in ways that are not permissible in English, such as the sentence initial و *and* and the second و *and*
in وللأسف *and unfortunately*, which conjoins a question and a statement.
The cohesive device ف- *then* in فالأفضل *then it is best* is also left out because
then is not needed to mark the result clause in this conditional construction.
These deletions do not lead to translation losses, and the translation is internally cohesive without them.

In (12), حتى cannot be translated as *until* either, because we are also
dealing with a causal rather than a temporal relation. But this causal relation is different from the one in (11), in that it is indirect causation. In other
words, the source text does not tell us that the culture is changing fast for
the purpose of challenging people; it is the pace of change that is causing
these challenges. Because this is an issue of degree, حتى *until* is better
translated using the *so . . . that* construction. The decision regarding which
English cohesive device to use is dependent on our analysis of the context
and, in many cases, the linguistic properties of cohesive devices. For example, if حتى is followed by a noun phrase that refers to a point in time or
interval, it is translated as *until*. Otherwise, we need to analyze the text to
determine the nature of the cohesive relation it encodes and to be able to
identify a true functional equivalent.

(12) زكي نجيب محمود، ١٩٨٧، "مجتمع جديد أو الكارثة"، دار الشروق، القاهرة، ص ٢٠٠.

أقول إن الفجوة بين الجيلين المتعاقبين أمر لا مفر منه، لكنها في عصرنا فجوة أوسع عمقا مما كنا نألفه، لأننا – أولا – في عصر تحول الحضارة إلى حضارة، وثانيا – لأن الحضارة الجديدة تعدو بالناس عدوا سريعا، **حتى** لتحدث لهم من التغيرات ما يتعذر على عقولهم أن تلاحقها وتواكبها إلا بعد رهق شديد.

Generation gaps, I believe, are inevitable, but the current gap is much wider than previous ones, for two reasons: First, we are in the middle of a cultural shift; and second, the new culture is so fast-paced that people can hardly keep up and cope with the changes it incurs.

In addition to their linking functions, many cohesive expressions gain additional contextual meanings and connotations that need be considered when translating. For example, the demonstrative هذا *this* at the beginning of (13) functions as a linking word that connects this paragraph to previous discourse, in which Amartya Sen's theory is first mentioned. Additionally, it serves the rhetorical function of signaling the author's negative attitude toward this theory. Basically, using a demonstrative in this context, rather than just a definite noun phrase, indicates that the author is distancing himself from Sen's views. Note that if the author used the demonstrative at the end of the phrase, as in إن المسلك الذي اختاره الأستاذ سن هذا, the negative attitude would be explicitly focused on Sen rather than on his theory.

The repetition of قد يبدو للوهلة الأولى *might initially seem* is a cohesive device that connects the two clauses in which the phrase occurs. At the same time, it emphasizes that the validity of the theory under consideration is only apparent and that it should be quickly discarded. The second and third sentences present the author's explanation for why this theory might look valid and appealing. He repeats هناك *there* at the beginning of each sentence to provide parallel structures, indicating that these two sentences form a rhetorical unit, whereas the use of the deictic distal expression itself suggests that the theory is not appealing on its merit, but because of external factors. Finally, the multiple repetitions of الحاجات والرغبات *needs and desires* is another cohesive device that establishes a referential chain holding the internal structure of the text. The author could use pronouns in place of some of these repetitions to achieve the same cohesive functions, but he chooses to use them to keep triggering the negative connotations associated with these expressions in a technique that aims at skewing the readers' perception of the theory in question. Note that every adjective in this text is followed by a synonym, thus creating parallel structures, which is another rhetorical technique to establish internal text cohesion. Maintaining these cohesive devices in the translation is not always the best option, as we can see in (13a).

(13) جلال أمين، ٢٠٠٥، "خرافة التقدم والتخلف"، دار الشروق، القاهرة، ص ٧٤.

هذا المسلك الذي اختاره الأستاذ سن قد يبدو للوهلة الأولى مقبولا ولا غبار عليه، بل قد يبدو للوهلة الأولى أيضا جذابا ومفيدا. فهناك بالطبع جاذبية رد أشياء كثيرة ومختلفة إلى أصل واحد، كما في رد إشباع كل الحاجات والرغبات الإنسانية إلى شيء واحد هو ((التمتع بالحرية)). وهناك أيضا الجاذبية المستمدة من فكرة الحرية نفسها، فالنظر إلى مختلف أنواع الإشباع لمختلف أنواع الحاجات والرغبات على أنها كلها تتضمن تحقيق هذا الهدف السامي والرفيع ((الحرية))، فيه إعلاء وتفخيم لهذه الحاجات والرغبات، ويزيد من مقتنا لأي صورة من صور الحرمان من إشباع أي حاجة أو رغبة من حاجاتنا ورغباتنا.

(13a) This approach that Sen has chosen not only might initially seem acceptable and sound, but it might, also initially, seem appealing and useful. That is, of course, because there is the appeal of explaining several diverse things by connecting them to one source, as in justifying efforts to satisfy one's needs and desires by connecting them to one thing, namely, "freedom." There is also the appeal drawn from the notion of freedom itself. Thinking that satisfying one's diverse needs and desires is an activity that involves achieving the noble and lofty goal of freedom elevates and glorifies those needs and desires. It also makes us abhor anything that deprives us from satisfying our needs and desires.

If we need to choose between the lexical meaning of a word and its function as a cohesive device, we are better off finding a different way of encoding cohesion. In the case of (13), we can leave out the demonstrative at the beginning of the first sentence because translating this phrase as *this approach that Sen has chosen* or *this approach of Sen* can be seen as aggressive or disparaging, which is not the author's intention. He is only distancing himself to give the impression of being objective. The definite article is enough to establish the connection with the previous discourse. We can avoid the repetition of *at first glance* by using it once at the beginning, where it immediately reveals the author's attitude toward Sen's view. Adding the demonstrative phrase *this appeal* at the beginning of the second sentence connects the introductory sentence with the following section that elaborates on it. Other repetitions can be replaced by using pronouns or by deleting the repeated words where possible. Note that the revised translation in (13b) is still cohesive, even though it uses far less cohesive devices than the close translation in (13a).

> (13b) Sen's approach might initially seem valid and sound, if not appealing. This appeal, of course, is due to its reductionist nature, as it reduces efforts to satisfy one's needs and desires to the pursuit of freedom. There is also the appeal of freedom itself; viewing efforts to satisfy one's needs and desires as attempts to achieve the noble goal of freedom glorifies them and makes us resist any attempt to stand in the way of their fulfillment.

Cohesion is a discourse phenomenon that is grounded in linguistic forms, whose function is to signal the connections between the sentences and clauses that make up a text. We need to make sure that these connections are clear in the translation, but not at the expense of the message, whether it is stated information or implied connotations.

5 Tone

Tone is the writer's emotional attitude toward the audience and the subject matter of the text. It constitutes an integral part of the message, as writers communicate their feelings, along with information, in order to influence readers' views and attitudes. If we are writing a description of an old house we are trying to sell, we are likely to use words such as *quaint* or *classic* rather than *old-fashioned* or *run-down* because we know that our choice of words has a significant effect on people's reactions. A writer sets the tone of a text according to the communicative objectives that he or she hopes to achieve. For example, an author might use a neutral tone to be perceived as objective and credible, or a sarcastic tone to be critical without being seen as aggressive. Tone is not directly signaled by any one particular type of linguistic forms or constructions. Instead, there are several clues that readers can follow to determine attitudes; tone is reflected in the choice of words, expressions, grammatical structures, metaphors, text design, and even punctuation.

Tone can be challenging to maintain in translation, because many emotion and attitude triggers are culture-specific. If we look at the satirical text in (14), we realize that many tone triggers can be easily lost or altered when the text is translated. In order to successfully preserve tone, we need to first analyze the text and determine how tone is set. This text is made up of three sections with different objectives. The first section uses two questions to make serious, yet indirect, accusations about an alleged plan to shut down a major public mental hospital and sell the land. Note that the questions, which are intentionally ambiguous between rhetorical and felicitous interpretations, do not point to who might be behind the plans or who intends to benefit from selling the land. The author, at this point in the text, has chosen to criticize the government without pointing fingers. The second section gradually increases the use of humor triggers, starting with إن ملاذنا الأخير شاء الله—which literally means *our last resort, God willing*—and ending with the sentence about casting demons out with flip-flops. Note that this section includes scathing criticism of the government, hence the reference to Muhammad Ahmed El-Razaz, Egypt's minister of finance at the time. The third section, which is represented in the source text as a separate paragraph, involves another shift in tone, marked with the shift in viewpoint from the third person (all the crazy people) to the first person (we, the citizens). This section presents the author's main thesis statement—that maintaining this hospital is the responsibility of the government. The big picture, of course, is that shutting down the hospital, despite the invaluable services it provides to the community, is just another example of the corruption and oppression that have gone out of control.

(14) أحمد رجب، ١٩٩٦، ''الفهامة''، الطبعة الثالثة، دار الشروق، القاهرة، ص ١٥.

هل هناك اتجاه لتصفية مستشفى العباسية؟ وهل صحيح أن المرضى يطردون منه الآن إلى الشوارع؟ مهما كانت قيمة متر الأرض في هذا الموقع، فنحن المواطنون نأمل التوسع في مساحة المستشفى لا تصفيته، فهو ملاذنا الأخير إن شاء الله ما دامت الحكومة تدفعنا إلى الجنون بكل أنواعه، ابتداء من الجنون الذهولي إلى الجنون الهياجي .. وهيئة الإحصاء لا تقدم لنا للأسف إحصائية عن عدد الذين أصبحوا يكلمون أنفسهم، أو عدد الآباء الوقورين الذين يجلسون أمام المرايا لتلعيب حواجبهم، أو عدد المصابين بالوسواس القهري والذين يعتقدون أن الرزاز يطاردهم في الشوارع المظلمة، أو يتصورون أنه يفتش جيوبهم وهم نيام .. أو يتخيلون أن الدنيا أصبحت مليئة بالعفاريت والجن الذي يسكن الأجسام ولا يخرج إلا بضرب الشباشب.

لقد رضينا بأن تسبب لنا الحكومة الجنون، وأصبح من حقنا على الحكومة أن
توفر لنا المأوى الذي نمارس فيه الهلوسة والتخريف.

Are there plans to shut down the Abbasiyya Mental Hospital?
Is it true that patients are being thrown out to the streets? No
matter how valuable this piece of real estate is, we, the citizens,
hope that the hospital will be expanded, not shut down, because
eventually we will all end up there as long as the government
continues to drive us into madness. We have no idea how
many of us have already gone over the edge. Unfortunately, the
Census Bureau does not tell us how many people are talking to
themselves or how many of our esteemed fathers are making
funny faces at themselves in mirrors. We have no idea how many
people are now paranoid, imagining El-Razaz, the minister
of finance, chasing them down dark alleys or going through
their pockets while they are asleep. We have accepted that the
government is going drive us crazy, but we have the right to
expect it to provide a place where we can exercise our madness.

Having analyzed the structure of the text, we also need to analyze the
tone triggers—or the sources of humor, in this case—because they can help
us generate translation candidates. The sarcastic tone in this text relies
heavily on lexical selection. For example, the author uses various colloquial
words and expressions with culture-specific connotations that easily create
the humorous effect, such as ضرب الشباشب *lit. beating with flip-flops* and
تلعيب حواجبهم *lit. making their eyebrows dance*. These colloquialisms are
used in contrast with very formal expressions, such as الوقورين *respectable*
and نحن المواطنون *we the citizens*. This contrast is a source of humor in its
own right. Moreover, the main theme of this passage—mental illness—can
be a rich source of humor, but making fun of mentally ill people is inappropriate and offensive. The author walks a tightrope by designing the text
in a way that allows the humor triggers to work only when they are appropriate and conducive to his goals. The first section of the text, with its
serious and accusatory tone, does not include any humor triggers related
to insanity, even though the Arabic name of that particular hospital has
the same connotations as *the loony bin*, *the booby hatch*, or *the cuckoo's
nest*. The name does not trigger humor in this section because it comes in
a context in which formal language is used. Any humor about mental illness in this section would undermine the author's plan. The other set of

lexical items, including تلعيب حواجبهم *lit. making their eyebrows dance* and يكلمون أنفسهم *talk to themselves*, is not offensive either, because it does not describe people who are actually mentally ill. Rather, these descriptions refer to the Egyptian people, including the author, who have metaphorically gone crazy because of the government's actions. This analysis helps us understand how humor is created, which in turn can help us recreate it in the translation.

The main challenge in translating this text is transferring the humor and sarcasm to English while making sure that the underlying message is communicated accurately, despite the culture-specific references. We need to maintain the accusatory tone of the first section, which is not a problem because its first two sentences are ambiguous questions that have the same rhetorical effects in English. The third sentence is also ambiguous, because it can be understood as an indication that the real estate value in this area is very low or very high; hence the rephrasing. The *no matter* construction presupposes that the land is now very expensive. The rephrased translation provides indirect affirmative answers to the preceding questions, and, as a result, the indirect accusatory tone is preserved. As for the name of the hospital, it is transliterated with an added definition because most of our readers are not expected to be familiar with the nature of the hospital or the connotations associated with its name—that is, the issue of triggering inappropriate humor does not arise.

The second section of the translation introduces humor in the same fashion as in the source text. The phrase إن شاء الله is translated as *eventually* rather than *God willing* or *hopefully*, neither of which would trigger humor in this context. Moreover, we can delete the phrase describing the range and types of madness to keep the sentences relatively short, which in turn adds to the humorous effect. Including this phrase in the translation would require technical terms that would be confusing in this context, especially if understood as references to real psychiatric conditions. As for the above-mentioned lexical contrasts, we can maintain them by translating الوقورين as *esteemed* and تلعيب الحواجب as *making funny faces* via cultural approximation. The last sentence of this section is particularly problematic; it is the humorous climax, but it can disrupt the rhetorical structure of the translation. The humor is triggered by the comical overexaggeration of the rituals associated with superstition, namely, exorcism by beating with flip-flops; however, it is not clear how this superstition relates to the main theme of government corruption and its effects on people. The rhetorical function of this sentence is to diffuse the author's sharp criticism of the government, especially after the direct attack on the minister of finance. In other words, it is meant to be funny and confusing. The challenge here is to maintain the humor without changing the tone. We cannot use *jinn* because it is an unfamiliar concept to many readers and the author is not attempting to make fun of people's religious or cultural beliefs or to even refer to a real cultural practice. We cannot use *demons* or *goblins* either, because these would alter the tone in different ways. Perhaps, it is best to leave out this sentence altogether, because including it would disrupt the rhetorical structure of the translation, and it might change the tone.

Misinterpreting tone is one of the most serious translation pitfalls, especially in complex argumentative texts in which different points of view are presented with different tones. To illustrate the seriousness of this issue, let us look at the text in (15) in some detail. The author of this text is giving his opinion on the outcomes of secular higher education in the Arab world: This education system is modeled after secular Western curricula; and as a result, students graduate with negative attitudes toward their religion and language. According to the author, these attitudes are motivated by what students see as a contradiction between the rational nature of science and the "superstitious and mythical" nature of religion, along with the perceived incompatibility of their language (Arabic) with scientific investigation. These attitudes are manifested in the following tendencies: (1) Students prefer to speak European languages over Arabic, (2) they have an elitist attitude toward others who do not share the same secular beliefs, and (3) they refrain from engaging in religious discourse or reading Arabic resources, especially the Qur'an. This is the information content that needs to be carried over in the translation.

(15) محمد قطب، ٢٠٠٦، "واقعنا المعاصر"، دار الشروق، القاهرة، ص ٢٦٥.
أما الكليات العملية فهي تخرج الفنيين من أطباء ومهندسين وزراعيين وغيرهم .. ولكنها تخرجهم على الطريقة الغربية البحتة، أي ((علمانيين)). لا يطيقون الحديث في أمور الدين – فضلا عن أن يتدينوا هم أنفسهم – لأنهم طلاب ((علم)) والدين خرافة، ولأنهم ((واقعيون)) والدين أساطير، ولأنهم ((عقول مفكرة)) لا ينبغي لها أن تتدنى إلى مستوى العوام الذين لم يطلعوا على ((الحقائق العلمية)) .. وفضلا عن ذلك فإنهم ((يتميزون)) عن أمثالهم من ((العلمانيين)) في الغرب، بكونهم يحتقرون لغة بلادهم، لأنها لغة متخلفة لا تصلح للعلم، ويتحدثون – من ثم – بلغة السادة المتحضرين، ويرفضون أن ينظروا في أي كلام مكتوب بالعربية، لأن العربية أصلا هي لغة الجمود والتخلف، ولو كان المكتوب بالعربية هو القرآن .. بل إن هذا الكتاب بالذات هو أشد ما ينفرون من قراءته أو النظر إليه.

superstition and myth   *always single*

One might assume that the explanations provided in this text are the author's own ideas, and consequently conclude that he is a staunch supporter of secularism. This attitude will need to be reflected throughout the translation. For example, we might interpret the double parentheses as emphasis markers and replace some of them with adjectives and adverbials that signal emphasis, such as *ardent* and *indeed*. We can also use a variety of word- and phrase-level strategies to ensure that this enthusiastic prosecularism tone is easily recognized, such as adding *nothing but* in *religion is nothing but superstitions and myths*. The most powerful translation strategy to express assertive attitudes is using the verb *to be* with attributive predicates, as in *they are rational students of science* and *Arabic . . . is incompatible with progress*. In fact, we might be tempted to tone down some of the expressions used in this passage, such as متخلفة *backward* and يحتقرون *despise*, because they might be too strong in the target language. This analysis gives us a translation along the lines of (15a).

> (15a) Those who study at colleges of applied sciences graduate
> to be physicians, engineers, agriculturalists, and the like—but
> their education follows what is essentially a Western curriculum.
> As a result, they become ardent secularists who cannot stand
> discussing religion, let alone being religious themselves, because
> they are rational students of science, whereas religion is nothing
> but superstitions and myths. Indeed, they are intellectuals
> who would not stoop to the level of the ignorant people who
> are unaware of scientific facts. These secularists surpass their
> Western counterparts in that they even look down on their own
> language because it is not suited for scientific pursuit. Instead,
> they prefer to speak the languages of civilized gentle people,
> and they refuse to read anything written in Arabic, which is
> incompatible with progress, even if it was the Qur'an. In fact, it
> is this book in particular that they avoid most.

The problem with the translation in (15a) is that it completely misses the point of the source text. The author is, in fact, strongly opposed to secular higher education, and the purpose of this text is to condemn what he sees as the disastrous repercussions of such an education. He does so by using two separate points of view (or voices) with independent tones. There is his own point of view, which he tries to keep objective, and the reported secularists' point of view, which he makes obviously biased against religion. The author's voice includes the first and last statements along with his observations, whereas the presumed secularists' voice includes the explanations of these observations. For example, the author states that those who graduate from colleges of applied sciences do not like to engage in religious discussions and they are not religious, but he does not provide his own explanation. Instead, he reports what the proponents of secular education would say—that these are rational students of science and that religion is nothing but superstitions and myths. In other words, it is not the author who thinks religion consists of superstitions and myths; it is his adversaries who think so. This rhetorical technique is common in argumentative discourse because it is effective in discrediting one side of the argument without being seen as biased.

The structure of this text is designed in a way that helps readers distinguish the author's own voice from that of his adversaries. Every subordinate clause that starts with لأن *because* reports the secularists' point of view, whereas the rest of the text reflects the author's voice. All the words and phrases in double parentheses reflect the ways secularists describe themselves—that is, these parentheses function as scare quotation marks that keep the two voices separate. The text's design keeps the two tones separate as well. For example, all the loaded words that would trigger negative attitudes are in the parts of the text that reflect the secularists' voice, whereas the parts that reflect the author's voice are neutral; they are merely descriptive. Note that most of the words and phrases in double parentheses can be seen as positive, but in this particular context, they evoke negative attitudes because they create the perception that secularists are arrogant. This gives the impression that if the reader is not a secularist, he or she would be viewed by them as an ignorant person—that is, secularists look down on Islam, Arabic, and the reader.

Any successful translation of this text needs to keep the points of view and tones separate and easily identifiable, as in (15b). This can be done by adding adverbial phrases, such as *so-called* and *in their view*, while reconstructing some sentences to include subjects and verbs that make it easy to know whose viewpoint is being represented, as in *they see* and *they claim*. The double parentheses can be converted to quotation marks to maintain the author's strategy of borrowing his adversaries' vocabulary to describe their views. Finally, there is no need to tone down the author's provocative words—such as *ignorant, backward,* and *masters*—because they play a crucial role in communicating the author's feelings and how he thinks his adversaries feel.

> (15b) Those who study at colleges of applied sciences graduate to be physicians, engineers, agriculturalists, and so on, but their education follows what is essentially a Western curriculum. As a result, they become so-called secularists who cannot stand any discussions of religion, let alone be religious themselves, because they see themselves as "rational" students of science, whereas religion, in their view, is nothing but "superstitions and myths." They even think of themselves as "intellectuals" who should not stoop to the level of "ignorant people" who are not aware of "scientific facts." Those secularists "surpass" their Western counterparts in that they despise their own language because they think it is "backward" and "unsuited for scientific pursuit." Instead, they prefer to speak the languages of their "civilized" masters. They would not read anything written in Arabic, which they claim to be "incompatible with progress," even if it was the Qur'an. In fact, it is this book in particular that they avoid most.

Just as there is no one particular construction or linguistic form that signals tone, there is no one particular strategy that can be used to reflect tone in our translation. Rather, we need to use several translation strategies to address as many tone triggers as possible. Our goal is to make sure the writer's attitudes survive the translation. If our translation fails to preserve the tone of the source text, we ultimately change the message. This is why it is imperative that we make sure our own feelings and attitudes about the content of the message do not affect the tone of the translation.

6 Genre

Writing, as I mentioned above, is a purposeful act of communication. But for a text to achieve its goals, it needs to meet certain social and cultural norms, or expectations, which help readers identify its type or genre.

Once we identify the genre of a text, we activate our relevant background knowledge, which we have developed by reading many similar texts in the past, to make assumptions that would help us understand the objectives of the particular text at hand. For example, when we read a text that has the name of a dish as a title followed by a list of food items and a series of relatively short sentences starting with imperative verbs such as *simmer* and *mix*, we recognize it as a recipe. When we recognize a text as a recipe, we realize that the food items on the list are ingredients and that the sentences, whether numbered or not, detail the steps of a cooking process that need to be followed in order. Moreover, we recognize that the author's use of imperative verbs is intended as a friendly way of giving directions rather than orders. As readers, we might not be consciously aware of the cognitive processes involved in identifying genres or the kinds of genre-driven information we use in analyzing texts. As translators, however, we need to be able to identify the linguistic and stylistic features that distinguish genres in the source and target languages because when we translate a text, we try to incorporate the genre features of the target language whenever possible.

There are many discourse genres with which we are all familiar—recipes, jokes, political speeches, religious sermons, newspaper editorials, and obituaries, among others—but there is no comprehensive list of all discourse genres. That is because discourse genres are dynamic by nature, in the sense that there are no necessary and sufficient linguistic or stylistic features that definitively determine whether a text belongs to a particular genre rather than another. In other words, there is quite a bit of variation within every genre or subgenre; writing is a creative endeavor, after all, and writers are always pushing the limits of stylistic conventions and manipulating linguistic patterns to better achieve their goals. For example, a political speechwriter might include jokes, religious quotations, anecdotes, and the frequent use of the inclusive first-person plural pronoun *we*, but the presence or absence of any one of these features does not by itself determine whether or not a text is a political speech. The deciding factor is whether the speech is delivered (or meant to be delivered) by a politician in a political context. Therefore, we can view genres as a less-than-perfect classification of text types that differ from each other in terms of linguistic and stylistic features as well as their communicative functions and participants. We do not need to find all the distinctive features of a genre in a text to classify it as such.

Identifying the genre of a text is a prerequisite to translating it, but the question remains: Which linguistic and stylistic features should be preserved when translating? We often take it for granted that the translation of a text should belong to the same genre as its source, and that both texts will thus share many of their genre features. For example, if we are translating a poem, we would use lines or verses, and if we are translating an official form, we would use the same format. This view presupposes that genres and their distinctive features are universal, but this is not always the case. Suppose we need to translate the following knock-knock joke into Arabic: A: *Knock, knock!* B: *Who's there?* A: *Police.* B: *Police who?* A: *Police stop making these knock-knock jokes.* This discourse genre has very specific stylistic features. It involves a strict turn-taking routine with predetermined exchanges, and it must include a pun. Neither of these features can be transferred directly to Arabic, because Arab cultures do not have this particular genre of jokes; therefore, our audiences or readers would not recognize their function. More important, puns often do not translate well because they rely on the sounds of words, which is the first thing that is lost when translating. If we use the genre features of knock-knock jokes in the translation, they would fail to achieve their communicative goals, for nobody would laugh. Knock-knock jokes might be an extreme example, but they demonstrate how genre-specific features can be problematic for translation. In the remainder of this section, we focus on the genre features of Arabic business letters and discuss different ways of translating them.

Business letters constitute a rather unique genre of writing because they fall at the intersection of three powerful cultural domains: the culture of the local speech community, the corporate culture of the organization, and the quickly globalizing international business culture. Each of these cultural domains plays an important role in shaping the linguistic and stylistic features of business letters. For example, letters addressed to local businesses or government agencies demonstrate more features that reflect the local culture, whereas letters addressed to a potentially international audience downplay these local features in favor of more internationally recognized standards. Moreover, the authors of business letters do not communicate on their own behalf as free agents. Rather, they play their roles within an organizational hierarchy to achieve specific procedural goals determined by the organization. For instance, a college representative who writes an admissions letter does not express his or her personal beliefs, emotions, or views. Rather, he or she only reports an institutional decision. The roles played by business letter writers are dictated by their institutional cultures, and they differ from one context to another depending on the procedural goals. For instance, the same employee would write differently when addressing his or her superior than when addressing a subordinate, a potential client, or a representative of another corporation. Therefore, to successfully translate a business letter, we need to identify its genre features, analyze them to understand the writer's motivations, and finally decide whether to incorporate these features in the translation.

One of the most distinctive features of business letters is their layout. Business letters have standardized conventions that govern where certain kinds of information are located, for purposes of clarity and institutional efficiency. However, Arabic business letters demonstrate some variation regarding their layout, especially when we compare letters from different Arabic-speaking countries. For example, the date is sometimes written at the top of the letter aligned to the right, left, or center; but in other letters, it is written at the bottom next to the signature, which is the more traditional format. We also see variation in the calendars used; some countries use only the Gregorian calendar, whereas others use both the Gregorian and the Hijra calendars, or the Gregorian and the Assyrian calendars. The layout itself is not a problem for translation, because all we need to do is follow the guidelines of English business letters. In other words, it does not matter where the date appears in the original letter, because in the translation it will be at the top aligned to the right or left, depending on which style manual we adopt. The internal structure of the date also needs to follow English standards—that is, it needs to start with the month rather than the day, whereas Hijra and Assyrian dates are either converted to the Gregorian calendar or are deleted altogether.

The reference line is the only structural element that involves significant regional differences in its content. In most Arab countries, the reference line (المرجع) includes a combination of numbers and/or letters used for filing purposes or to facilitate identifying the letter in future correspondence. In North Africa, however, there can be a bibliography line (المراجع), which, like a bibliography, includes a list of the documents, correspondence, and policies mentioned in the body of the letter, whereas a serial number (الرقم or العدد) is used for reference and filing purposes. The problem with the bibliography is that it does not have a standard structural equivalent in English business correspondence. One way of dealing with this issue is to delete the list and incorporate this information in the body of the letter itself.

Almost all Arabic business letters include a salutation line, but unlike English business letters, the salutation may either precede or follow the subject line and/or the reference line. Again, no matter where the salutation is located in the source letter, the translation needs to follow the conventions of English: two lines below the addressee's mailing address or the attention line, if there is one. There is a wide range of acceptable salutations in Arabic business letters, for the choice of salutation depends on many factors, including where the writer and the addressee fall within their institutional hierarchies, how formal or informal the letter is meant to sound, and whether the author is familiar with the addressee. The standard Arabic salutations are السيد *Mr.*, السيدة *Ms.*, and their plural forms السادة and السيدات, followed by the addressee's full name. The name is sometimes separated from the salutation with a slash, as in السيدة / كريمة مندور and السيد / محمد المصري, and followed by the adjective الفاضل or المحترم, both of which mean *respected*. If the addressee has a professional title, such as الدكتور *Dr.* or المهندس *Engineer*, it immediately precedes the name—for example, السيد الدكتور / محمد المصري. Honorary titles are added at the beginning of the salutation, and they can be stacked with other terms of address, depending on the addressee's status. For example, a cabinet minister with a doctoral degree might be addressed as معالي *Excellency* معالي السيد الأستاذ الدكتور الوزير / يوسف البدري, whereas is the title for a minister, and الأستاذ الدكتور is the title for a professor. When translating salutations, we need to follow the target language standards and use cultural approximation to identify functionally equivalent titles and terms of address.

It is common in very formal letters to keep the addressee's name out of the salutation line and use only his or her position, as in السيد/الأستاذ مدير البنك العربي, or to keep the name but add the position on the next line. In impersonal correspondence, in which the writer is unfamiliar with the addressee, the phrase إلى من يهمه الأمر or لمن يهمه الأمر *lit. To whom it matters* is used in the salutation line, but it is translated as *To Whom It May Concern*. Note that the modal verb *may* is added to the translation because we are using a functionally equivalent formulaic expression. Finally, the salutation عزيزي *lit. my dear*, is considered a term of endearment that is inappropriate for business correspondence. However, most Arabic salutations can be translated as *Dear*, in addition to the appropriate honorary title, if applicable.

The salutation line is almost always followed by a greeting line, which traditionally includes a formulaic expression, such as السلام عليكم ورحمة الله

وبركاته *lit. Peace be upon you and God's mercy and blessings.* But religious expressions in general are becoming less common in Arabic business correspondence. Even the opening phrase بسم الله الرحمن الرحيم *lit. In the Name of God, Most Merciful, Most Gracious,* which used to be written at the top of every letter, is becoming more restricted in use. Instead, it is becoming more common to see the standard greeting تحية طيبة وبعد *lit. Kind greetings* and then immediately followed by the body of the letter. The length of the greeting line reflects the power relations between the writer and the addressee; longer greeting lines indicate that the addressee is higher than the writer on the institutional hierarchy. The greeting line is often left out when translating, because it does not have a functional equivalent in English business letters. Nevertheless, we need to maintain the power relations and the level of formality in the translation while adhering to the target language's conventions. For example, we can use a colon after the addressee's name, instead of a comma, to signal a higher level of formality.

Every business letter ends with a complementary close, such as *Thank you, Yours,* or *Respectfully yours,* among others. Arabic has a large inventory of formulaic expressions that can be used as complementary closings. These expressions range from lengthy formulas that reflect the addressee's higher status, such as وتفضلوا بقبول فائق الاحترام والتقدير *lit. and please accept the utmost respect and appreciation,* to the very formal مع الشكر *lit. with thanks,* which reflects the writer's higher status. Similarly to other formulaic expressions, we can substitute the Arabic complementary closings with appropriate English functional equivalents that reflect the same power differentials between the writer and the addressee and the intended level of formality.

The sample letter in (16) and its translation demonstrate some of the structural changes we can implement to make sure our translation complies with the conventions of English business letters. These changes include relocating the date line, the reference line, the inside address, and the enclosures line. The bibliography is omitted from the translation, and the document listed there in the Arabic version is mentioned in the body of the letter instead. The greeting line is also deleted, and a formal salutation line is used in its place, whereas the formulaic complementary closing is replaced with a typical English one. All such changes are dependent on the letter format we decide to adopt in the translation, and they all need to reflect the same level of formality of the source text.

(16)

الرابطة العربية لعلوم البحار
۱۲۰ ش التاج، العباسية
القاهرة، ج م ع
رقم: ٦٦/٢٠٠٩

السيد الأستاذ الدكتور / إبراهيم سلامة
رئيس الرابطة العربية لعلوم البحار ـ القاهرة

الموضوع: الاجتماع السنوي الحادي عشر للرابطة العربية لعلوم البحار
المرجع: رسالتكم رقم ۱۸۲ بتاريخ ٢٠٠٩/٨/٢٤
المرفقات: السيرة الذاتية وملخص ورقة العمل

تحية طيبة وبعد،
تبعا لرسالتكم المشار إليها في المرجع أعلاه، يشرفني أن أحيل عليكم سيرتي
الدراسية والمهنية وكذلك ملخص ورقة البحث التي أقترحها للمؤتمر بعنوان:
تأثير خطوط الإنترنت البحرية على البيئة البحرية، للعرض على لجنة التحكيم.
وتفضلوا بقبول فائق الاحترام والسلام.

تحريرا في ٢٠٠٩/٩/١٥

September 15, 2009
Ref: 66/2009

Professor Ibrahim Salama
President, Arab Association for Marine Sciences
120 Al-Taj St., Al-Abasiyya
Cairo, Egypt

Dear Professor Salama:

Subject: AAMS 11th Annual Meeting
In response to your message of August 24, I am pleased to
enclose my curriculum vitae and abstract. The paper I am
proposing for the 11th Annual Meeting of the Arab Association
for Marine Sciences is titled "The Effects of Underwater Internet
Cables on Marine Environment."

Sincerely yours,

Enclosures: Curriculum vitae
               Abstract

We now turn to the cultural and linguistic features of Arabic business letters as reflected in the body of the message. Generally speaking, conciseness, directness, and clarity of objectives are defining characteristics of business correspondence. Writing in an efficient way that helps the reader save time is seen as a considerate and tactful way of communicating. This is why writers try to get to the point immediately, without additional pleasantries or personal remarks. Many contemporary Arabic business letters follow this pattern; but more traditional styles emphasize a more cordial approach, especially when addressing someone of a higher status or a potential client. From an Arab point of view, business is always personal, and it is important to establish a positive tone before getting to business, as we can see in the letter excerpt in (17). The problem here is that if this traditional style is carried over into English, as in the translation candidate in (17a), it has the potential of causing misunderstandings. A potential client who is not aware of traditional business norms in the Arabic-speaking cultures might find the tone of this letter to be "over the top" and consequently think that the writer is unprofessional (by the target culture's standards), or even worse, untrustworthy. To avoid such complications, it is best to keep the translation in line with the standards of the target language, thus leaving out what would be seen as unnecessary pleasantries and by toning down the wording accordingly, as in (17b).

(17)

أنتهز هذه الفرصة لأعبر لكم ولمؤسستكم الموقرة عن تقديرنا وتمنياتنا القلبية بالمزيد من التقدم والازدهار، ويسرني أن أتقدم لكم بخالص الشكر على رسالتكم الكريمة المذكورة أعلاه.

استمرارا لتطوير الخدمات التي نقدمها إلى عملائنا الكرام، تتشرف الشركة الكويتية لنظم المعلومات بأن تضع بين أيديكم قائمة بأحدث تقنيات الشبكات التي ندعمها والخدمات التي نقدمها.

(17a) I would like to seize this opportunity to express our gratitude to you and your esteemed organization and our heartfelt wishes for more progress and prosperity. I am pleased to thank you wholeheartedly for your above-referenced kind letter.

As a continuation of our efforts to further develop the services that we offer to our generous clients, the Kuwaiti Company for Information Systems

is honored to provide you with a list of the latest networking technologies
we support and the services we provide.

> (17b) Thank you for your inquiry about the network systems we
> support at the Kuwaiti Company for Information Systems. Please
> find enclosed a list of our latest products and services.

We often find certain Arabic cliché phrases with English referential
equivalents that cannot always be used in translation because they might
violate the standards of English business communication. For example, the
phrase يتشرف *to be honored* is commonly used in almost all types of Arabic
business letters. We can use its English equivalent when translating invitations and announcements, but Arabic business letters include this phrase in
contexts in which *to be honored* might sound a bit awkward, such as يشرفني
أن أحيل عليكم سيرتي الدراسية والمهنية *lit. I am honored to present to you my ré-
sumé* in (16). In English business communication, the phrase *to be honored*
is usually used to show modesty, but in Arabic, the honor has to do with
communicating with the addressee and his or her organization. In these
contexts, English favors *to be pleased*, which we can use in our translation
as a functional equivalent as يشرفني.

Another common cliché in Arabic business correspondence is the phrase
برجاء التكرم بـ, which roughly means *hoping you would be generous enough
to*, as in (18). Being faithful to the wording of this phrase when translating
it might make the writer sound as if he or she was pleading, which in this
case is not the original intention at all. The writer of this particular letter is
only asking the addressee to fill out a form and send it to human resources.
It is simply a polite way of making requests, regardless of the power relations
between the writer and the addressee; therefore, we can translate it as *please*.

> (18) برجاء التكرم بإكمال النموذج المرفق طيه وإرساله إلى مكتب شؤون
> العاملين.
>
> Please fill out the enclosed form and send it to the Human
> Resources Office.

Business letter writers pay special attention to the way they use pronouns.
For example, it is perfectly appropriate in English business correspondence
to use the first-person singular pronoun *I* because it makes the writing less
formal while helping distinguish personal and organizational views and

decisions. The first-person plural pronoun *we*, conversely, is used to express the commitments of the organization rather than the writer—that is, it clarifies the writer's role in the communication context. Of course, there is the referential ambiguity of whether *we* refers to the writer and his or her organization or the writer and the reader(s), but there are always enough contextual clues that reduce the risk of miscommunication. The second-person pronoun *you* is used frequently in English business communication. In fact, some business manuals encourage writers to count the instances of second-person reference to make sure they exceed the number of references to the writer and his or her organization to establish the "you attitude."

These genre-specific linguistic features can be problematic when one translates Arabic business letters because they have different cultural restrictions on the use of pronouns. Many Arabic business letter writers try to avoid the first-person singular pronoun أنا *I*, especially when addressing someone of a higher status. Perhaps the only contexts in which we see this pronoun are formulaic expressions in legally binding forms, such as أقر أنا الموقع أدناه *I, the undersigned, certify that*, and in very personal letters, such as complaints and appeals. To avoid this potentially offensive pronoun, writers opt for morphologically dependent referential forms, such as affixes on verbs. Writers also prefer to make reference to themselves in subordinate clauses and embedded constructions, such as يسرني أن أرسل *lit. it pleases me to send* as opposed to أنا سعيد لأني أرسل لك *I am happy to send you*. Another way to avoid direct reference to the writer is to use the first-person plural pronoun, which does not necessarily refer to the organization, as in يسعدنا أن ندعوكم *lit. we are pleased to invite you* instead of يسعدني أن أدعوك *I am pleased to invite you*, which might sound arrogant. This is not the "royal" *we*; it is simply a communicative strategy that helps the writer sound modest. Of course, we need to change the pronoun in the translation to avoid miscommunication.

Second-person references are even more complicated in Arabic business letters. Using the singular second-person pronoun أنت *you* when addressing someone of a higher status is considered disrespectful, whereas using it when writing to someone of equal or lower status in a business setting is considered condescending. This is why business letter writers often use plural second-person pronouns to show respect, especially when affixed to a polite form such as سيادتكم. When addressing someone of an equal or lower status, the passive voice is used to avoid second-person references.

The problem here is that some of the strategies used in Arabic business writing to avoid first- and second-person references—namely, *it*-clefts and the passive voice—are discouraged in English business writing because they negatively affect the clarity and directness of the letters, as in the close translation in (19a).

(19)

تحية طيبة وبعد،

السلام عليكم ورحمة الله وبركاته ونهديكم أطيب تحيات مكتب البعثات الخارجية، أما بعد، فإن أسرة المكتب تهنئكم بالحصول على منحة دراسية شاملة لإكمال برنامج الدراسات العليا بالخارج وترجو لكم التوفيق ودوام النجاح.

نتشرف بأن نرفق طيه استمارات ونماذج يرجى استيفاؤها وإعادتها للمكتب في أقرب فرصة ممكنة مع خطاب من الأستاذ المشرف يوضح البرنامج الزمني المقترح للبحث، كما نرجو الاطلاع على التعليمات الموضحة بها والالتزام بما جاء فيها.

وتفضلوا بقبول فائق الاحترام والتقدير

(19a)
Greetings,

   Peace be upon you and God's mercy and blessings. We offer you the kindest greetings from the Study Abroad Office. The Office family congratulates you on receiving a full scholarship to complete your graduate studies abroad, and wishes you continuous success.

   We are honored to enclose forms and applications that are wished to be filled out and returned to the office at the earliest possible opportunity, along with a letter from the academic adviser indicating the proposed research schedule. We also wish for a review of the instructions clarified herewith and a close adherence to them.

(19b)
On behalf of the Study Abroad Office, I would like to congratulate you on receiving a full scholarship to complete your graduate studies abroad. Please complete the enclosed forms

and return them to our office at your earliest convenience, along with a letter from your academic adviser indicating the proposed schedule for your research. The forms include instructions that you might find helpful.

Although business letters are rather restrictive in their format and content, many other genres have more room for creativity and diversity, such as essays, political speeches, and memoirs. In fact, no matter how restrictive a genre might be, writers are constantly pushing the limits of genre features to find ways that better achieve their communicative goals. Genres, after all, do not have rules that determine what writers can and cannot do. They are mere classifications of already-existing texts, and therefore their defining features are constantly changing. Nevertheless, the concept of genres is quite helpful for translation; identifying the genre of a text helps us know what to expect and how to make our translation meet the readers' expectations.

Exercises

Translate the following texts into English and pay special attention to their rhetorical structure. Discuss the translation problems you encounter and the strategies you propose to use to resolve them.

(١) عبد الفتاح محمد شبانة، ١٩٩٦، ''اليابان: العادات والتقاليد''، مكتبة مدبولي، القاهرة، ص ٩.

يكفل الدستور الياباني حرية الأديان، ولا يوجد دين رسمي للدولة، وغالبا ما تتم احتفالات الميلاد والزواج وفقا لمراسم ((الشنتو))، أما ما يتعلق بالوفاة والجنازات ومراسمها فتتم وفقا للمراسم البوذية، والطريف أن الياباني عندما يسأل عن دينه فإنه يرد بأنه ((لا ديني))، ولا يكتب شيئا في خانة الدين باعتبار أن مذهب ((الشنتو)) ما هو إلا عادات اجتماعية يابانية تقليدية ومتوارثة عبر الأجيال، وأن البوذية تعتبر فلسفة أكثر منها دينا، والياباني يأخذ أمور الدين ببساطة، فهو يزور معبد الشنتو والمعبد البوذي وقد يزور الكنيسة المسيحية أيضا، كل ذلك في نفس الوقت ويقدم لكل مكان الاحترام والتقديس.

(٢) أحمد زكريا الشلق، ١٩٩٩، ''فصول من تاريخ قطر السياسي''، مطابع الدوحة الحديثة، الدوحة، ص ١٥٦.

وفي يوم الثلاثاء الأسود، كما أسمته المعارضة البريطانية، ١٦ يناير ١٩٦٨ أعلن السير هارولد ويلسون رئيس الوزراء العمالي أن بريطانيا سوف لا تنسحب من الشرق الأقصى فحسب، بل ومن الخليج أيضا قبل نهاية عام ١٩٧١ بعد أن تحدث في مجلس العموم عن

حجم المشكلات الاقتصادية وتكاليف الوجود العسكري، وقد اتخذ القرار البريطاني طابعا دراميا مفاجئا بالنسبة للمنطقة، لأنه كان يعني بطبيعة الحال، انتهاء معاهدات الحماية القديمة، التي فرضتها بريطانيا على إمارات الخليج، وقد يبدو هذا الأمر منطقيا، بعد أن ضعفت قبضة بريطانيا على المنطقة بشكل عام في أعقاب الحرب العالمية الثانية، وانسحابها من شبه القارة الهندية، حين أصبحت علاقات بريطانيا مع إمارات الخليج العربي تخضع بشكل مباشر لإشراف وزارة الخارجية في لندن، بعد أن أنهيت خدمة الضباط السياسيين البريطانيين في الهند، على الرغم من بقاء المعاهدات والاتفاقيات القديمة.

(3) إبراهيم سعدة، ١٩٩٧، ''مقالات ساخنة''، الهيئة العامة المصرية للكتاب، القاهرة، ص ٥٩. لقد أصبحت كل شبكات التليفزيون في كل دول العالم – ماعدا دول العالم الثالث طبعا – ملكا لشركات القطاع الخاص. سواء شئنا أو أبينا – في دول عالمنا الثالث – فإن الحكومات ستضطر إلى رفع يدها عن أجهزة الإعلام – صحافة وإذاعة وتليفزيون – وتتركها للقطاع الخاص إن لم يكن اليوم فخلال سنوات قليلة قادمة على الأكثر.

[margin handwritten note:] wanted or not like it or not

(4) أحمد بهجت، ١٩٩٤، ''أهل اليسار يا ليل''، دار الشروق، القاهرة، ص ١٦. يرسم توفيق الحكيم في كتابه ((يوميات نائب في الأرياف)) صورة سريعة لما كان يحدث في الانتخابات أيام زمان.. كشف انخفاض منسوب النيل عن صندوق من صناديق الانتخابات في إحدى الترع، وسأل وكيل النيابة – وهو توفيق الحكيم – أحد ضباط الإدارة عن قصة هذا الصندوق، فقال الضابط إنه رجل حر ويؤمن بالحرية وهو لا يحب الضغط على الفلاحين، وإنما يترك لهم حرية إبداء رأيهم بالكامل، فإذا انتهوا من ملء بطاقات الانتخاب وضعها في صندوق وأمر بحمله وإلقائه في الترعة، وفي نفس الوقت الذي يكون فيه صندوق الآراء الحقيقية في طريقه إلى مثواه في الترعة، يكون هناك صندوق آخر يحمل بطاقات مزيفة تضم النتيجة التي تريدها الحكومة .. ويذهب هذا الصندوق المزور ويتم فرز بطاقاته فإذا بأصوات الناخبين تجمع على انتخاب مرشح الحكومة رغم أن أحدا لم يعطه صوته.. هذه الصورة السريعة الواردة في كتاب أدبي تكشف القناع عن تدخل الحكومة في نتائج الانتخابات ((زمان))، وتكشف عن تزويرها لهذه النتائج.

(5) إملي نصرالله، ٢٠٠١، ''نساء رائدات من الغرب''، الجزء الخامس، الدار اللبنانية المصرية، ص ٢٠٠. مرحلة استقرار جديدة في حياة أجاثا كريستي. رواياتها منتشرة، وتترجم. وهي تجرب حظها في كتابة المسرحيات. والرواية الكلاسيكية الوحيدة، التي كتبتها وعنوانها ((خبز العمالقة)) كانت حول الموسيقى وقعتها بإمضاء مستعار. أما المسرحيات التي اشتهرت لها فهي ((عشرة عبيد صغار)) وقد ترجمت إلى العديد من اللغات، أما مسرحيتها ((مصيدة الفئران)) فقد ضربت رقما قياسيا في الاستمرار إذ أنها تقدم كل ليلة، فوق أحد مسارح لندن، ومنذ العام ١٩٥٢.

Annotated Texts for Translation

Annotated Text 1

جبل الزنابق[1] لسمر يزبك[2] في الزيتون الأدبية[3] بالقاهرة

ناقشت ‘‘ورشة الزيتون الأدبية’’ في العاصمة المصرية[4] القاهرة، كتاب ‘‘جبل الزنابق’’ الصادر عن[5] ‘‘دار المدى’’ للكاتبة السورية[6] سمر يزبك، وهو كتاب متوسط الحجم يقع في ١٦٦ صفحة.

ويمكن تصنيف مضمون الكتاب بالكتابة[7] التي لا تلتزم بشكل أو نوع أدبي[8] بعينه[9]، وإن كان يتراوح بين القص[10] والشعر النثري في رصد الأحلام والمنامات، مستلهما[11] في ذلك تجارب عظيمة ككتاب ‘‘منامات الوهراني’’، وكتاب ‘‘١٢ قصة عجيبة’’ لجابرييل جارثيا ماركيز. ويضم الكتاب ٧٩ نصا قصيرا حلميا عبارة عن نقل شعري سوريالي أحيانا[12] يمزج بين الواقع والحلم في رصده للعديد من الأحلام والمنامات المتفرقة، حيث[13] قالت الكاتبة إنها استغرقت شهرين في كتابته[14]، غير أنها وصفت أحلامها فيه بـ ‘‘الدفقات المفاجئة’’، وإن فكرة كتابة المنامات بدأت لديها[15] عندما أرادت التحرر من ثقل يرهقها مثل أي شخص يعيش حياتين نهارا مع أناس طبيعيين وكائنات مفكرة[16] وليلا يبدأ استدعاء حياته الداخلية ‘‘العقل الباطن’’، فكانت هذه المنامات أشبه[17] بعملية التصفية.

وناقشته الكاتبة هويدا صالح والناقدان الدكتور شريف الجيار وسيد الوكيل والشاعر شعبان يوسف وأدارت النقاش[18] الروائية أمينة زيدان. وقالت الكاتبة هويدا صالح إن كتاب ‘‘جبل الزنابق’’ يتراوح بين السرد واللغة الشعرية، وهو يفجر[19] قضية قديمة جديدة في الأدب وهي قضية الشكل والمضمون، ويعلي شأن[20] حرية الكاتب[21] في أن يكتب ما يشاء دون الالتزام بقالب أدبي معين، وهذا ما دفع الكاتبة لوصف الكتاب بأنه مجموعة ‘‘منامات أحلام’’ فهذا يريح القارىء[22] ويحرره من إطار[23] الشكل والنوع ويهيئه لكتابة حرة لا تلتزم إلا[24] بما يعتمل[25] داخل الكاتب من الأحاسيس والمشاعر والرؤى والأفكار.

جريدة الاتحاد (الإمارات)، ١٠ يوليو ٢٠٠٨، العدد ١٢٠٥٨.

Annotated Text 2

مستقبل الثقافة في مصر

كتاب "مستقبل الثقافة في مصر"[1] ينبغي[2] أن نقرأه لأنه لم يقرأ جيدا من قبل، أقصد أنه لم يقرأ قراءة موضوعية أمينة متفهمة[3] حتى الآن. ولا شك في أن القراء الأفراد الذين أحسنوا قراءة هذا الكتاب كثيرون[4] لكن الذين أساؤوا قراءته[5] وأشاعوا في الناس قراءتهم الفاسدة المتحاملة أكثر بكثير[6]. والسبب في هذا هو الظروف السياسية والمناخات الفكرية والنفسية المصرية والعربية والدولية التي أعقبت ظهور[7] الكتاب وظلت سائدة طوال العقود الستة الأخيرة[8].

لقد ظهر "مستقبل الثقافة في مصر" كما هو معلوم[9] عام ١٩٣٨ بعد أن عاد للبلاد دستورها[10] الذي كان صدقي[11] قد أوقف العمل به، ثم أجريت انتخابات لتأتي[12] بوزارة النحاس التي وقعت مع الإنجليز معاهدة ١٩٣٦ التي استردت بها مصر جانبا جديدا من حقوقها وقطعت شوطا بعيدا في طريق الاستقلال، كما وقعت مصر مع الدول الأوروبية اتفاقية منترو[13] التي تمكنت بها[14] من إلغاء الامتيازات الأجنبية[15] وإخضاع الأجانب المقيمين فيها لقوانينها الوطنية التي يخضع لها المصريون. هذه التطورات الإيجابية أعطت الانطباع بأن مرحلة من التاريخ كانت فيها مصر مكبلة بالقيود توشك أن تنتهي[16]، وأن مرحلة جديدة من الحرية والاستقلال توشك أن تبدأ[17]. فما هو المستقبل الذي تتصوره مصر لنفسها وكيف تعد العدة[18] لتحقيقه والوصول إليه[19]؟

وقد أجاب طه حسين على هذا السؤال فقال: إن مستقبل مصر مشروط[20] بمستقبل الثقافة فيها، إذا كانت الثقافة المصرية ستنهض وتتقدم وتتمثل روح العصر الحديث[21] وتجيب على أسئلته وتلبي حاجاته ومطالبه فستنهض مصر وتتقدم وتتصل بالعصر وتلحق من سبقوها وإلا ستظل ضعيفة خاملة متخلفة ولن يغني الدستور والاستقلال عنها شيئا[22]. بل إن مصر ستفقدهما إذا فقدت الثقافة، لأن الثقافة هي الشرط الذي تتحقق به الثروة والقوة والمنعة. كيف إذا[23] تكون هذه الثقافة المصرية الحديثة؟ كيف تكون مصرية وكيف تكون حديثة؟

أحمد عبد المعطي حجازي، ٢٠٠٦، "مستقبل الثقافة في مصر"، من كتاب "طه حسين معلم الأجيال"، تحرير لطفي عبد الوهاب، مكتبة الأسكندرية، ص ٣٩.

Annotated Text 3

التنوع الحيوي[1] عند نقطة اللاعودة[2]

في العام[3] ٢٠٠٢، تعهدت حكومات العالم بتحقيق تخفيض كبير[4] في معدل فقدان التنوع الحيوي بحلول[5] العام ٢٠١٠. وبالرغم أنه من الصعب[6] قياس حجم التنوع الحيوي على

كوكبنا، فإننا على يقين[7] من أن هذا الهدف لم يتحقق. فالوطأة (بصمة القدم)[8] الإيكولوجية لنا ـ ما نأخذه من كوكبنا ـ ٣٫١ مرة القدرة البيولوجية للأرض.

وهو ما يعني[9] أننا على حافة[10] نقطة اللاعودة. وبالتالي فإن ما سنفعله في العقدين المقبلين سيحدد ما إذا[11] كانت البيئة المستقرة التي عاشت عليها[12] الحضارات الإنسانية منذ العصر الجليدي[13] الأخير، أي[14] قبل ١٠ آلاف سنة، ستبقى على حالها أم لا؟

وتتعرض[15] النظم الطبيعية التي تساند الاقتصادات والحياة وسبل العيش[16] في جميع أنحاء كوكب الأرض[17] لخطر التدهور والانهيار السريعين، إلا إذا[18] اتخذ إجراء سريع وجذري وخلاق لحفظ تنوع الحياة واستخدامه المستدام[19] على كوكب الأرض.

وهذا[20] استنتاج أساسي لتقييم رئيسي جديد[21] للحالة الجارية للتنوع البيولوجي وآثار ضياعه المستمر على رفاهية الإنسان.

ويؤكد ثالث تقارير «التوقعات العالمية للتنوع البيولوجي[22]»(٣-GBO) ، الذي تصدره «اتفاقية التنوع البيولوجي»، أن العالم فشل في الوفاء بهدفه بتحقيق خفض ملموس[23] في معدل فقدان التنوع البيولوجي بحلول العام ٢٠١٠.

ويستند التقرير إلى التقييمات العلمية والتقارير الوطنية المقدمة من الحكومات[24]، والدراسة عن السيناريوهات المستقبلية للتنوع البيولوجي. ورهنا بعملية استعراض علمي مستقل موسع، فإن إصدار الطبعة الثالثة من تقرير التوقعات العالمية للتنوع البيولوجي يمثل واحدا من المعالم الرئيسية للسنة الدولية للتنوع البيولوجي[25]، التي تحتفل بها الأمم المتحدة في العام الحالي.

أحمد خضر الشربيني، ''التنوع الحيوي عند نقطة اللاعودة''، مجلة العربي (الكويت)، ١ أغسطس ٢٠١٠، العدد ٦٢١.

Annotated Text 4

ثقافة التسامح عند المسلمين[1]

من أشد الأمور خطرا[2]، والتي تهدد المجتمعات بالتمزق[3] والتعادي، بل[4] قد تفضي إلى اشتعال الحروب بين المجتمعات بعضها ببعض، بل[5] بين أبناء المجتمع الواحد، والوطن الواحد: التعصب[6].

وليس المراد[7] بالتعصب اعتزاز الإنسان[8] بعقيدته أو بأفكاره التي اقتنع بها بمحض اختياره[9]، فهذا لا يمكن أن يعاب[10]. إنما المراد بالتعصب انغلاق المرء على عقيدته أو فكره[11]، واعتبار الآخرين جميعا خصومه وأعداءه، وتوجس الشر منهم، وإضمار السوء لهم،

وإشاعة جو من العنف والكراهية لهم، مما يفقد[12] الناس العيش في أمان واطمئنان. والأمن نعمة من أعظم نعم الله على الإنسان، لهذا امتن الله على قريش فقال:

«فليعبدوا رب هذا البيت الذي أطعمهم من جوع وآمنهم من خوف»[13] (قريش: ٣-٤). واعتبر[14] القرآن الجنة دار أمن كامل: «ادخلوها بسلام آمنين» (الحجر: ٤٦). واعتبر شر ما تصاب به المجتمعات[15]: الجوع والخوف، فقال تعالى: «فأذاقها الله لباس الجوع والخوف بما كانوا يصنعون» (النحل: ١١٢).

ومن الناس[16] من يتصور أن الإيمان الديني ملازم للتعصب لا يفارقه لا محالة[17]، لأن المؤمن بدينه يعتقد أنه على الحق، وما عداه[18] على الباطل، وأن إيمانه هو سبيل النجاة، ومن لم يتمسك بعروته الوثقى[19] لم يهتد إلى طريق الخلاص، وأن من لم يؤمن بكتابه المنزل[20]، وبنبيه المرسل، فهو ذاهب إلى الجحيم، ولا تنفعه أعمال الخير التي قدمها، لأنها لم تبن على الإيمان، فلا قيمة لها عند الله. كما قال تعالى[21]:

«والذين كفروا أعمالهم كسراب بقيعة يحسبه الظمآن ماء حتى إذا جاءه لم يجده شيئا» (النور: ٣٩)، وكقوله تعالى: «مثل الذين كفروا بربهم أعمالهم كرماد اشتدت به الريح في يوم عاصف لا يقدرون مما كسبوا على شيء» (إبراهيم: ١٨). وهذه التصورات للآخرين تنشيء العداوة والبغضاء بين الناس بعضهم وبعض[22]، وكثيرا ما تؤدي إلى حروب دموية بين الطوائف والشعوب المختلفة دينيا[23].

يوسف القرضاوي، "ثقافة التسامح عند المسلمين"، مجلة الدوحة (قطر)، ديسمبر ٢٠٠٧، العدد ١٤٢٨، ص ٦٩.

Annotated Text 5

آثار الأزمة المالية العالمية: الإطار العام للأزمة

تعتبر سنة ٢٠٠٨ كإحدى السنوات السيئة[1] في التاريخ من حيث[2] التنمية البشرية. فمن ناحية[3] سجلت الارتفاع الصاروخي[4] لأسعار المواد الخام، مما تسبب في وضع[5] أكثر من ١٥٠ مليون شخص في فقر مدقع[6] في مختلف أرجاء العالم ومن ناحية أخرى[7] فإن الأزمة المالية حتى الآن في العديد من البلدان ساهمت[8] في تعطيل مستوى التنمية[9] الذي سطرت لبلوغه عديد البلدان[10] ضمن مخططاتها التنموية[11].

وقد ضربت الأزمة المالية في المقام الأول[12] أسواق الأسهم في البلدان المتقدمة قبل أن تمس بشكل غير مباشر[13] اقتصادات البلدان النامية. وفي الواقع، وعلى الرغم من[14] انخفاض مستوى الاندماج المالي لاقتصادات البلدان النامية فإنها تعاني من تأثير الوضع السلبي السائد في البلدان المتقدمة.

وبالنسبة لسنة ٢٠٠٩، فهناك قلق[15] من أن مستوى التجارة العالمية سيتقلص بشكل كبير. ولذلك، فإن معدل نمو الناتج القومي الإجمالي[16] للبلدان النامية سينخفض وضمن عدة عوامل أخرى[17] بتراجع وانخفاض الصادرات. وبالإضافة إلى ذلك، وحسب[18] تقرير محدث للاقتصاد السويسري فإن التشدد في الائتمان في الأسواق العالمية سوف يحد من تدفق رؤوس الأموال إلى بلدان الجنوب بما يقرب من ٥٠% مقارنة مع عام ٢٠٠٨، مما سيحد من الحصول على القروض لرجال الأعمال وأصحاب المقاولات المحليين[19].

وأخيرا فإن إجمالي التحويلات[20] من المهاجرين إلى أسرهم بالبلدان النامية أو في طريق النمو سيسجل كذلك انخفاضا كبيرا.

محمود قطوس وتيري ماكلين، ٢٠٠٩، "الاتفاقية العربية المتوسطية للتبادل الحر، الدراسة القطاعية التفصيلية المتعلقة بإمكانيات التكامل والاندماج الاقتصادي المتاحة في قطاع الجلود والأحذية لبدان اتفاقية أغادير: التقرير النهائي"، الأردن، ص ١٣-١٤.

Annotated Text 6

قضايا مستحدثة في الزواج: الزواج العرفي[1]

تعريفه[2]: عرفته[3] مجلة البحوث الفقهية، باعتباره علما على معنى محدد[4]، فقالت: "هو اصطلاح حديث يطلق على عقد الزواج غير الموثق بوثيقة رسمية[5]، سواء أكان مكتوبا أو غير مكتوب[6]"، ومن التعريف يتضح أن الزواج العرفي هو زواج شرعي مستوف للأركان والشروط الشرعية[7] مع غياب التوثيق الرسمي[8] لهذا العقد، ومن المعروف أن التوثيق ليس من الأركان ولا من الشروط، وبغيابه يكون العقد صحيحا[9]، وهذا ما جرى عليه المسلمون لفترات طويلة، بل إن زواج النبي صلى الله عليه وسلم لم يكن موثقا على الورق بوثائق رسمية، إنما[10] اتخذ زواجه صلى الله عليه وسلم وزواج الصحابة أيضا الصفة الشرعية من[11] استكمال أركان وشروط العقد، ومن شيوع أمر الزواج بين الناس (الإشهار والإشهاد)[12]، يقول[13] شيخ الإسلام ابن تيمية: (لم يكن الصحابة يكتبون "صداقاتهم"[14] لأنهم لم يكونوا يتزوجون على مؤخر[15]، بل يعجلون المهر[16]، وإن أجلوه فهو معروف، فلما صار الناس يزوجون[17] على المؤخر والمدة تطول وينسى، صاروا يكتبون المؤخر وصار ذلك حجة في إثبات الصداق وفي أنها زوجة له[18]).

شرط توثيق الزواج[19] هو شرط قانوني من باب السياسة الشرعية[20]، والشروط القانونية هي شروط يضعها المشرع الوضعي[21] لجلب مصلحة أو دفع مفسدة ومضرة، والشرط القانوني ليس شرط صحة ولا نفاذ ولا لزوم، لأن المشرع الوضعي ليس له[22] أن ينشئ حكما شرعيا دينيا، يحل حراما أو يحرم حلالا[23]، بل هو شرط يترتب عليه أثر قانوني[24] لا دخل له في الحكم الشرعي. ومن المعروف أن للخليفة (للدولة)[25] أن تنظم المباح، وإلزام الرعية بتوثيق العقود هو من هذا الباب[26]، ومن ذلك الإلزام بفعل مباح للقيام بحكم شرعي أو بأمر أمر به الشرع ومنع غيره من قبيل التبني في الأساليب وهو جائز للإمام – الحاكم – أو من يفوضه.

زياد أحمد سلامة، "قضايا مستحدثة في الزواج"، مجلة هدى الإسلام، الأردن، المجلد ٥١، العدد ٦، ٢٠٠٧، ص ٩٨–٩٩.

Annotated Text 7

الانقضاض وموضوع ((الليبرالية)) عند بوش وديكاكوس[1] و((الأفنديات)) عند السادات!!

إذا[2] كانت ظاهرة الانقضاض[3] تتمثل في التركيز على [4]حرفية المعنى أو جزئية المعرفة وتجاهل السياق، فمن المهم[5] أن نستعرض معا المعاني المتعددة للمصطلح[6] في السياق الأوروبي والأمريكي الذي نشأ فيه أولا، وهنا أبدأ هذا العرض الموجز باستدعاء حدث من أطراف الأحداث[7] التي شاهدتها أثناء وجودي في الولايات المتحدة وقت الحملة الانتخابية بين الرئيس السابق جورج بوش ومنافسه مايكل ديكاكوس، حيث[8] اتهم جورج بوش منافسه بأنه ليبرالي[9] (liberal) وكان جورج بوش يشدد في نطقه على مقاطع الكلمة أثناء حملته[10]، وكنا نندهش ونترقب رد فعل المنافس (مايكل ديكاكوس) الذي كان يقول أنا لست ليبراليا[11] (بالمعنى[12] الذي كان يقصده بوش) وكأنه يدفع عن نفسه تهمة[13]. وتدور المناقشة ونكتشف أن المعنى (بشكل التهمة) قد دخل إلى حيز الوجود والاستعمال اللغوي[14] على الساحة الأمريكية (رغم أن أمريكا هي معقل المبادئ الليبرالية) بسبب سياق مسبق وخاص في الحملة الانتخابية حينما هاجم بوش مايكل ديكاكوس قائلا إنه[15] ((ليبرالي)) يبيح الإجهاض ويتعاطف مع المثليين. فالسياق الذي حدد معنى التهمة هنا هو سياق[16] فرضه أحد المحافظين الأقوياء (بوش)[17] والذي كان يعارض إباحة الإجهاض[18] ويحتقر المثليين من منطلق القيم الدينية التي تربى عليها في مؤسسة واسب المسيحية. وبدلا من أن يردد بوش[19] كل هذه القصة كل مرة أثناء حملته قرر أن يركز على كلمة ((ليبرالي)) بتشديد صوتي جعل للكلمة معنى التهمة.. (نتذكر هنا أن السياسيين يستطيعون فرض الكثير من المعاني المستجدة على ألفاظ قديمة، فالرئيس السادات قد جعل من كلمة ((الأفنديات)) [20] إشارة للنخبة المعارضة له والتي اتهمها بانعزالها عن فهم وقائع العالم والسياسة) فإذا[21] كان هذا هو معنى كلمة ليبرالي في سياق حملة انتخابية شهيرة تركت بصماتها[22] على الاستعمال اللغوي للفظ إلى الآن في الولايات المتحدة.. فهناك معان كثيرة ومتعددة للمفهوم في السياق الأمريكي والأوروبي نستعرض منها الآتي: (liberal education) وهو يعني أساسا التعليم غير الحرفي[23]، أي تعليم الثقافة والإلمام بالمعارف الإنسانية والفنون والموسيقى ومن جامعات أو مدارس ذات سمعة عريقة، الأمر الذي[24] ارتبط أساسا بالطبقة التي كانت دائما ممثلة لدعائم الحكم، فالمصطلح في سياقه الأمريكي (التعليم الليبرالي) يختلف أساسا عن مصطلح التدريب الحرفي، وهذا المفهوم في حالة خفوت الآن على ساحة التفاعلات. أما تعبير الليبرالية الفردية أو ليبرالية الفرد فهو يعود إلى المفكرين جون لوك وهوبز[25]، واتباعهما، والمفهوم هنا مرتبط بصعود فكرة الرأسمالية واقتصاديات السوق.

حسن وجيه، ١٩٩٤، "مقدمة في علم التفاوض الاجتماعي والسياسي"، عالم المعرفة، المجلس الوطني للثقافة والفنون والآداب، الكويت، ص ١٨٢–١٨٣.

Annotated Text 8

الشريعة الإسلامية والموقف من الديموقراطية والمجتمع المدني عام ١٩٨٣–١٩٨٥

نجحت جماعة الإخوان المسلمين السودانية في الاستفادة من مصالحة نظام مايو[1] أكثر من الأحزاب الأخرى التي دخلت المصالحة[2]. فقد نقض حزب الأمة بقيادة[3] الصادق المهدي اتفاقه، أما الهندي[4] فلم يعد أصلا إلى السودان. المفارقة الرئيسية في هذه المصالحة هي قبول الأحزاب[5] التقليدية الكبيرة لصيغة الحزب الواحد أو التنظيم الواحد[6]. فالأحزاب عارضت انقلاب مايو في البداية ليس بسبب إلغائه الديموقراطية والتعدد الحزبي[7]، ولكن بسبب ميوله اليسارية، وهذا نقد يوجه للأحزاب السودانية لأنها لم تتحول حقيقة إلى مؤسسات ديموقراطية تمارس الديموقراطية في داخلها وبين أعضائها قبل أن[8] يكون ذلك في البرلمان واختيار الحكومات. دخلت الأحزاب الثلاثة الاتحاد الاشتراكي[9] حسب الصيغة التي تعطي رئيس الجمهورية سلطات مطلقة وتلغي أي تعدد حزبي أو نقابي، بالإضافة إلى وجود[10] قوانين أمن الدولة المقيدة للحريات[11]. كل ذلك[12] لم يكن عقبة في سبيل التعاون[13] مع نظام النميري، لأن الأولوية عند الأحزاب كانت للتوجه الإسلامي ((للنظام)) الذي ظهر في السنوات الأخيرة[14]، ولم تكن للديموقراطية. ويقول منصور خالد عن هذا الموقف الذي عبر عنه الصادق المهدي في لقاء بورتسودان باعتباره بداية المصالحة[15]:

((وكعادته[16] آثر النميري أن يرمي بطعمه لما حسب صيدا ثمينا[17]، كانت هذه الطعمة هي إعلانه للتوجه الإسلامي كأساس للحكم، بعد أن حكم السودان قرابة التسع سنوات تحت ظل دستور علماني دون أن ينتقص ذلك شيئا من إسلامه أو إسلامية أهل السودان[18]. وما كان من السيد الصادق إلا أن قال[19] للرئيس (المؤمن): ((لقد أثلج صدرنا[20] أن نسمع عنك مؤخرا مثل هذا الحديث عن التوجه الإسلامي.))

كان على السيد الصادق[21] أن يبرر أو يسبب قبوله للمصالحة[22] مع نظام عارضه بالسلاح حتى قبل عام من هذا اللقاء، أي العمل العسكري المعارض في يوليو ١٩٧٦[23]. ذكر هذه الأسباب في شرحه للعودة والمشاركة:

- إن الظروف التي قادت لانطلاق المعارضة من الخارج قد انتفت[24]، بل إن المعارضة كادت أن تصبح جزءا من استراتيجيات الدول المضيفة لها، ((ليبيا وأثيوبيا))، مما قد يؤدي إلى هيمنة خارجية على الإرادة السودانية الذاتية[25].
- ضرورة تضافر[26] الجهود الوطنية للحيلولة دون نمو تيارات للتظلم الإقليمي بالصورة التي تهدد الوحدة.

حيدر إبراهيم علي، ١٩٩٥، ''المجتمع المدني والتحول الديموقراطي في السودان''، مركز ابن خلدون، القاهرة، ص ٦١-٦٢.

Annotated Text 9

العرب وحوار الثقافة والتقانة
يا له من مخاض عسير[1]!! نهايات ومابعديات[2]

في البداية، ليكن حديث النهاية[3]، وليس ثمة تناقض في ذلك مع عصرنا هذا[4] الذي نسعى إلى تمثله، عصر يلهث فيه قادمه يكاد يلحق بسابقه[5]، وتتهاوى فيه النظم والأفكار على مرأى من بداياتها[6]، وتتقادم فيه الأشياء وهي في أوج جدتها[7]، عصر تتآلف فيه الأشياء مع أضدادها. فالمعرفة قوة والقوة أيضا معرفة، معرفة تفرزها هذه القوة لخدمة أغراضها وتبرير ممارساتها وتمرير قراراتها[8]. ولهذا التضاد المعرفي رفيق اقتصادي؛ فالمعلومات مال بعد[9] أن أصبحت موردا تنمويا يفوق في أهميته الموارد المادية، والمال بدوره أوشك أن يكون[10] مجرد معلومات؛ نبضات وإشارات وشفرات تتبادلها البنوك في معاملاتها المالية الإلكترونية. وثمة علاقة بين هذا التضاد المعرفي – المعلوماتي[11]، والتضاد الحاكم في عصرنا، الذي أصبح فيه العلم هو ثقافة المستقبل، في حين اقتربت الثقافة من أن تصبح[12] هي علم المستقبل الشامل، الذي يطوي في عباءته[13] فروعا معرفية متعددة ومتباينة.

ودعنا نستطرد في حديث الأضداد[14]، فما أعجب أضداد عصرنا، ذلك الذي تتعلم فيه الأجيال اللاحقة من أجيالها السابقة، مثلما[15] تتعلم السابقة من اللاحقة، بعد أن أصبحت معرفة من سبق تتهالك بمعدل يفوق في سرعته معدل اكتسابه لها[16]. وثمة صلة ما بين هذا ومعكوس التاريخ لدى ميشيل فوكو[17]، الذي يزعم أن الماضي لا يؤدي إلى الحاضر، والحاضر هو الذي يهب الماضي معناه[18] وجدواه. لقد اختلطت الأضداد وتداخلت في أيامنا حتى أعلن جان بودليار[19] «نهاية الأضداد ٢٣٣:٢٦٧» نهاية تضاد الجميل والقبيح في الفن، واليسار واليمين في السياسة، والصادق والزائف في الإعلام، والموضوعي والذاتي في العلم، بل ونهاية تضاد «هنا وهناك» أيضا بعد أن كاد «طابع المكان[20]» أن ينقرض وقد سلبته عمارة الحداثة خصوصيته وتميزه. إنها بالقطع، وبكل المقاييس، ثورة مجتمعية عارمة. لقد دان العالم لسيطرة الصغير متناهي الصغر[21]، من جسيمات الذرة وجزيئات البيولوجيا الجزيئية[22]؛ والأخطر من ذلك أنه قد دان لسيطرة «ذرة» المنطق الصوري التي بلغت ذروتها في ثنائية «الصفر والواحد[23]»، الثنائية الحاكمة التي قامت عليها تلك التكنولوجيا الساحقة الماحقة[24]: تكنولوجيا المعلومات.

حقا ... نحن نواجه عالما زاخرا بالمتناقضات، يتوازى فيه تكتل دوله مع تفتت دويلاته، ولا يفوق نموه الاقتصادي إلا زيادة عدد فقرائه[25]. وها هي شبكة الإنترنت، التي أقيمت أصلا لاتقاء ضربة نووية محتملة ربما يقدم عليها الخصم السوفيتي[26] آنذاك، ها هي تلك الشبكة، وليدة الحرب الباردة[27]، يروجون لها كأداة مثلى لإشاعة ثقافة السلام، ونشر الوفاق والوئام بين الأنام[28]. إنها البشرية تمارس هوايتها الأبدية[29] في مزج الآمال بالأوهام، فلا حرج ولا تناقض بين حديث السلام هذا، والمائة والخمسين حربا التي نشبت منذ الحرب العالمية الثانية (١٦:٦٥) الأمر الذي يبدو[30] وكأن كبار عالمنا يصدرون لصغاره[31] حروبهم وصراعاتهم وأزماتهم، يفتتونها حروبا أهلية، وصراعات عرقية ودينية ولغوية، وبطالة

وتغريبا وتهميشا واستبعادا، وكل درجات هذا الطيف القاتم لاستغلال أيامنا. وربما تساير نزعة تفتيت الكوارث تلك نزعة اللامركزية التي تسود هذا العصر، وتتبدى أكثر ما تتبدى[32] في شبكة الإنترنت، شبكة بلا محور وبلا قمة وبلا هرمية أو تراتبية.

نبيل علي، ٢٠٠١، "الثقافة العربية وعصر المعلومات: رؤية لمستقبل الخطاب الثقافي العربي"، عالم المعرفة، المجلس الوطني للثقافة والفنون والآداب، الكويت، العدد ٢٦٥، ص ٩-١٠.

Answer Key

Chapter 1

Exercise 1: Identifying Translation Problems

1. The adjective واضح means *clear*, and so does جلي. The phrase واضحا وجليا is a synonymous couplet—that is, two synonyms conjoined for emphasis. This is an acceptable emphasis technique in Arabic, but it is considered redundant in English. We can leave out واضحا or جليا and translate them as one word, namely, *clear*. To maintain the emphasis, we can add a modifier, as in *quite clear*, or use an idiomatic phrase that already signals emphasis, such as *crystal clear*.

2. The verb ضمن represents a case of morphological complexity that results in a lexical gap. It is a Form II causative verb that means *to make something include something*. We cannot unpack the semantic content of this verb and translate ضمنته بعض المعلومات as *I made it (the letter) include some information*. But we can apply substitution and use the basic verb *include*, while making the necessary changes, such as deleting the direct object pronoun referring to the letter. This gives us *I included some information about Churchill Bek*.

3. العوام is a Classical Arabic collective noun that describes the masses of people who do not belong to the intellectual elite. The problem here is that candidate translations—such as *commoners*, *yokels*, and *rustic folks*—are not true functional equivalents because they reflect different social hierarchies or add connotations that are not available in the

source sentence. Alternatively, we can paraphrase العوام as *uneducated
/lay people*, which also maintains the author's negative attitude.

The name داروين is repeated to maintain the text's cohesion, which
is disrupted by an appositive phrase and two embedded clauses. This
cohesion strategy is not acceptable in English; therefore, the second instance of *Darwin* needs to be deleted. This, of course, requires additional changes to the structure of the translation.

4. الترابية is an attributive (*nisba*) adjective derived from the noun تراب,
    which means *dust* or *dirt*. In this particular context, the meaning of تراب
    is metaphorically extended to refer to land. This adjective constitutes
    a lexical gap because there is no English adjective derived from *land*,
    whereas the adjectives derived from *dust* and *dirt* describe very different
    properties. Because there is no suitable functional equivalent, we can re-
    sort to substitution and translate وحدته الترابية as *its territorial integrity*.

5. Qaraqoosh (died AD 1200, 597 AH) was a sultan who ruled Egypt shortly
    before the rise of the Mamluk Dynasty. In Arab folk history, he is seen as
    a dictator who unfairly applied severe punishments for minor offenses,
    and his name has come to symbolize oppression and tyranny. Because
    his name has specific social meanings attached to it, we cannot simply
    transliterate it. We can either spell out these associations, as in *unfair
    rules*, or use an English adjective derived from a name with similar social
    meanings, as in *draconian rules*.

Exercise 2: Definiteness

1. King Faisal
    الملك فيصل is a proper noun with a title; therefore, we cannot include the
    definite article, as in *the King Faisal*, which is not grammatical.

2. chapter—observations—the countries of origin
    The definite articles in الفصل and الملاحظات need to be left out be-
    cause English does not allow the use of the definite article following
    demonstratives or quantifiers. With بلدان المنشأ, we need to maintain the
    definiteness marking because the referent of the source word is made
    specific by the possessive construction. However, we cannot incorporate
    the definiteness marking on *origin* because it is a generic term.

3. men—women
    Both الرجل *lit. the man* and المرأة *lit. the woman* are definite singular
    generic terms. They should be translated as bare plurals without the
    definite article: *men* and *women*.

4. a divorce

   In this sentence, the definite noun الطلاق *lit. the divorce* must be translated as an indefinite noun. This is because *divorce* in English is made definite only when there is a restrictive relative clause—that is, *she got the divorce she wanted*—which is not the case in the source sentence. In Arabic, however, طلاق is typically used as a definite noun because it is contextually specific.

5. tea—fluoride

   Natural kind terms are always definite in Arabic, just like generic nouns, but English does not mark these nouns for definiteness or indefiniteness.

Exercise 3: Adverbs

1. قدما is a Classical Arabic adverb that means *straight* (for walking). The literal translation of المضي قدما is *going straight*, but this is a false equivalent because it is not what the source sentence means. We need to substitute the adverb and the verb with *move forward* or *go ahead*.

2. أبدا is a polarity item that functions as an adverb whose meaning depends on its grammatical context. If it is used in a negative sentence, it means *never*; but in questions and affirmative sentences, it means *ever*. Because English does not allow the use of *ever* as an adverb in affirmative sentences—as in *he enjoyed her voice ever*, which would be ungrammatical—we can instead apply substitution and translate أبدا as *always* and make the other necessary changes.

3. يوما is an adverb derived from the noun يوم *day*, but it also functions as a polarity item. When used in affirmative sentences, it means *one day* or *someday*; but when used in negative sentences, it means *never*, which is the functional equivalent needed to translate this sentence.

4. مترأسا is an adverb generated by adding the *tanween* suffix to the active participle مترأس, which is derived from the Form V verb ترأس *to become the head of*. This derivation chain stems from the noun رأس *head* via the Form I denominal verb رأس *to head*. This adverb constitutes a lexical gap because English does not allow the derivation of adverbs from the noun *head* or the verb *to head*. In this sentence, مترأسا functions as an adverb of manner; therefore, we can use the gerund form in a relative clause, as in *heading the Sudanese delegation*, or we can use a prepositional phrase, as in *at the head of the Sudanese delegation*.

5. ماركسيا is an adverb of manner derived from the adjective ماركسي *Marxist*. Morphological unpacking gives us *in a Marxist way*, but this is not a

common expression. We can resolve this lexical gap by paraphrasing the clause as *how to think like Marxists*. Note that we cannot translate the adverb as *how to think as Marxists*, because this candidate would mean that the writer was a Marxist, which is additional information that is not available in the source text.

Exercise 4: Lexical Gaps

1. تدجين is an event nominal (مصدر) derived from the Form II causative verb دجن *to cause someone to act like a chicken*. Although there are English predicates associated with chicken, such as *chicken out* and *be a chicken*, there is a crucial difference in meaning: In English, acting like a chicken indicates being cowardly; but in Arabic, it means being harmless. What we need here is a noun or a gerund derived from a causative verb that means *making someone act peacefully*, such as *taming, domesticating*, or, in this particular context, *pacifying*.

2. يبطن is a verb that literally means *to stomach*, but it does not share any of the meanings associated with its English counterpart; it is a false equivalent. This verb is best translated as *hide* or *conceal*. Of course, it can be translated differently, depending on how the rest of the sentence is translated. We might use paraphrasing and substitution to end up with *had sectarian and nationalistic undertones/hidden agendas*.

3. دية is a traditional legal practice in some Arab communities, where someone who committed manslaughter pays money to the family of the victim instead of being incarcerated or subjected to other forms of punishment. English has two close equivalents—*wergild* and *blood money*—but neither term is a true functional equivalent in this context. This is because *wergild* is rather outdated, if not archaic, and *blood money* is ambiguous; it also means *money gained at the expense of someone else's livelihood*. Instead of using referential equivalents, we can apply substitution or paraphrasing and translate دية as *restitution*.

4. In Arab folk tales, الغول is a human-eating mythical creature that dwells in graveyards and deserted places. The word was borrowed into English as *ghoul*, which does not fit well in this context. We can apply lexical substitution and translate الغول as *monster*. The adverb عينيا is derived from the adjective عيني, which is in turn derived from the noun عين *eye*. In this context, the adverb is used in contrast with ماديا *in cash*, and it is best translated as *in kind*.

5. العارف is an active participle derived from the verb عرف *know*, and it means *someone who knows*. There are no -*er* or -*ant* agent nouns derived from *know*, but there are related adjectives, such as *cognizant, knowledgeable*, and *aware*. Although these are valid substitution candidates, none of them fits in the grammatical context of the possessive construction, in which a noun phrase is needed. We could apply substitution and use *expert*, but it would not fit with the rest of the sentence—*with the confidence of an expert in what the future holds*. Alternatively, we could apply morphological unpacking to العارف and translate the whole possessive phrase with the embedded relative clause, as *with the confidence of someone who could tell the future*.

Exercise 5: Advanced Translation

1. This sentence describes major events in the history of the Baha'i faith. We need to make sure that the terms we use in the translation are the ones commonly used in English texts on the subject. Encyclopedia entries and introductory textbooks on the subject are good sources for such information. If we use transliterations with the titles الميرزا and الباب, we need to include their definitions as well. فتنة is a rather difficult word to translate because, even though it is common in Islamic texts, it is used to describe many things. Basically, it refers to any social unrest or threat to the faith; therefore, it can be translated as *civil war, secession, anarchy*, and *temptation*, among many other possibilities.

2. المحبظين are actors who perform a traditional form of street theater in Morocco. الحواة is a Modern Standard Arabic term that describes street performers who perform magic tricks for an audience of bystanders.

3. حاج is used in this sentence as a title, so it should not be translated as *pilgrim* or morphologically unpacked as *someone who is performing (or has performed) the Muslim pilgrimage to Mecca*; it can only be transliterated. شلخة is a colloquialism borrowed from Gulf Arabic. It describes a story that is completely false but is told as if it were true. This kind of story is not intended to misinform, but to entertain—that is, it is a tall tale.

4. Historically, a تكية was a charitable organization or a shelter for the disadvantaged. However, it has come to mean a place where undeserving individuals receive free services. We can translate it as *a charity*, but we need to make some changes to maintain the connotations, such

as adding the phrase *for freeloaders*, which also maintains the author's negative attitude and cynicism.

5. In folk religious narratives, ناكر and نكير are the names of two angels who are believed to come to dead people soon after their burial to tell them about each and every good and evil deed they did in their lives. Transliterating these names with or without definitions would not provide the best translation because the phrase is used metaphorically. We need to paraphrase or substitute with an idiomatic expression that describes meticulous and unforgiving treatment.

Chapter 2

Exercise 1: Identifying Translation Problems

1. The frozen expression على ما يرام *lit. on that which is desired* is a modifier phrase that means *favorably*. We can use any adverb with the same meaning that fits in the context, such as *fine* or *going well*. Alternatively, we can reconstruct the whole clause using an appropriate collocation or idiom, as in *we had a smooth sailing*.

    The phrase أمر لا يمكن أن يصدقه عقل *lit. a matter that no mind can believe* is made up of a noun and a negated modifying relative clause. We can apply morphological packaging and translate it as *unbelievable*.

2. The intransitive predicate تم *became complete* is an aspectual verb that tells us that the event described by the subject noun phrase took place in the past. In other words, this verb is functionally equivalent to the English past-tense suffix *-ed*. We can apply substitution and use a lexical past-tense verb to translate تم دخول موكلي as *my client entered a hospital* instead of the literal candidate *my client's entering of a hospital was complete*. The collocation دخل المستشفى *entered the hospital* can be translated word for word, but this translation candidate does not tell us why he did that. To improve the quality of the output phrase, we can apply lexical substitution and use a common English collocation, as in *my client, Mr. Mukhtar Hammoud Al-Shabbuty, was admitted to a public hospital*. This candidate makes it clear that the client went to the hospital as a patient, not as a visitor or a doctor.

    The phrase لإجراء عملية استئصال الزائدة الدودية literally means *for the performance of the operation for excising the appendix*. We can use lexical and morphological packaging and translate عملية استئصال الزائدة الدودية as *appendectomy*. As for لإجراء, we can delete it because the context makes it clear that the client went to the hospital to undergo the surgery, rather than to perform it, especially if we use the predicate *was admitted* in the first clause.

3. The phrase الفقر المدقع *lit. the poverty that pins one's face to the ground* is an idiomatic expression that describes extreme poverty; therefore, we can translate it using the functionally equivalent idiomatic phrase *abject poverty*. The phrase الغنى الفاحش *lit. sinful richness* is an idiom that describes extreme wealth, but unlike *filthy rich*, it is used as a noun; therefore, we cannot consider it functionally equivalent. Moreover, the successful translation candidate needs to describe extreme wealth without adding negative connotations because the source text is defending economic disparities, provided that the rich pay their taxes. We also need to make sure the translations of the two idioms are compatible, because they are conjoined. One solution is to apply literalization, as in *excessive wealth side by side with extreme poverty*.

4. The locative noun محمل is derived from the verb حمل *carry*; therefore, it constitutes a lexical gap. This is not a problem, however, because the phrase يأخذ على محمل الجد is a semantically noncompositional open collocation, in which يأخذ على محمل is fixed, except for the verb inflection, whereas the generic definite noun that follows is variable. Because the whole expression is used as a manner modifier, it can be translated as *taken*, followed by an adverb derived from the equivalent of the noun after محمل. In this sentence, we can translate the whole clause يؤخذ على محمل الجد as *taken seriously*.

    The prepositional phrase في أقصاه *lit. in its furthest* is another modifying collocation. It profiles the scalar attribute of seriousness as a physical domain where the referent of the possessive pronoun is located at the higher end. This is a functional mismatch issue that can be resolved by applying substitution and using a suitable modifier, such as *very* in *taken very seriously*.

5. The prepositional phrase بشكل من الأشكال *lit. in a form from the forms* has an indefinite noun followed by من *from* and the definite plural form of the noun; therefore, we can ignore the embedded prepositional phrase من الأشكال. This leaves us with the main prepositional phrase بشكل *in a form*, which is used as an adverbial. We can apply substitution and translate it as *in a way*, but because the source phrase is a degree

modifier, we are better off translating it as *to some degree/extent*. Note that بشكل من الأشكال is an ambiguous polarity item, which can also mean *never* or *under no circumstances* in negative sentences, but this is not the case here.

Exercise 2: Light Verbs

Light verbs are verbs that form semantically noncompositional collocations with their direct objects. What distinguishes these collocations is that the semantic focus of a light verb construction is the direct object, which is used literally, whereas the verb is used figuratively, as in *pay a visit* and *take a look*. When it comes to translating light verbs, we focus on the direct object and find a target language verb that collocates with it:

1. Tell a joke
2. Made a decision
3. Made a promise/promised
4. Give an example
5. Posed a question/raised a question/asked
6. Filed a lawsuit
7. Offered an apology/apologized
8. Buy a ticket
9. Died
10. Compare.

Exercise 3: Idioms

1. The idiom وجهان لعملة واحدة *lit. two faces of one coin* describes two things that are quite different yet closely related. Obviously, it is a borrowing from English corresponding to *two sides of the same coin*. The wording of the idiom is changed slightly because of the internal collocation restrictions; in Arabic, the round side of a coin is considered its "face," whereas its edge is considered its side. Because the Arabic idiom and its English counterpart use similar metaphors in the same contexts, we can simply back-translate it.

2. The idiom جاءت الريح بما لا تشتهي السفن *lit. the wind came with what the ships do not desire* describes a situation in which things go wrong. There are many functionally equivalent English idioms that describe

the same situation, even though they do not use the same metaphor. However, in this particular sentence, the idiom can be left out altogether because it is preceded by the clause ولكن الأمور لم تسر كما يجب *things did not go as they should have*, which conveys the same meaning as the idiom. If we want to maintain the metaphorical language, we can use a functionally equivalent idiom, such as *things took a wrong turn*, and leave out the preceding clause to avoid the redundancy of *things did not go as they should have and took a wrong turn*.

3. The idiom ندا لند *lit. opponent to opponent* is an adverbial phrase that describes two people facing each other in a fair and equal competition. The repetition of ند *opponent* and the context might mislead us into translating it as *head to head*, which carries the connotations of confrontation and conflict. Because the Arabic idiom does not have these connotations, we must discard this candidate and instead choose an idiomatic expression that is functionally equivalent, such as *on an equal footing*.

4. The idiom على قدم وساق *lit. on a foot and a leg* is rather opaque, given that neither the metaphor nor the functional meaning can be easily understood from its constituents in isolation. However, there are enough clues in the sentence that can help us realize that it is functionally equivalent to *in earnest* or *in full swing*.

5. The Arabic idiom رأسا على عقب *lit. head on heel* uses the same metaphor as the English idiom *head over heels*, but they are not functional equivalents because they describe very different situations. The Arabic expression describes a situation that involves radical change, and it is functionally equivalent to *upside down*.

Exercise 4: Structural Mismatches

1. غض النظر is a prepositional phrase that means *by looking down*. When used literally, it means *by averting one's eyes*; but in this particular sentence, it is used as a figurative frozen expression that encodes the semantic function of exclusion. This has the same function as the adverbial phrase *regardless*.

2. بناء على ذلك *lit. building on this* is an idiomatic modifier phrase. In terms of structure, it is headed by the event nominal بناء *building*, which is used as an adverb by adding the *tanween* suffix, followed by a prepositional complement with a demonstrative referring to the situation described in the preceding sentence. As for its function, this expression is a cohesive

device that establishes logical relations between sentences; the sentence that follows it is a conclusion based on the one that precedes it. We can ignore the building metaphor altogether and translate the expression using a functional equivalent, such as *accordingly* or *therefore*.

3. لسوء الحظ *lit. for the badness of luck* is a prepositional phrase used adverbially to modify the whole clause rather than just the verb phrase. The issue here is that the word-for-word candidate does not collocate in English; therefore, we need to apply substitution. We can use *unfortunately*, which is functionally equivalent to the source phrase.

4. The frozen expression إن آجلا وإن عاجلا *lit. if soon and if later* is made up of two conjoined conditional clauses, but it functions as a temporal adverbial. This expression is functionally equivalent to *sooner or later*, despite the structural differences.

5. وهي تتحلى بالثقة *lit. and they are adorned with confidence* is an idiomatic adverbial clause modifying the preceding verb phrase تخوض المنافسة *compete* (*lit. wade through the competition*). The metaphor does not transfer well in this context; therefore, we can apply literalization and use a nonfigurative functional equivalent, such as *confident*. The prefix و *and* functions here as a temporal conjunction profiling the situations described in the adverbial and main clauses as contemporaneous. This is the function of the conjunction *while*; but if we maintain the biclausal structure, we end up with *compete while confident*, which does not collocate well either. One possible solution is to apply reconstruction and translate the embedded clause as an adverb, as in *compete confidently* or even better, *compete with confidence*.

Exercise 5: Advanced Translation

1. The difficulty in translating منظم بشكل لا يتوه فيه الحمار *lit. organized in a way that the donkey cannot get lost in it* has to do with its structure and the donkey metaphor. In terms of structure, the phrase is essentially an adjectival predicate headed by the passive participle منظم *organized*, followed by the modifier phrase بشكل *in a way*, which is in turn modified by a reduced relative clause. The problem is that the pronoun in فيه *in it* refers to the head noun شكل *way* rather than مطار لندن *London airport*. Note that two word-level translation strategies are necessary here. First, the word for *donkey* is a generic definite noun that is better translated as *a donkey* in this particular context. Second, the English equivalent

of منظم *organized* does not collocate with *airport*; therefore, it is better translated as *laid out*. This gives us the close translation *the London airport is laid out in a way in which a donkey cannot get lost in it*, which is ungrammatical and thus requires reconstruction. The donkey metaphor is based on the fact that donkeys represent low intelligence in Arab cultures. The function of the whole phrase is to demonstrate that the airport is so well laid out that nobody can get lost in it. We can achieve this function by applying literalization, but this solution comes at the expense of the humor that is a defining characteristic of the author's style. We can maintain the humor by applying metaphorical approximation, as in *the London airport is so well laid out that a monkey would not get lost in it*.

2. The verb phrase نتج بصورة غير متعمدة من جانب علماء literally means *resulted by an image that is not intentional from the side of scientists*, which obviously does not make sense in English. The prepositional phrase بصورة غير متعمدة is a modifying collocation used as a manner adverbial, which can be translated as *unintentionally* or *inadvertently* via morphological packaging. The second prepositional phrase من جانب علماء is also a collocation, but it marks the agent of an event; thus, it can be translated as *by scientists*. These strategies give us *The H1N1 swine flu virus resulted unintentionally by scientists who were working on eggs*, which still falls short of sounding natural, even though the constituent phrases collocate internally. In this case, we need a more holistic approach; the phrase *lab accident* is usually used to describe a situation in which something goes wrong with an experiment; therefore, we can reconstruct the translation around this phrase. The word *accident* semantically means that it is not intentional, thus rendering the first modifier redundant. The second modifier, with its embedded relative clause, can be reconstructed as a temporal adverbial clause, as in *The H1N1 swine flu virus was the result of a lab accident while scientists were working on eggs*.

3. The phrase من الأهمية بمكان *lit. from importance in a place* is a semantically noncompositional open collocation. This expression profiles the scalar attribute of importance as a spatial domain where items are arranged according to their degree of importance. The function of the collocation is to place the subject, *using modern technologies*, at the top of the importance hierarchy; therefore, the phrase من الأهمية بمكان is equivalent to *of utmost importance*. However, the subordinating conjunction

حتّى *until* establishes a causative relation between the collocation and the following clause—that is, using modern technologies is at a high position on the scale of importance, which causes many universities to adopt them. The two clauses can be translated together as *using modern technologies has become so important/of such importance that many universities are keen to adopt them.*

4. The phrase في المقام الأول is a frozen expression that literally means *in the first place.* However, we cannot translate it as such because the Arabic expression and its English counterpart are not functionally equivalent. The English expression places a situation in relation to others in terms of temporal sequence, whereas the Arabic expression has nothing to do with temporal sequence; it metaphorically places a situation in the first place in terms of importance. In this particular context, we can translate في المقام الأول as *first and foremost.*

5. The phrase أكثر مشكلة is rather challenging because it means *the most problem*, where the attribute that is being compared is not immediately clear. The key to understanding this phrase is the word الفتاة *lit. the young woman*, which is used in this sentence as a generic term—that is, it refers to all young women rather than a particular one. We can think of it as a plural noun, and this will lead us to realize that the function of the superlative adjective is to compare this problem with others in terms of their frequencies of occurrence among young women. The phrase أكثر مشكلة تواجهها الفتاة can be translated as *the most common problem that young women face.*

The phrase عدم الفهم الكامل is made up of the possessive construction عدم الفهم *the lack of understanding* and the adjective الكامل *complete*. Because the two nouns have the same grammatical gender, the phrase is structurally ambiguous because the adjective could modify either noun. In other words, the phrase could mean *the complete lack of understanding* or *the lack of complete understanding*. The difference is that the latter reading suggests that there is some degree of understanding, but it falls short of full understanding. The context itself does not provide sufficient clues to help us decide which reading is the intended one; however, the structure indicates that the intended reading is *the lack of complete understanding*. The adjective الكامل *complete* is conjoined to الواعي *aware*; therefore, they need to modify the same noun. The two adjectives collocate with الفهم *understanding*, but الواعي *aware* does not collocate with عدم *lack*, suggesting that they both modify الفهم

understanding. Various word- and phrase-level strategies can be applied to improve the close translation *the most common problem that young women face with their families is the lack of complete and aware understanding of the reality of the problems they suffer from.* For example, the adjective الواعي *aware* can be deleted because its equivalent does not collocate with *understanding,* and the noun phrase عدم الفهم الكامل can be reconstructed as a verb phrase, as in *the most common problem young women suffer from is that their families do not fully understand the true nature of their issues.*

Chapter 3

Exercise 1: Temporal Reference

1. سوف is the future marker in Arabic; therefore, it is usually translated as *will* or some other expression that encodes future time reference. However, in this particular sentence, we need to translate it as *would* because it is used in reported speech, and the temporal reference of the embedded clause is dependent on that of the main clause. In other words, the temporal reference of سوف يعقد اجتماعا *he would hold a meeting* is future relative to the past time reference of the perfective verb قال *he said.* The whole sentence can be translated as *Taha Hussein said that he would hold another meeting to answer all our questions.*

2. The conjunction سواء *whether* is a conditional expression; therefore, the verb كان is used in the perfective form. In other words, the perfective verb كان is used only for grammatical purposes and has nothing to do with temporal reference. Because the source sentence is stating a fact, it should be translated using the present simple tense, as in *a cellular phone can be located, whether it is turned on or off.*

3. The subordination conjunction كلما is a compound made up of the quantifier كل *every* and the relative pronoun ما, which refers to the situation described in the following clause. This conjunction encodes quantification over times, and it is usually translated as *whenever.* However, when we have two instances of كلما in conjoined clauses, we get a construction that describes correlation, which is functionally equivalent to the English construction *the more . . . the more.* This correlation is essentially a conditional relation, and like other conditional expressions in Arabic, كلما

requires a perfective verb. Therefore, the verbs كانت and كان in this context do not describe past situations, and the temporal reference of the conjoined clauses depends on the rest of the sentence. Because the author is using this sentence to make a factual statement, we can translate these two verbs in the present tense, as in *the bigger the fish is, the more mercury it has*.

4. The verb يضم *include* is ambiguous between an inchoative and a stative interpretation, but the perfective form can only have the inchoative meaning. In other words, it describes adding those names to the list as a complete event with no commitment to the termination of the resultant state of their being on the list. The present adverbial حتى الآن *until now/thus far* indicates that the resultant state holds at speech time. The English past tense does not allow present-tense adverbials; therefore, we need to translate ضمت using the present simple or the present perfect, as in *thus far, the National Progressive Unionist Party list includes sixty-eight candidates in seventeen provinces*, in which the adverbial phrase is moved to the sentence's initial position. If we want to avoid the repetition that would result from translating منهم as *including*, we can substitute the first instance of *include* with *has*, to end up with *thus far, the National Progressive Unionist Party list has sixty-eight candidates in seventeen provinces, including nine women*.

5. The phrase كان سيكون is a complex aspectual construction in which the perfective verb كان sets the time reference to the past, whereas the prospective verb سيكون expresses a future time reference. Together, these two verbs encode the future in the past, which can be translated as *was going to be*. The appositive clause with كان سيكون has a contextually driven conditional interpretation: If Jacques Chirac had attended the meeting, he would have been the first French president to do so. This interpretation justifies reconstructing the appositive clause as a relative clause with an implied conditional clause, as in *Jacques Chirac, who would have been the first French president to participate, had to miss the meeting*.

Exercise 2: Negation

1. The particle لم encodes both negation and past time reference; therefore, the phrase لم تستمر by itself can be translated as *did not last*. However, سوى *except* interacts with negation to set an upper bound on the focus

of negation, which is the duration of the game. Accordingly, we can translate سوى as *more than*, as in *this game did not last more than 15 minutes*, or as *only* with negation left out, as in *this game lasted only 15 minutes*.

استطاعة استطاعة is a noun derived from the modal verb of possibility استطاع *can*, whereas عدم *lack* is a noun that encodes negation in noun phrases. The possessive construction عدم استطاعته إكمال المباراة can be translated as *his inability to finish the game* or *he could not/was not able to finish the game*. Note that إكمال *finishing* is translated as a verb with temporal reference is set to the past, because the whole text is reporting on a past story. The choice of the optimal translation candidate will, of course, depend on how we translate the rest of the sentence because this phrase is conjoined with مع إصابة حارس المرمى *with the injury of the goalkeeper*, and together they are bound by a causal relation to the following clause about the referee calling off the game. Our final translation needs to either have the same grammatical structure in the two conjoined phrases or have the second phrase translated as an embedded relative clause, as in *with the injury of the goalkeeper, who could not finish the game*. There are many ways to translate this sentence, but perhaps our best option is to translate عدم استطاعته as an adjective, as in *With the goalkeeper injured and unable to finish the game, the referee had to call the game off*.

2. The phrase ليس من غير المعروف has two instances of negation. The first is sentential negation encoded by ليس, and it denies the relation between the clausal subject starting with أن يأمر *that he orders* and the predicate من غير المعروف. The second is phrasal negation encoded by غير, and it negates only the passive participle المعروف *known*. To avoid ending up with double negation in the translation, we can incorporate phrasal negation morphologically and translate غير المعروف as *unknown*. This gives us *it is not unknown*. The construction made up of the preposition من *from* followed by a definite adjective or participle and a sentential subject is typically translated using the *it*-cleft construction, as I discussed early on. These strategies give us *it is not unknown for him to order a vehicle ready in the early morning hours*, in which we leave out عنه *about him* and translate أن as *for*. The issue now is that ليس من غير المعروف *it is not unknown* does not mean *it is not a secret* in the source sentence. Rather, it refers to the frequency of the event described in the subject clause; he orders a vehicle ready in the morning often enough

that he is known for it. Therefore, we can revise the translation by applying lexical substitution in a way that makes this interpretation easily
accessible, as in *it is not unusual for him to order a vehicle ready in the
early morning hours.*

3. تنتفي is a lexically passive verb that means *to be negated*; therefore, it
entails the meaning of negation. This verb constitutes a functional gap,
because the close translation *a journey where the differences between
fact and fiction are sometimes negated* does not collocate internally. We
can express negation explicitly in the translation, as in *a journey where
sometimes there is no distinction between fact and fiction* or *a journey
where sometimes the differences between fact and fiction do not exist.*
The issue with these candidates is that they might be understood as
negative criticisms of the novel. To make sure that our translation reflects
the author's neutral attitude toward the book, we can use an idiomatic
phrase that fits in the contexts and entails the meaning of negation, as in
a journey where the line between fact and fiction is sometimes blurred.

4. يخفى is a stative verb that means *to be hidden.* أحد is a polarity item
that means *someone* in affirmative sentences and *anyone* in negated
sentences. The subject of يخفى *be hidden* is the clause starting with أن
نظام فرانكو الديكتاتوري *that Franco's dictatorial regime*, but English does
not allow sentence initial clausal subjects, which requires an *it*-cleft in
the translation, as in *it is not hidden from anyone that Franco's dictatorial regime.* Note that we used the passive voice to translate يخفى,
but this is problematic because this translation candidate suggests that
there is someone who can potentially hide that information. To resolve
this issue, we need to reconstruct the translation in a way that does not
involve the passive voice. We can do this by moving the polarity item
to the subject position, changing it to the plural, reversing the polarity
by deleting negation, and applying lexical substitution to get an active-
voice verb that entails the negation of the problematic verb. These strategies give us *everyone knows that Franco's dictatorial regime.*

5. لم يكن هناك أي شيء is a negated clause in which the polarity item أي
شيء *anything* functions as the subject, whereas the negated existential
phrase لم يكن هناك *there was not* functions as the predicate. Together, لم
يكن هناك أي شيء can be translated as *there was not anything*, which we
can rephrase as *there was nothing.*

The real issue in this sentence has to do with the conjoined phrasal
negation in لا في أسرة بهاء، ولا في البيئة المحيطة به، ولا في مصر كلها، ولا

في ذلك الوقت بالذات. Conjoined phrasal negation is usually translated as *neither . . . nor*, but only if we have two phrases to conjoin; the source sentence has four negated conjuncts. One way to resolve this issue is to leave out all instances of conjoined phrasal negation and use only one instance of *or*, as in *there was nothing in his family, his surroundings, or all of Egypt, especially at that time*, in which the sentential negation in *there was no* takes scope over all these conjoined phrases, thus maintaining the original meaning. Note that we reduced the number of conjuncts by translating ولا في ذلك الوقت بالذات *lit. and not in that time in particular* as the adverbial appositive phrase *especially at that time*, while reducing the prepositional phrases to noun phrases to avoid repetition.

Finally, the subject of this negated sentence, أي شيء *nothing*, is modified by the relative clause starting with ينبئ *predicts/foretells*; but the relative clause is separated from the noun it modifies by a series of negated conjuncts, which motivated the author to repeat the subject phrase. This type of repetition is ungrammatical in English; therefore, we need to delete the second instance of *nothing*, to end up with *there was nothing in his family, his surroundings, or all of Egypt, especially at that time, that would predict*.

Exercise 3: Modals

1. ربما is an adverbial modal of possibility, whereas يجب is a lexical modal verb of necessity. Together, ربما يجب is a structure that has a modal of possibility taking scope over a modal of necessity; therefore, this phrase is usually translated as *might have to*. The problem is that the subject in the source sentence is an event nominal with a prepositional complement—namely, البحث عن حل آخر *the search for another solution*—whereas the predicate is the modal verb itself, yielding the literal translation *the search for another solution might have to* or *perhaps, the search for another solution must*, both of which are ungrammatical because English modals require complements. One solution is to use the modal *must* as a noun or to rephrase it as the adjective *necessary*, both of which can be used as predicates, as in *the search for another solution may be a must/necessary*, but neither option sounds natural in this context. The source sentence purposefully does not state or provide clues about the logical subject, or the entity or person who would search for

another solution. We often use the passive voice when a logical subject is missing, as in *another solution might have to be found*, which avoids the modal predicate problem. Alternatively, we can use the *it*-cleft construction as in *it may be necessary to find another solution*.

2. لا بد is a negated frozen expression of modal necessity that encodes deontic modality (obligation for the lack of options) or epistemic modality, whereby one makes an informed guess. We can tell the intended function of لا بد from the structure of the sentence. If there is an object pronoun with أن *that*, which is the case in this sentence, we have epistemic modality. Epistemic modality is usually expressed in English using *must* (e.g., *You must be hungry*), but it is negated using cannot (e.g., *You cannot be hungry*). This gives us *we cannot know exactly the secret of the family's immigration to Egypt*, which can be revised as *we cannot know exactly why the family immigrated to Egypt*. This translation is grammatical, but it does not have the epistemic reading. To avoid this problem, we can translate the epistemic necessity using a modal adverbial of possibility, as in *we probably do not know exactly why the family immigrated to Egypt*. Alternatively, we can apply lexical substitution, as in *it seems that we do not know exactly why the family immigrated to Egypt*, in which the verb *seem* entails the epistemic modality.

3. The phrase يمكن أن يستطيع is made up of the modal verb of possibility يمكن and its subject clause, which has a modal of possibility of its own, resulting in a structure that literally means *can be able to*. Having two modals of possibility in the same sentence is semantically redundant; therefore, we can delete one modal expression and translate يمكن أن يستطيع as *can*. From a pragmatic perspective, those two modals have different interpretations; يمكن encodes probability, whereas يستطيع encodes ability. Usually, we translate these constructions as *may/might be able to*, but this candidate would suggest that the author has doubts about the outcomes of these meetings and workshops, which is not what the source sentence indicates. To avoid these complications, we can either delete one modal, as suggested above, or apply lexical substitution and translate يمكن أن يستطيع as *has the opportunity to*, which lexically entails the meanings of probability and ability.

4. ضرورة لا بد منها is a noun phrase made up of ضرورة *necessity* and the modifying relative clause لا بد منها *that is necessary*, yielding a structure that means *a necessity that is necessary* or *a necessary necessity*, which is obviously redundant. We can resolve this issue by leaving out

one modal expression, as in *confronting this danger is necessary* or *it is necessary to confront this danger*. Although both candidates are valid, we might want to reconstruct the translation in a way that maintains the first-person plural reference to have a parallel structure with the preceding sentences, as in *we have to confront this danger*.

5. الذي ألزم التزكية أن تكون خطية is a causative verb derived from لزم, which is a modal verb of necessity. The relative clause means *which makes it necessary for nominations to be made in writing* or *which necessitates that nominations be made in writing*. Note that we shifted the temporal reference to the present simple because the sentence describes a fact. We also changed the voice of أن تكون خطية to the passive because the logical subject (the person who will make nominations) is unknown. Even though these close translations are grammatical, we need to apply further sentential reconstruction. For example, we can use lexical substitution and translate ألزم as *requires*, which collocates better with *the registration law* and lexically entails the meaning of necessity. These strategies give us *the registration law which requires nominations to be made in writing*.

The verb يجب is a modal expression of necessity that is usually translated as *have to*, *must*, *need*, or *should*, depending on the context. The main problem in this sentence is that يجب *is* used in the subjunctive mood following كي *in order to*, whereas most English modals are auxiliaries that cannot be used in similar contexts, as in the ungrammatical structure *in order to must/should*. We can use a different conjunction or a nonauxiliary modal expression that would be grammatical in this context—that is, *in order for the public notary to have to notarize nominations*—but this candidate is not optimal because *have to* encodes obligation but the source sentence does not. The source sentence means that the law requires a nomination to be made in writing because this is the only way for it to be notarized; therefore, we can translate the modal of necessity as a modal of possibility, as in *the registration law which requires nominations to be made in writing so that the public notary can notarize them*. In fact, we can leave out the modal of necessity altogether, as in *the registration law which requires nominations to be made in writing for the public notary to notarize them*, which can be further improved by converting it to the passive voice, yielding *the registration law which requires nominations to be made in writing to be notarized*.

Exercise 4: Voice

1. المزعومة is a passive participle derived from the verb زعم *claim/allege*, and it is used as an adjective modifying the noun العلاقة *relationship*. The adjectival passive *alleged* is a perfect equivalent for المزعومة in this context; it is commonly used in journalistic discourse describing this kind of story, and it is typically used as an adjective.

    القيل والقال is a frozen expression that literally means *that which was said and that who said*, and it describes spreading rumors and making unfounded accusatory remarks. Even though this frozen expression has a passive voice verb, we can apply literalization and translate it as *gossip*, which fits well in this context.

    ما قيل is a free relative clause that literally means *that which was said*, and it functions as the direct object of the verb نفى *denied*. We can improve this translation candidate by deleting *that* to get *Putin denied what was said*, but this would yield unwanted redundancy because the following prepositional phrase with the embedded clause states what Putin denied. Instead, we can delete the whole passive relative clause to end up with *Putin denied that he*.

2. خيف is the perfective passive form of the verb خاف *feared*, and it is equivalent to the passive verb phrase *was feared*. However, we cannot translate إذا خيف منه المرض as *if illness was feared from it*, even though it is a grammatical structure. We can improve the translation slightly by deleting the odd prepositional phrase, as in *if illness was feared*, but it still falls short of sounding natural. We can delete the passive voice altogether and apply lexical substitution to translate إذا خيف منه المرض as *if it poses health risks*.

3. The clause تم الانتهاء من استكمال ٥١٧ مركز شباب is made up of the aspectual verb تم *completed*, followed by the event nominal subject الانتهاء *finishing* with its prepositional complement من استكمال *from completing* and the rest of the possessive phrase describing the entity that was completed. This clause literally means *The finishing of completing 517 youth centers is complete*, which is obviously redundant. This redundancy is structurally and semantically motivated; the تم construction is used to avoid the passive form of the verb phrase انتهى, which is rarely used, but this construction requires a subject, hence الانتهاء. Still, the subject phrase is ambiguous because تم الانتهاء من ٥١٧ مركز شباب

517 youth centers were finished does not clearly describe the nature of the "finishing," whereas استكمال *completing* by itself, as in تم استكمال ٥١٧ مركز شباب *517 youth centers were completed*, might suggest that these youth centers were already built. Because the redundancy is motivated by linguistic issues in the Arabic source sentence rather than rhetorical ones, we can apply deletion and translate تم الانتهاء من استكمال ٥١٧ مركز شباب using the passive voice, as we usually do with this construction, resulting in *517 new youth centers were built*. The added adjective makes it unambiguously clear that these centers did not exist before.

4. المبالغ التي تم الفوز بها is a noun phrase modified by a relative clause with the تم construction. If we apply the sentence-level strategy of translating the تم construction using the passive voice, we get *the amounts of money that were won*, which is grammatical but not optimal. Because the source sentence is about a game in which contestants win money, we can apply morphological packaging and translate the whole noun phrase with the modifying clause as *winnings*.

5. مشكورة is a passive participle derived from the verb شكر *to thank*, and in this particular sentence, it is used as an adverb modifying the verb عملت *worked*. The closest possible equivalents for this participle are *thankfully* and *appreciatedly*, which are not optimal in this context; therefore, we are better off treating it as a lexical and structural gap. In some cases, مشكورة can be translated as *graciously*, but it does not work well in this context because this adverb usually describes doing something nice when one does not have to, whereas the Ministry of Education is expected to provide teacher training. Translating مشكورة using the passive voice is not an option either, because it will not give us the adverbial reading we need, and the passive would cause the deletion of the logical subject *a number of school district directors*, which we need to keep. To translate this participle, we need to make a few changes across the sentence. The verb in the main clause عبر *expressed* has the subject *a number of school district directors*, whom we can assume to be the same people who thanked the ministry for its support. Therefore, we can conjoin the two clauses using the active voice in a completely reconstructed sentence as in *a number of school district directors expressed their pleasure . . . and their gratitude for the Ministry of Education's efforts to support teachers*. We would need to leave out مشيرين *indicating* while substituting the verb *worked* with the noun *efforts*.

Exercise 5: Advanced Translation

1. The phrase المطلوب إنشاؤها is made up of the passive participle المطلوب *required* and the event nominal إنشاؤها *constructing them*, and together, they modify the noun phrase الوحدات السكنية *the housing units*. We can reconstruct the modifier phrase as a relative clause to get *the number of housing units whose construction is required to end the crisis*. To improve the translation, we might consider using a modal expression of necessity, which is lexically implied by the passive participle, while maintaining the passive voice because the source sentence does not specify who would build these housing units. These strategies give us *the number of housing units that need to be constructed/built to end the crisis or the number of new housing units needed to end the crisis.*

2. The imperfective verb يمكن is a modal expression of possibility, whereas the perfective verb كان sets the temporal reference of the whole sentence to the past. Any translation of this sentence needs to have a construction that encodes past possibility, such as *could have*. The phrase يشفى منه is a passive construction that constitutes a structural gap; it literally means *to be healed from it*. We could use *recover* or *heal* in the active voice, as in *he could have easily recovered from it (the eye infection)* or *it (the eye) could have healed easily*, but these candidates indicate that the eye infection could have healed without medical intervention, which is not suggested anywhere in the source sentence. Alternatively, we can apply lexical substitution and translate يشفى منه as *was treated*, as in *he had a simple eye infection that could have been easily treated.*

3. يستطاع is the rarely used passive form of the modal verb of possibility يستطيع *can/be able to*, and obviously, it constitutes a structural gap because English modals do not have passive forms. The subject of this passive verb is the clause أن يعوض *lit. to be compensated for*, which has a passive verb of its own. Translating this sentence requires using only one passive verb following a negated modal of possibility, as in *this professor cannot be compensated for*. This translation candidate can be improved by substituting *compensated for* with *replaced*, which fits better in this context, as in *this professor cannot be replaced*. However, this interim translation is vague when it comes to the reasons why Taha Hussein cannot be replaced. The context suggests that no other professor can take his place because of his qualifications and skills rather

than external factors. We can maintain this interpretation by morphologically packaging *cannot be replaced* as *irreplaceable*, in which modality and negation are incorporated morphologically in an adjective that describes Taha Hussein. These strategies give us *this professor is irreplaceable.*

4. The complement clause أنه لم يكن يجب إلقاء القبض عليها أو إدانتها has a complex grammatical structure in which لم encodes negation and the past time reference and يجب encodes modal necessity. There are several possible translations for لم يكن يجب, including *should not have* and *did not have to*. The context indicates that the optimal candidate is *should not have*. The subject of the source sentence is إلقاء القبض عليها أو إدانتها *lit. arresting her or convicting her*, but its equivalent must be the complement of the modal verb to avoid the ungrammatical structure in *arresting or convicting her should not have.* Because the source sentence does not name the agency that arrested and convicted Lubna, we need to use the passive voice in the translation to get *she should not have been arrested or convicted.*

5. The verb يملك *own* is used metaphorically in this sentence to express ability; therefore, we can translate it as *can* or *be able to*. The negated verb is followed by an adverbial phrase with إلا *except* and a clausal complement that specifies the interpretation of possibility. In this context, we can translate إلا as *but* or *only*. The latter option gives us *a journalist can only ask questions*, whereas *but* gives us *a journalist can but ask questions*, which is grammatical but rather awkward.

Chapter 4

1. The Japanese Constitution guarantees freedom of religion, and it does not recognize an official state religion. Births and marriages are usually celebrated according to Shinto rites, whereas death rituals and funerals are arranged according to Buddhist customs. However, if asked about their religion, the Japanese tend to say they do not have one. They even leave the religion line blank on official forms. In Japanese culture, Shinto is viewed as a set of age-old traditions and customs, whereas Buddhism is seen as more of a philosophy than a religion. Generally speaking, the Japanese take a relaxed approach toward religion; they visit Shinto

shrines and Buddhist temples, but may also go to Christian churches, with the same respect and reverence.

Translation notes:

- This paragraph is made up of one sentence that comprises several conjoined independent clauses that would be considered comma splices if this structure were maintained in the translation. Some conjunctions can be replaced with context-appropriate connectors to maintain cohesion. For example, أما *as for* in أما ما يتعلق بالوفاة *lit. as for that which is related to death* can be replaced with *while* to make it easy to recognize the contrastive function of this sentence. Other conjunctions are deleted and replaced with periods.

- A close translation of ولا يوجد دين رسمي للدولة, as in *there is no official state religion*, lacks a topic phrase; therefore, it has the potential to disrupt the text's cohesion. In order to link this sentence to the previous one, a referential chain is created by using a pronoun that refers to an already-established topic, namely, the Japanese Constitution, along with an appropriate predicate.

- The word «الشنتو» *Shinto* is between chevrons because it is a foreign proper noun. We do not need the chevrons in the translation because proper nouns in English are easily recognized; they start with capital letters.

- The negated adjective لا ديني is a relatively new coinage that means *of no religion* in a neutral way. The author does not want to trigger the negative connotations associated with the other synonyms, such as كافر and ملحد. Using the phrase *has no religion*, rather than *atheist* or *agnostic*, achieves the same function. The chevrons function as scare quotation marks that help avoid value judgments, but we need to leave them out because they would undermine the neutral tone if included in the translation as quotation marks.

- The translation tones down some of the author's statements by adding discourse hedges, such as *generally speaking* and *tend to*. These hedges help avoid making sweeping overgeneralizations that might be perceived negatively in English.

- The clause والياباني يأخذ أمور الدين ببساطة can be translated literally as *Japanese people take religion lightly/have a simplistic view of religion*, but these mean very different things from what the Arabic text suggests. We need to rephrase this clause in a different way, as in

Japanese people take a relaxed approach toward religion, to avoid any negative connotations.

2. On January 16, 1968, which the British opposition dubbed "Black Tuesday," Sir Harold Wilson, then Britain's labor prime minister, announced that by the end of 1971 Britain would withdraw, not only from the Far East, but also from the Arabian Gulf. This announcement came after a speech he gave before the House of Commons, in which he talked about the nation's growing economic problems and the cost of maintaining a military presence abroad. The announcement took the Gulf region by surprise because it meant the end of the old protectorate treaties that Britain had imposed on the Gulf emirates. However, this shift in policy was rather predictable, because Britain's control over the region had been significantly weakened in the aftermath of World War II and its withdrawal from the Indian subcontinent. Even before Wilson's announcement, while the old treaties and agreements were still in effect, the British political officers in India, who administered the Gulf region, were relieved of their duties, and Britain's official relations with the Arabian Gulf emirates were transferred to the Foreign and Commonwealth Office in London.

Translation notes:

- The first clause in this text is quite complex in terms of structure. The initial adverbial phrase في يوم الثلاثاء الأسود *on Black Tuesday* is modified by the clause كما أسمته المعارضة البريطانية *as the British opposition dubbed it* and the date phrase. These phrases need to be reordered in the translation according to the English conventions of adjunct phrase order.

- The adverbial clause starting with بعد أن تحدث *after he spoke* can start a new sentence in the translation; but to maintain the text's cohesion, this clause needs to be reconstructed to start with the topic phrase *this announcement*. The same strategy is used throughout the translation to establish a referential chain; hence, the use of the co-referential topic phrases *the decision*, *this shift in policy*, and *Wilson's announcement*.

- The second half of the text, starting with وقد يبدو هذا الأمر منطقيا *and this matter may seem logical*, requires comprehensive reconstruction because a close translation would be incoherent. The tense shift in قد يبدو *may seem* divides the text into two distinctive parts: a descriptive account of a past event, Britain's decision to withdraw from the Gulf region, and an analysis of why this event took place. We cannot maintain this shift in the translation because English does not allow tense shifts within sentences. The tense shift also contrasts this sentence with the previous one that describes how Wilson's announcement was received in the Gulf region. This contrast can be maintained by using the discourse marker *however* and the added clause that functions as the thesis statement of the author's analysis. These changes also help avoid the modality reading in which the author describes the decision as possibly illogical.

- The author provides two arguments in support of his thesis. First, the decision to withdraw was motivated by Britain's weakened position in the Gulf region. Second, Britain was already not adhering to the old treaties, even though they were still in effect, at least officially. Each argument is supported by two stated details. World War II and the withdrawal from India explain Britain's weakened position in the region. The information about the political officers in India and the change of the government agency that handled Britain's relations with the Gulf emirates demonstrate the change in Britain's policy toward the region before the withdrawal announcement. The logical structure of the author's argument presupposes some information that is not stated in the text, namely, that the British political officers in India administered the Gulf region. We need to add a clause to this effect to maintain the logical structure of the translation. The translation needs to make the structure of the analysis clear, especially the temporal and causal relations.

3. Television networks all over the world are now owned by private corporations, except, of course, in "third-world countries." Whether we like it or not, governments in the third world will need to give up control of all media outlets and leave them to the private sector—if not today, then within the next few years at most.

Translation notes:

- The first parenthetical phrase ما عدا دول العالم الثالث طبعا *except, of course, in third-world countries* separates the verb أصبحت *has become* from its complement ملكا *property*. Although the parallel structure is grammatical in English, the parenthetical material breaks the structure of the sentence, as in the close translation *all television networks in the world have become, except, of course, in third-world countries, owned by private corporations.* This issue can be resolved by reconstructing the sentence to move the adverbial parenthetical to the end.

- The second sentence has two parenthetical phrases marked with hyphens in addition to a sentence initial adverbial phrase and a sentence final modifying clause. The first parenthetical phrase في دول عالمنا الثالث *in the countries of our third world* can be easily integrated within the sentence structure, whereas the second parenthetical phrase can be safely deleted to avoid redundancy. The phrase وسائل الإعلام *the media* already refers to the press, radio, and television, but the parenthetical phrase lists them for emphasis, which is maintained in the translation by adding the quantifier *all*.

- The Arabic expressions العالم الثالث *the third world* and الدول النامية *developing countries* are functionally equivalent to their English counterparts. In fact, they were introduced to Arabic through translation from English. The author chooses the العالم الثالث *the third world* on purpose, as it better serves his objective of establishing a critical tone. To avoid changing the author's tone and attitude, we can maintain العالم الثالث *the third world* in the translation even though it is no longer politically correct.

4. In his semiautobiographical novel, *Diary of a Country Prosecutor*, Tawfik Al-Hakim gives a glimpse of what used to happen during elections in the old days. He tells the story of a ballot box that was found at the bottom of a canal when the Nile River was low. Al-Hakim, who was then a district attorney, asked a police officer about that box. The officer explained that he was a free man who believed in freedom, and that he would never pressure the peasants to vote for any particular candidate. Instead, he would let them fully exercise their voting rights at the polls. But once they were done casting their votes, he would order the ballot box dumped in the canal. While the ballot box was on its way to its final resting place, another box stuffed with fraudulent ballots, which guaranteed the results the government wanted, would go to the counting station. Suddenly, the government candidate got all the votes, even though nobody voted for him. This story exposes how the government used to rig elections in the "old days."

Translation notes:

- This text is divided into four paragraphs: an introduction, the narrative of a story, the conclusion of the story, and commentary. We can merge them into one paragraph to maintain thematic unity.

- The double periods at the end of the first and third paragraphs separate the summary of Al-Hakim's story from the author's introduction and commentary, whereas the double periods at the end of the second paragraph signal a pause before the end of the story for rhetorical effects. In order to merge these paragraphs, we need to reconstruct the first sentence of the second paragraph to make it serve as a transition.
- The double parentheses in ((يوميات نائب في الأرياف)) help identify this phrase as a book title. We can delete them and write the title in italics with initial capital letters. The double parentheses in ((زمان)) function as scare quotation marks. They hint to the readers that the government is still involved in such fraudulent practices. We can convert these parentheses to quotation marks.
- There are two instances of the subordinating conjunction إذا *if* in this text, but both are used as cohesive devices rather than logical operators. The conditional conjunction in فإذا انتهوا من ملء بطاقات الانتخاب *lit. if they were done filling out the ballots* has a temporal function, and is therefore translated as *once*. The second instance of إذا *if* is used with the preposition ـب in a construction that encodes immediate and unexpected temporal sequence, which justifies translating it as *suddenly*.

5. This was a new period of stability in Agatha Christie's life. Her novels were widely read, and several were being translated into other languages. She was even experimenting with new literary genres; she wrote her only classical novel, *Giant's Bread*, under a pseudonym, as well as several well-received plays, including *And Then There Were None* and *The Mousetrap*, which broke the record for the longest-running play, as it has been performed every night in London since 1952.

Translation notes:

- The text starts with a noun phrase followed by a period, which is essentially a sentence fragment. This structure is ungrammatical in English, but Arabic allows it at the beginning of rhetorical units in which it functions as a title or subheading, provided that the rest of text elaborates on it. We can reconstruct this fragment as a sentence by adding a demonstrative as a subject.
- The three clauses following the subheading are all in the present tense, even though the text describes past events. This technique keeps the descriptive section of the text static; the popularity of

Christie's novels, their being translated, and her experimenting with plays are represented as parts of the new stage in her life. This technique also separates the section that describes her life from the one that describes her literary works, which starts with a tense shift to the past. To maintain the cohesion of the translation, we need to use the past tense throughout the text.

- The clause وهي تجرب حظها في المسرحيات *lit. and she is trying her luck with plays* introduces a new referent, the plays, which are the topic of the following sentences. The problem is that there is an intervening sentence about a novel, which might disrupt the cohesive structure of the translation. We can reconstruct the text to maintain cohesion by moving the part about the novel to the preceding clause so that all the clauses about the plays are together in one section of the translation.

- The title of Christie's play is عشرة عبيد صغار in the Arabic text, but in our translation it is *And Then There Were None*. This play was published under different titles, and we chose the one that is most commonly known.

Notes on the Annotated Texts

Annotated Text 1

جبل الزنابق لسمر يزبك في الزيتون الأدبية بالقاهرة

1. This is the title of a book. It needs to be in italics and/or underlined with the initial letters capitalized: *The Tulips Mountain*.

2. سمر يزبك is the name of the author, and it is preceded by the prefix preposition لـ *for*, which is functionally equivalent to *by*. We can translate this phrase as *The Tulips Mountain by Samar Yazbak*.

3. الزيتون *olives* is the name of a literary club in Cairo. It can only be transliterated and defined as in *Al-Zaytun Literary Club*.

4. The phrase العاصمة المصرية *the Egyptian capital* can be left out because it would be redundant when used to define *Cairo*.

5. الصادر is a definite active participle derived from the verb صدر *come out*, and it literally means *that which has come out*. We can translate it by applying lexical substitution and reconstruction to get the passive voice in a reduced relative clause, as in *published by*.

6. The phrase requires reconstruction to change the order of its constituents. The translation can start with the book title followed by the author's name along with its modifying adjective and then the publisher, as in *The Tulips Mountain by Syrian author Samar Yazbak, published by Dar Al-Mada.*

7. The definite singular noun الكتاب *the book* is rather vague, as it could refer the physical properties of the book (its size, number of pages, etc.), the materials it includes (stories, essays, etc.), or the writer's style. To avoid this vagueness, the author uses the possessive phrase مضمون الكتاب *lit. the content of the book*, which can be translated as *the book*, in which we delete *the content*. However, this translation gives us *the book can be classified as writings*, which does not sound natural in this context because it inherits the vagueness of the source phrase. We can apply lexical substitution to get a more specific translation, as in *the author's style can be classified as free writing.*

8. The term نوع أدبي *lit. a literary type* is functionally equivalent to *a literary genre.*

9. The phrase بعينه *lit. by its eye* is a frozen adverbial phrase that is functionally equivalent to the reflexive pronoun *itself.* In this particular sentence, we need to apply substitution and reconstruction to translate the source phrase as an adjective, as in *a particular genre.*

10. القص is an event nominal that means *telling stories*. In this context, it is equivalent to *narrative.*

11. مستلهما is an active participle derived from استلهم *get inspiration*, and it is used as an adverb. To maintain its function as a modifier, we can translate it using the passive voice in a reduced relative clause, as in *inspired by.*

12. سوريالي is a borrowed adjective that means *surrealistic*. The Arabic adjective also means *surrealist,* but because we are describing the art rather than the artist, we need to use *surrealistic.* The adverb أحيانا *sometimes/at times* is structurally ambiguous, given that it can modify the preceding phrase, as in *surrealistic at times*, or it can modify the following verb, as in *that sometimes mixes dreams and reality.* Based on our understanding of the context, we can conclude that the author intended the former interpretation.

13. حيث *where* is a relative pronoun, but in this context, it only serves a way of encoding indirect causation. More specifically, it indicates that

the writer's description of the book in the preceding clause is based on what Samar Yazbak said in an interview. We can translate حيث using the conjunction *as* or leave it out and start a new sentence.

14. في كتابته *in writing it* is a prepositional phrase used as a modifier for the verb phrase استغرقت شهرين. This phrase can be reconstructed as an infinitival clause, as in *it took her two months to write the book* or *the book took two months to write*. Alternatively, we can reconstruct the whole clause using the passive voice, as *the book was written in two months*, or we can maintain the active voice, as in *she wrote the book in two months*. These are all valid candidates that profile the same situation differently, depending on which constituent is in the prominence subject position, but the optimal choice will depend on what we do with the rest of the sentence.

15. بدأت لديها cannot be translated word for word as *started at her* because it does not collocate internally. We can either leave out لديها and translate the whole clause as *the idea of writing dreams started* or rephrase it as *the idea of writing dreams came/occurred to her*.

16. نهارا is an adverb derived from the noun نهار *day*, and it can be translated as *during the day* or *by day* (not *daily*). The sentence at this point is structurally ambiguous because of the conjunction in أناس طبيعيين وكائنات مفكرة, as it could mean *like anyone who leads a double life during the day with normal people and also with sentient beings* (two lives during the day) or *like anyone who leads a double life, living during the day with normal people and at night with his subconscious*. The second interpretation is one intended in the source text, and the phrase *with sentient beings* is left out to avoid ambiguity and confusion. Note that we need to substitute the pronoun *his* with a plural reference to avoid sexist language.

17. أشبه *most like* is a superlative adjective derived from the verb يشبه *resemble/look like*. In this context, it is not used to make any comparisons; this morphological form is used only for emphasis. Therefore, we can translate it as a noncomparative adjective, such as *were similar to*. However, this strategy fails to maintain the emphasis; hence, the need for other strategies, such as metaphorization to get *served as*.

18. أدارت النقاش is a light verb construction that is functionally equivalent to *moderated the discussion*.

19. يفجر *blow up* is a causative verb used in this sentence figuratively to describe the critics' responses to the novel. We can use a different

figure of speech that fits the context, such as *sparks/ignites the old–new controversy*.

20. The figurative expression يعلي شأن *lit. raises/elevates the status* can be translated as *underscores*.

21. The definite singular masculine noun الكاتب *the writer* is a generic noun that is functionally equivalent to the bare plural noun *writers*. We can use a singular definite generic noun in the translation, but this would lead to ambiguity, as it can refer to Samar Yazbak or all authors.

22. The definite noun القارئ is generic; therefore, it is functionally equivalent to its bare plural counterpart *readers*. The verb phrase يريح القارئ means *makes the readers comfortable* or *relieves the readers*, neither of which fits in this context because they presuppose that the readers are already under some kind of stress. One way of translating this phrase is to add negation and apply lexical substitution, as in *does not burden the readers with the restrictions of literary form*. The problem, however, is that negation can be interpreted to take scope over the two conjoined verbs يريح and يحرر *liberate*. This gives us a reading in which the author's description does not burden the readers with the restrictions of literary form and does not liberate them. One solution is to leave out the phrase يريح القارئ to avoid redundancy and ambiguity. In fact, this deletion does not cost us anything because *liberate* entails the meaning of relieving and not burdening.

23. إطار is *frame*, and it is used here as a metaphor. It can be literalized as *restrictions*.

24. The phrase لا تلتزم إلا *lit. does not adhere except to* has negation and إلا *except*. We can delete negation and translate إلا as *only* to get *adheres only to*, which can be rephrased and reconstructed in the passive voice to get *limited/restricted only by*. Another option is to delete negation and apply lexical substitution to get *reflects only*, but this depends on what we do with the rest of the sentence.

25. يعتمل is a Form VIII verb derived from عمل *work*, and it is used figuratively to add a dynamic dimension to writers' emotions and ideas. For emotions, we can use *stir*, *churn*, or *swell*; and for ideas, we can use *germinate* or *float*. What we need in this particular context is a verb that can be used in the same way to figuratively describe both ideas and emotions, such as *swirl*. We can also apply literalization to get *free writing style that reflects only the author's feelings and ideas*.

Annotated Text 2

مستقبل الثقافة في مصر

1. The phrase "مستقبل الثقافة في مصر" كتاب, can be reconstructed as *The Fu-*
   ture of Culture in Egypt is a book that, which allows us to keep the book
   title in the sentence initial topic position while providing a grammatical
   structure needed for the following relative clause.

2. ينبغي is a modal verb of necessity that means *must, have to, should,*
   or *need*. In this context, it is best translated as *should* because the discourse function of modality in the source sentence is making a recom-
   mendation rather than expressing obligation. The problem here is that
   the topic phrase of this sentence (the book title) is different from its
   subject (the clause starting with أن). This construction is not allowed in
   English; therefore, we need to apply reconstruction. We can use the passive voice to resolve this issue and maintain the sentence initial position of the book title, as in *The Future of Culture in Egypt is a book that*
   should be read.

3. The phrase قراءة موضوعية أمينة متفهمة *lit. an objective, honest, and un-*
   derstanding reading includes a noun functioning as a cognate object
   followed by three modifying adjectives. We can delete the cognate object
   and translate the adjectives as adverbs modifying the passive verb يقرأ—
   as in *it was not read objectively, honestly, and understandingly*—which
   can be further revised as *it was not read objectively and open-mindedly.*

4. كثيرون *many* is the predicate of القراء الأفراد *individual readers*. A word-
   for-word translation would give us *the individual readers who read this*
   book well are many. We can translate *many* as a quantifier, as in *many*
   individual readers read this book well, but this candidate falls short of
   sounding natural; it is rather vague. We can substitute *read* with *appre-*
   ciated to improve this translation.

5. The verb phrase أساؤوا قراءته involves a lexical gap, namely, the verb أساء,
   which means *to do something wrong*. This verb is functionally equivalent to the prefix *mis-*, as in *misread it*. However, because this clause is
   in contrast to the preceding one, we can use ellipses, as in *while many*
   readers appreciated this book, many more did not.

6. أكثر بكثير *lit. more with a lot* is a frozen expression that is functionally
   equivalent to *many more*.

7. The verb أعقب means *to immediately follow*, and it is usually translated as *in the aftermath of* or *came on the heels of*, which might not fit well in this context because they would suggest that the book was in some way responsible for the events described in the preceding phrase. Instead, we can translate it as *which emerged soon after the appearance of the book*, and we can revise it as *which emerged soon after the publication of the book*.

8. The conjoined clause وظلت سائدة طوال العقود الستة الماضية means *and remained prevalent throughout the last six decades*. One way to improve this close translation is to replace *throughout the last six decades* with *ever since*.

9. كما هو معلوم *as it is known* can be restructured as a sentence initial it-clef construction, as in *it is well known that*, or as a quantified subject phrase, as in *everyone knows that*. However, these candidates would come at the cost of moving the book title from the sentence initial topic position. This phrase does not add much in terms of content. It is used only as a rhetorical device that signals the beginning of a background account. Because this function is not recognized in English, we can simply delete the phrase altogether.

10. The verb–first word order allows the pronoun in the subject phrase دستورها *its Constitution* to come after its referent البلاد *the lands*. If the order of the pronoun and its referent is maintained in the translation, we would get *after its Constitution returned to the lands*. The pronoun needs to come after its referent, and *the lands* can be substituted with *Egypt*. These strategies give us *after the Constitution was returned to Egypt*. We can also substitute *returned* with *reinstated/restored* and use reconstruction to modify *the Constitution* and incorporate the passive voice. These strategies give us *after the Egyptian Constitution was reinstituted/restored*. The relative clause, which follows this phrase in the source sentence, will need to come in the middle, right after the noun it modifies, as in *after the Egyptian Constitution, which Sidqi suspended, . . . was reinstated*. Further reconstruction can yield a noun phrase after the preposition, as in *after the reinstatement of the Egyptian Constitution*.

11. This is the name of the Egyptian prime minister at the time. We can add this information, as in *Prime Minister Ismail Sidqi*.

12. The prefix preposition لـ *for* is ambiguous in this sentence. It can suggest that the elections were held for the purpose of bringing Al-Nahhas Pasha's government to power (direct causation) or simply that the elections

resulted in the formation of this government (indirect causation). The context suggests that the latter interpretation is the one intended here, and we can use reconstruction to make the translation unambiguous, as in *following the elections that brought Al-Nahhas Pasha's government to power.*

13. The Montreux Treaty.

14. The structure of the relative clause التي تمكنت بها من إلغاء is equivalent to *with which Egypt managed to abolish/cancel.* We can rephrase this candidate as *which allowed Egypt to abolish.*

15. الامتيازات الأجنبية is *capitulations*, but this political term might not be familiar to many readers. We can use the next sentence as a definition while adding a conjunction, as in *capitulations, thus making foreign nationals subject to the same laws as Egyptians.*

16. The verb توشك is often translated as *almost*, but in this particular sentence we are better off translating it as *coming to.* Note that the author is using the imperfective form of the verb, but this is an embedded clause in which temporal reference is dependent on that of the main verb, namely, أعطت الانطباع *gave the impression.* Therefore, the translation needs to be in the past tense, as in *gave the impression that an era . . . was coming to an end.*

17. The translation of توشك أن تبدأ needs to be compatible with the translation of توشك أن تنتهي *was coming to an end* because they are conjoined. We can translate توشك أن تبدأ as *was about to begin.*

18. تعد العدة is a frozen expression that means *to get ready*, and we can metaphorize it as *gear up.*

19. The phrase لتحقيقه والوصول إليه *lit. to achieve it and reach it* is a synonymous couplet, and the second conjunct can be deleted because it means the same thing as the preceding word.

20. مشروط is a passive participle derived from the verb شرط *to make a condition*, but its counterpart *conditioned* means something completely different (false equivalents), and therefore we need to use another word, such as *depends on.*

21. The whole phrase تتمثل روح العصر الحديث *lit. embody the spirit of the modern era* can be literalized as *modernize.*

22. The verb phrase يغني عن constitutes a lexical gap. It literally means *to cause someone to be in no need for something.* We can incorporate negation while applying lexical substitution to get *will be of no use* or use the idiom *in vain.*

23. The question word كيف in this context means *what* because the predicate of the question clause is يكون *be*. The particle إذا here is not the
conditional marker. It is a discourse marker that signals a conclusion,
which is functionally equivalent to some uses of *then*. This sentence can
be translated as *what will this modern Egyptian culture be like,* in which
then is deleted to avoid ambiguity.

Annotated Text 3

التنوع الحيوي عند نقطة اللاعودة

1. التنوع الحيوي is a recent coinage that means *biodiversity.*
2. نقطة اللاعودة is a frozen expression that means *the point of no return.*
3. We can leave out العام *the year,* and translate this phrase as *in 2002.*
4. The phrase تحقيق تخفيض كبير means *achieving a big reduction,* but this
candidate does not collocate well. In this context, this phrase can be
reconstructed as *to significantly slow down the rate.* Note that the prefix preposition بـ *with* is translated as *to,* and the translation is reconstructed accordingly.
5. بحلول *by the arrival of* can be translated as *by.*
6. The construction made up of the preposition من *from* followed by a
definite adjective is typically translated as an *it*-cleft followed by an
infinitive clause, as in *it is difficult to measure.*
7. على يقين *lit. on truth* is an idiomatic expression that describes a very
high degree of certainty. We can translate it as *certain* or *know for sure.*
8. الوطأة is *footprint,* which is a newly adopted sense of this word. This is
why the author offers a synonym in parentheses and a definition in an
appositive phrase separated from the rest of the text with hyphens. Because the English equivalent is a well-known expression, we can delete
the synonym to end up with *our ecological footprint.*
9. وهو ما يعني is a complex structure that means *and it is that which means,*
and we can reconstruct it as *this means.* Because this sentence elaborates on the previous one, there is no need to start a new paragraph, and
we can optionally substitute *and this means* with *in other words.*
10. حافة is *edge,* but the expression على حافة in this context is equivalent
to *on the verge of* or *on the brink of.* If we want to avoid *on the verge
/brink of the point of no return,* we can substitute *on the verge of* with
almost.

11. ما is a relative pronoun, but when used with the conditional particle إذا, they can be translated together as *whether*.

12. From a structural point of view, the relative clause التي عاشت عليها الحضارات الإنسانية means *on which human civilizations lived*, but the preposition *on* does not collocate with the head noun *the stable environment*. One way of restructuring this relative clause is to use the relative pronoun *where*. The perfective verb عاشت should be translated using the present perfect, as in *where human civilizations have lived* to accommodate the modifier phrase headed by the preposition منذ *since*.

13. العصر الجليدي is *Ice Age*.

14. أي is a discourse marker that is functionally equivalent to *in other words* or *that is (i.e.)*, but we can delete it in this context to end up with *the last Ice Age 10 thousand years ago* to avoid disrupting the structure of the translation.

15. تتعرض is a lexically passive verb that means *to be exposed*. The subject of this sentence is the noun phrase النظم الطبيعية *natural systems /ecosystems*, whereas the prepositional phrase starting with لخطر *to the danger of* functions as a complement of the verb. We can improve the close translation *the ecosystems, which, . . . are exposed to the danger* by changing it to *the ecosystems, which, . . . are in danger of*.

16. The phrase سبل العيش means *ways of living*, but it could be interpreted as *ways of making a living* or as *cultures*. Nothing in the context supports one reading over the other, but the *ways of making a living* interpretation would be redundant in this context because this phrase is conjoined to الاقتصادات *economies*, which means the same, more or less. Therefore, we can translate سبل العيش as *cultures*.

17. كوكب الأرض is *Planet Earth*. The word كوكب *planet* is used in the Arabic text to avoid the ambiguity of الأرض, which could mean *land*, *ground*, *floor*, or *Earth*. We can leave out كوكب *planet* because the issue of lexical ambiguity does not arise in English.

18. إلا إذا *except if* is functionally equivalent to *unless*.

19. المستدام is a new coinage that means *sustainable*.

20. This sentence is presented as a paragraph by itself to keep it separate from the preceding paragraph, which is paraphrased or quoted from *The Third Global Biodiversity Outlook Report*, but we can use it as a conclusion for the previous paragraph with the conjunction و *and* left out.

21. The phrase استنتاج أساسي لتقييم رئيسي جديد is structurally ambiguous. Instead of trying to guess the intended structure, we can research the

original document referred to here and translate it as *the conclusion of a new basic assessment report.*

22. *The Third Global Biodiversity Outlook Report.*

23. The passive participle ملموس *touchable* is used figuratively, and it is functionally equivalent to *tangible* or *concrete.*

24. The reduced relative clause المقدمة من الحكومات *presented by the governments* might sound redundant because it modifies the noun التقارير *reports*, which is already modified by the adjective الوطنية *national.* The added modifier phrase is included in the Arabic text to make it clear that these reports come from different governments, not just one. If we delete the adjective *national*, we can add *participating* and get *scientific assessments and reports presented by participating governments.*

25. The International Year of Biodiversity.

Annotated Text 4

ثقافة التسامح عند المسلمين

1. التسامح is a noun derived from the reciprocal Form VI verb تسامح, which means *to forgive one another.* In this context, we can apply lexical substitution to translate التسامح as *tolerance.* The preposition *at*, the equivalent of عند, does not collocate with *Muslims*; therefore, we can change the close translation *the culture of tolerance at Muslims* to *the culture of tolerance in Islam.*

2. The phrase من أشد الأمور خطرا functions as a predicate for the subject التعصب, which comes at the very end of this short paragraph. The preposition من *from* and the superlative possessive phrase أشد الأمور *lit. the toughest of matters/things* encode a set membership relation, whereas the adverb خطرا *in terms of danger* identifies the membership criteria for this set. We can express this relation as *one of the most dangerous things*, which can be rephrased as *one of the most insidious dangers.* Alternatively, we can tone down the sentence by avoiding the superlative construction and adding a degree adverb, as in *very dangerous.*

3. The conjunction و in والتي *and which* needs to be left out. The relative clause can be reconstructed as an infinitive clause, as in *that threaten to tear societies apart.*

4. The conjunction بل signals contrast. In this context, it encodes a contrast of degree; it shows that the following clause describes a situation

that is more insidious than the one described in the preceding clause. We can translate بل as *and even*; however, because بل is repeated in the next clause, we can use a different contrast marker, such as *in fact*.

5. This instance of بل has the same function as the previous بل. To avoid repeating *and even*, we can use the *not only . . . but also/as well* construction, as in *it may even lead to wars, not only among societies, but within societies as well*.

6. التعصب in this context refers to *religious intolerance*, and it functions as the subject of the first clause. The author puts the subject at the very end of the paragraph to build up suspense and create a sense of expectation. This rhetorical technique is common in spoken English discourse, especially when introducing a speaker to an audience at a public event, but not in written discourse. Therefore, we need to move the subject to its sentence's initial position. Also, we can merge the first and second paragraphs because they deal with the same topic.

7. The passive participle المراد means *what is wanted*, but in this context it refers to *meaning*. We can reconstruct this whole phrase in the active voice as *Religious intolerance does not mean/refer to*.

8. الإنسان is a generic noun that refers to all human beings. We should avoid translating it as *man* because it would sound sexist, which is not intended in the source text. Instead, we can use the generic pronoun *one*, as in *religious intolerance does not mean being proud of/taking pride in one's religion*.

9. The adverbial phrase بمحض اختياره is a collocation that is functionally equivalent to *willingly*.

10. The negated modal phrase لا يمكن أن يعاب functions as the predicate of هذا *this*, which can start a new sentence. The negated modal verb يمكن *can/be able to* takes a clausal subject with the passive verb يعاب *be shamed*. We can use an adjective to translate يعاب, such as in *shameful* or *disgraceful*, but that would make it difficult to incorporate negation and modality, as in *this cannot be shameful/disgraceful*. One solution is to reconstruct the whole sentence as *this is not something to be ashamed of* or *there is not nothing wrong with this*.

11. When translating انغلاق المرء على عقيدته وفكره *lit. being closed up on one's religion and ideology*, we can reconstruct it using nonfigurative expressions, as in *to be dogmatic about one's religion or ideology*.

12. مما is a grammatical compound made up of من *from* and the relative pronoun ما *which*. We can leave out the preposition and translate the

compound as *which*. The causative verb يفقد means *to make someone lose something*, and it can be translated as *takes . . . away from people* or *deprives people of*.

13. This is a direct quotation from the Qur'an used to support a statement the author makes in the last sentence of the previous paragraph. We can move the translation of the quotation to the previous paragraph. Generally speaking, we do not need to translate verses from any scripture in Arabic. We can find the same quotation in a well-established translation and cite the translator.

14. The perfective verb اعتبر *considered* should be translated in the present tense because it describes a static situation.

15. The noun شر by itself means *evil*, but here it functions as a superlative expression that means *the most evil*, and it forms a possessive construction, with the relative clause starting with ما. The phrase شر ما تصاب به المجتمعات literally means *the most evil thing that societies are afflicted with*, which can be revised as *the Qur'an considers hunger and fear to be the worst social evils*.

16. The prepositional phrase ومن الناس *and from the people* is the predicate of this sentence, whereas the clause starting with the relative pronoun من *who* functions as the subject. This word order is a rhetorical technique the author uses to isolate himself and the readers from the group of people referred to in the subject clause. We can use the same technique in our translation, as in *among people are those who believe that, . . .* but this style is rather archaic. Instead, we can reconstruct the word order to get *some people believe that*.

17. The frozen expression لا محالة functions as a modal of necessity. The scope of the negation marker لا is limited to this phrase—that is, it does not affect the rest of the sentence—but the modal expression as a whole takes scope over the entire sentence, resulting in a structure that means *it is always/necessarily true that faith is attached to intolerance*. We can revise this close translation as *faith and intolerance are inseparable /two sides of the same coin*, in which the modal expression is deleted and *attached to* is substituted with a functionally equivalent adjective or an idiomatic expression. Note that لا يفارقه is semantically redundant in this context because it means the same thing as ملازم *attached*.

18. The frozen expression ما عداه is a relative clause with a verb that means *to be other than*. We can reconstruct it as *others* or *everyone else* because the object pronoun in عداه refers to a generic noun.

19. The idiomatic phrase يتمسك بعروته الوثقى describes holding on to one's beliefs. The idiom is negated with لم *did not*, but the translation needs to be in the present tense. The past tense in the source sentence is required only because of the conditional expression من *whoever/anyone who*.

20. In this context, كتاب means *scripture* or *holy book*. The passive participle منزل is derived from the causative verb أنزل *to send down*, and it is functionally equivalent to *revealed*. We can leave out the participle because *holy book* or *scripture* would be sufficient; it is needed in Arabic to avoid the ambiguity of كتاب.

21. تعالى is an honorific expression used to refer to God, but instead of translating كما قال تعالى as *as God Almighty says*, we can delete the whole phrase and use a colon followed by the quotation, thus merging the two paragraphs.

22. The frozen expression بعضهم وبعض means *each other*, but we can leave it out because it would be redundant in the translation.

23. The adverb دينيا is derived from adjective ديني *religious*, but we cannot translate it as *religiously* because it is not functionally equivalent in this context. This adverb specifies the nature of the differences between communities, which we can express using a prepositional phrase, as in *of different faiths/religions*.

Annotated Text 5

آثار الأزمة المالية العالمية: الإطار العام للأزمة

1. The quantified phrase إحدى السنوات السيئة means *one of the bad years*, but the modifying prepositional phrase في التاريخ *in history* suggests a superlative relation, which we can make explicit in the translation while substituting *in history* with the adverb *ever*, as in *one of the worst years ever*.

2. The frozen expression من حيث *lit. from where* is a phrasal conjunction that is functionally equivalent to *in terms of*.

3. This is a new sentence that does not need a conjunction to indicate its rhetorical function as an elaboration on the previous statement; therefore, we can leave out the prefix ـف. The frozen expression من ناحية is functionally equivalent to *on one hand*.

4. الارتفاع الصاروخي *lit. the rocket-like increase* is an idiomatic expression used in this context to describe the significant increase in the prices of

raw materials. We can use the idiomatic phrase *sharp increase* or reconstruct the sentence to accommodate the idiomatic verb *skyrocketed*.

5. The verb phrase تسبب في وضع means *resulted in placing/positioning*, but this close translation does not collocate with the complement phrase. We can use *pushed* as in *pushed more than 150 million people into poverty*.

6. The collocation فقر مدقع is functionally equivalent to *abject poverty*.

7. The sentential conjunction من ناحية أخرى is equivalent to *on the other hand*. We need to leave out the conjunction و *and* to start a new sentence.

8. حتى الآن *thus far/until now* and في العديد من البلدان *in many countries* are two prepositional phrases that separate the subject الأزمة المالية *the financial crisis* from the predicate ساهمت *contributed*. These prepositional phrases have different functions; حتى الآن is a sentential adverb, whereas في العديد من البلدان modifies the subject phrase. We need to change the order of these phrases to maintain their functions, as in *the financial crisis in many countries has thus far contributed*. Note that the perfective verb ساهمت is translated using the present perfect because of the present adverbial حتى الآن *thus far/until now*.

9. A close translation of تعطيل مستوى التنمية, such as *hindering the level of development*, does not fit well in this context with *contributed to*. We can rephrase it as *contributed to a slower growth rate*.

10. The possessive phrase عديد البلدان can be reconstructed as the quantified phrase *many countries*. However, this would be redundant because we already have *many countries* in the preceding clause. We can keep *many countries* in the translation of this relative clause if we take it out of the main clause. This gives us *the global financial crisis has thus far contributed to a slower growth rate than what many countries*.

11. The prepositional phrase ضمن مخططاتها التنموية *within their developmental plans* can be translated as *had planned for*, in which the past perfect sets the reference time before the financial crisis and the verb gives us a predicate for the relative clause.

12. The frozen expression في المقام الأول is an adverbial phrase that is functionally equivalent to *first and foremost*.

13. The modifier phrase بشكل غير مباشر *lit. in a way that is not direct* can be translated by applying morphological packaging yielding *indirectly*.

14. In this context, في الواقع *in fact* is a sentential conjunction that expresses contrast between two sentences, whereas على الرغم من *even though /despite* is a subordination conjunction that expresses contrast between the clauses that make up the second sentence. To avoid having two

conjunctions of contrast together in the translation, we can move the clausal conjunction to the beginning of the second clause. We also need to substitute *in fact* with *however*, which is better suited for this particular context. These strategies give us *however, developing countries are suffering . . . even though/despite*.

15. The singular noun قلق means *worry* or *concern*. We need to use the bare plural form of *concern*, as in *there are concerns*.

16. The phrase معدل نمو الناتج القومي الإجمالي is equivalent to *GDP* (gross domestic product).

17. The phrase وضمن عدة عوامل أخرى *among several other factors* is a modifier used as an appositive phrase. It can be moved to the end of this sentence in the translation.

18. بالإضافة إلى ذلك *additionally/in addition/moreover* is a sentential adverbial that connects this sentence to the previous one. It is followed by the adverbial حسب *according to*. To avoid having a sequence of two adverbial phrases in the translation, we can leave out *according to* and reconstruct the translation using a verb that entails the meaning of the adverbial, as in *Moreover, a recent report . . . predicts that*.

19. This entire relative clause can be reconstructed as *which would make it difficult for local entrepreneurs and contractors to get loans*.

20. In this context, التحويلات *lit. transferences* is best translated as *remittances*. Also, this sentence should be moved to the previous paragraph to serve as its conclusion.

Annotated Text 6

قضايا مستحدثة في الزواج: الزواج العرفي

1. The culture-specific term الزواج العرفي refers to a type of marriage that is not officially documented—that is, it does not require a written legal contract recognized by the state or the authorities. We can transliterate the word عرفي followed by the close equivalent *common-law marriage*.

2. The subheading تعريفه *its definition* signals the function of the first sentence, which is easily recognized because of the verb عرفت *defined*. We can leave out the subheading and start the translation with the sentence following the colon.

3. The perfective verb phrase عرفته *defined it* should be translated in the present tense because it describes a static state of affairs. We should

also replace the object pronoun with the equivalent of الزواج العرفي if we delete the subheading.

4. The prepositional phrase باعتباره literally means *by its consideration*, which can be rephrased as *by considering it*, but it is functionally equivalent to *as*, yielding *defines it as*. The grammatical term علم means *a proper noun*, and the phrase علما على معنى محدد means *a proper noun with a specific meaning*, which we can leave out because it is clear in the translation that the definition concerns a term.

5. The negated adjectival phrase غير الموثق بوثيقة رسمية *lit. nonregistered by an official document* can be reconstructed as a relative clause, as in *which is not officially registered*. We should avoid maintaining the lexically negated adjectival structure because the term *unregistered marriage* refers to a different type of marriage common in Southeast Asia and Eastern Africa.

6. The adverbial phrase سواء أكان مكتوبا أو غير مكتوب *whether it is written or not written* can be reconstructed as the legal phrase *expressed in writing or not/otherwise*, used as an appositive phrase separating the head noun *agreement* and the relative clause, as in *a marriage agreement, whether expressed in writing or otherwise, that is not officially registered*.

7. The active participle مستوفي is derived from the verb استوفى *fulfill /meet the requirements*; along with its complement, it modifies the noun phrase زواج شرعي *legal marriage*. The function of the participial phrase is to elaborate the meaning of شرعي, which refers to Islamic Sharia law rather than civil law. We can maintain this function by reconstructing the participial phrase while adding a phrase that specifies Islamic law, as in *a legal marriage in accordance with the Islamic law*.

8. The preposition مع *with* functions here as phrasal conjunction that encodes contrast. We can use any clausal conjunction with the same function—such as *even though, even if, despite*, and so on—while reconstructing the noun phrase complement accordingly. For example, if we use *even though*, we end up with *even though it is not officially registered*.

9. The construction made up of من *from* and a definite adjective is functionally equivalent to *it*-clefts, as in *it is known that official registration/documentation is neither a necessary nor a sufficient condition*. However, this sentence serves as a reiteration of the author's main argument stated in the previous sentence; therefore, we can leave it out to

avoid repetition. The same applies to the clause وبغيابه يكون العقد صحيحا *and in its absence, the contract is valid.*

10. The sentential conjunction إنما is a contrast marker that is functionally equivalent to *in fact*, but its translation in this context depends on what we do with the rest of the sentence. For example, if we translate بل in the previous sentence as *in fact*, we can translate إنما using contrastive *but* to get *In fact, the marriages of Prophet Muhammad PBUH and his companions were not officially documented in writing, but.* Alternatively, we can use the sentential adverb *rather*, which also encodes contrast.

11. The light verb construction اتخذ الصفة الشرعية *lit. took the legal property* is functionally equivalent to *acquired/had legal status*, which we can reconstruct as *were legally valid*. The preposition من *from* can be translated as *because* with the following noun phrase reconstructed as a full clause.

12. The two words in the parentheses list the legal requirements stated in the previous phrase: الإشهار is *announcing a marriage publicly*, whereas الإشهاد is *having witnesses*.

13. We need to start a new sentence here, delete the colon, and convert the parentheses to quotation marks. The reported speech verb يقول *says* can be substituted with *states* or *according to*.

14. In this context, يكتبون *write* is functionally equivalent to *document*. The culture-specific term صداق is better translated as *dowry* rather than *bride price*, which means something completely different from the source phrase and has negative social meanings in the target language.

15. The culture-specific term مؤخر is *lit. delayed* is *deferred dowry*, which is a portion of the dowry paid to the wife in case of divorce.

16. In this sentence, بل is functionally equivalent to *instead/rather*. يعجل is *speed up*, but we can translate it as *paid the dowry in advance*. We can also reconstruct the translation by reversing the order of the clauses, deleting negation, and changing the conjunction, as in *because they paid the full dowry in advance rather than deferring part of it (to be paid in case of divorce).*

17. The causative verb يزوجون *to marry someone to someone else* needs to be translated as a reflexive verb while reconstructing the sentence to accommodate the prepositional phrase على مؤخر, as in *when people started getting married with deferred dowries.*

18. The clause أنها زوجة له *that she is his wife* includes two generic pronouns with no identifiable referents in previous discourse. To make sure the

translation is clear, we can apply reconstruction to get *and the marriage itself*.

19. The noun phrase شرط توثيق الزواج *the condition of registering marriage* functions as the subject of this sentence, but شرط *condition* is repeated as the head of the predicate phrase. We can delete this noun from the subject phrase and reconstruct it as *registering marriages is a legal requirement*.

20. The term السياسة الشرعية is used in Islamic texts to refer to laws that are not directly derived from the main sources of Islamic jurisprudence, namely the Qur'an and Prophet Muhammad's teachings. This term is equivalent to *civil/positive law*, which is developed by a government or a legal system and not necessarily based on religion. The main argument of the source text is based on the distinction between civil law and Islamic law. The translation needs to maintain this distinction and provide a definition of civil law, which is offered in the next sentence. The phrase من باب can be reconstructed using the passive voice, as in *set/mandated by*.

21. In this context, we can translate المشرع الوضعي as *legislature* because it does not trigger religious connotations.

22. The preposition لـ *for* functions as a modal of possibility in this sentence, and with negation, it can be translated as *cannot*. However, this particular use of لـ *for* suggests that possibility is based on legal rights, which we can express using the collocation *does not have the authority to*.

23. The relative clause يحل حراما أو يحرم حلالا *lit. allows something that is a sin or forbids something that is permissible* serves as a definition of the head noun phrase حكما شرعيا دينيا *a religious ruling*. Because the head noun is already modified by an adjective that specifies its nature, the definition can be left out.

24. The phrase يترتب عليه أثر قانوني is equivalent to *has legal consequences*.

25. خليفة is *caliph*, which is the classical title for the ruler of a Muslim state. The term does not apply to modern governments, but it is included in this context because it is the term used in the classical literature on the topic, which is the main source of the author's argument. Because this title is no longer relevant, the author also includes the modern equivalent, namely, الدولة *the state*, in parentheses. We can incorporate *the state* in the translation and leave out *caliph* to avoid confusion.

26. The predicate phrase هو من هذا الباب is equivalent to *within its legal powers*.

Annotated Text 7

الانقضاض وموضوع ((الليبرالية)) عند بوش وديكاكوس و((الأفنديات)) عند السادات!!

1. The preposition عند is usually translated as *at* or *have*, but neither option works in this context. We can consider *on* as in *Bush and Dukakis on Liberalism*, but this translation candidate misleadingly suggests that the text discusses Bush's and Dukakis's positions on liberalism. Because the text discusses how they used the term, we can use a possessive construction to translate عند and end up with *Bush's and Dukakis's "liberalism."* The double parentheses in the source text should be converted to double quotation marks, موضوع *topic/issue* along with the conjunction can be deleted, and a colon can be added after the first word to make the rest of title function as a subtitle.

2. The conditional relation encoded by إذا *if* is rhetorical rather than logical; it serves to establish the definition presented in the conditional clause, which is the premise of the whole text. The result clause states the next step in the rhetorical structure, namely, elaborating on the issue under discussion. Because English conditionals do not encode this rhetorical function, we can leave it out and start the translation with the definition. We also need to use the present tense in the definition because the perfective aspect is used in the source text only for grammatical reasons.

3. In this particular context, the event nominal الانقضاض *pouncing* is used as a genre-specific term that describes preemption in discourse, in which one interlocutor hijacks the meaning of a word. We can translate the whole phrase as *preemption is a discourse phenomenon/strategy* followed by the definition.

4. The nouns حرفية and جزئية are derived from the adjectives حرفي *literal* and جزئي *partial*. The English counterparts *literality* and *partiality* are not optimal because *literality* is not a very common word, whereas *partiality* is a false equivalent; it has to do with bias rather than being a part of something. We can use substitution to get *literal or particular aspects of meaning while ignoring the context.*

5. من المهم means *it is important*. However, starting the new sentence this way disrupts the rhetorical structure of the text because it is not clear how this sentence relates to the previous one after eliminating the conditional relation. We might need major reconstruction here to explicitly

state this relation. For example, we can add *in order to understand how preemption applies to the term "liberalism," it is important to*.

6. Here, المصطلح *the term* refers to "liberalism," which is mentioned in the title. We can either use the possessive pronoun *its*, if *liberalism* is used in the beginning of the sentence, or translate المصطلح as *liberalism* to avoid confusion.

7. The phrase حدث من أطرف الأحداث means *an event that is one of the most interesting events*, which can be revised as *one of the most interesting events*. However, this use of the superlative is rather odd in this context. We are better off leaving out the superlative construction to end up with *an interesting story*.

8. The relative pronoun حيث means *where*, but in this context it is functionally equivalent to *when* because it locates the event described in the following clause as taking place within the duration of the event described in the preceding clause. We can also apply deletion and start a new sentence.

9. We need scare quotation marks here.

10. We can leave out the adverbial phrase أثناء حملته *during his campaign* to avoid repetition or substitute it with *in his speeches*.

11. We can translate كان يقول as *kept saying* to make sure the translation maintains the repeated action interpretation. As for أنا لست ليبراليا *I am not a liberal*, we can translate it word for word and add quotation marks, or we can reconstruct it as reported speech and change temporal references accordingly, as in *kept saying he was not a liberal* or *kept denying he was a liberal*. Note that the following modifier phrase is in parentheses because it is not part of what Dukakis said.

12. In this context, بالمعنى is equivalent to *in the sense*.

13. The verb يدفع *push* in يدفع عن نفسه تهمة *lit. push an accusation away from himself* is used figuratively to mean *fend off an accusation* or *defend himself*.

14. The phrase دخل إلى حيز الوجود والاستعمال اللغوي *lit. entered into the space of existence and linguistic usage* can be translated as *came into usage*.

15. We can apply lexical substitution to translate قائلا إنه *lit. saying that he is* as *calling him* because the word "liberal" is used in the context as an accusation rather than a statement.

16. The predicate phrase هو سياق *it is a context* repeats the subject phrase, and therefore, we can delete it to avoid redundancy.

17. The relative clause فرضه أحد المحافظين الأقوياء (بوش) *a strong conservative, Bush, imposed it* modifies the head noun سياق *context*. In addition

to switching the order of the subject and the verb, we need to change the order of *Bush* and the appositive phrase. These strategies give us *a context that Bush, a strong conservative, imposed*. However, this clause is followed by another relative clause modifying the noun *Bush*, resulting in having the verb *imposed* separating the noun *Bush* from its modifying relative clause. To resolve this issue, we can use the passive voice, as in *a context imposed by Bush, a strong conservative, who*. Note that we already deleted the predicate phrase هو سياق *it is context*; but this is not a problem, because the preceding clause is also a relative clause modifying the same noun. We end up with *the context, which, . . . was imposed by Bush, a strong conservative, who.*

18. This relative clause has two conjoined verb phrases. The first one, namely, يعارض إباحة الإجهاض *opposes allowing abortion*, can be morphologically repackaged and moved to the appositive phrase in the previous clause, as in *was imposed by Bush, an antiabortion strong conservative*. This way, we avoid having too many relative clauses in the same sentence.

19. Having a sentence in the complement position after the adverbial phrase بدلا من *instead of* constitutes a structural gap that can be resolved by using the gerund form of the verb, deleting the subject, and spelling it out in the next clause, as in *instead of repeating this story in every speech, Bush decided to focus on the word "liberal."*

20. The term أفندي was a personal title given to educated middle-class bureaucrats in Egypt. It was officially eliminated in 1952, but continued to be used an honorific title equivalent to *Mr.* or *Sir*. Transliterating the title would not help our readers understand its connotations, whereas trying to explain how Anwar el-Sadat used it would require incorporating much additional information. One solution would be to apply cultural approximation and use a term that is familiar to the expected readers, such as *bourgeoisie*. Of course, this term is inaccurate in this context, but it has the connotations that Sadat wanted to misleadingly associate with members of the opposition.

21. The conditional relation in this sentence is rhetorical rather than logical. The conditional clause serves as a conclusion for the Bush–Dukakis example, whereas the result clause functions as the introduction to the next segment of the text. We can delete the conditional marker and use the result clause as the beginning of a new paragraph. We can also present the conditional clause before the sentence about Sadat to keep the rhetorical structure clear.

22. تركت بصماتها *lit. left its finger prints* is an idiom that is functionally equivalent to *left its mark*.

23. التعليم غير الحرفي is *liberal education*; but in this context, it is used to define the English phrase. We can either delete the whole clause or translate this phrase word for word as *nonvocational education* to maintain its function as a definition.

24. الأمر *lit. the matter* is a placeholder, a definite noun that allows for the incorporation of the relative clause starting with الذي *which*. We can leave it out and start a new sentence starting with the referent of the relative pronoun, as in *This type of education*.

25. The noun المفكرين *the two thinkers/intellectuals* is needed in the Arabic text to introduce John Locke and Thomas Hobbes. We can leave it out in the translation and use only the names.

Annotated Text 8

الشريعة الإسلامية والموقف من الديموقراطية والمجتمع المدني عام
١٩٨٥–١٩٨٣

1. نظام مايو is a proper noun—*the May Regime*—which came to power under the leadership of Gafar Numeri in 1956 through a military coup; but the possessive phrase مصالحة نظام مايو *the May Regime reconciliation* is not a name. We can paraphrase it as *the national reconciliation initiated by the May Regime*, in which the possessive phrase is reconstructed using the passive voice in a reduced relative clause. This way we keep the reconciliation in the prominence position within the phrase and provide the necessary background information.

2. One way of translating the relative clause التي دخلت المصالحة *lit. which entered the reconciliation* is to apply lexical substitution while reconstructing the whole structure as an adjectival phrase, as in *the participating parties*. This also helps us avoid the ambiguity of *other*, which would suggest that the Sudanese Muslim Brotherhood participated in the reconciliation.

3. حزب الأمة is *the Ummah Party*. The prepositional phrase بقيادة *lit. with the leadership of* can be translated as *under the leadership of* or *led by*.

4. We need to do some background research to incorporate additional information that would facilitate comprehension—for example, *Sharif Hussein Al-Hindi, exiled leader of the Democratic Unionist Party*.

5. The possessive noun phrase قبول الأحزاب *the acceptance of the parties* needs to be reconstructed as a new clause, as in *the irony is that the major traditional parties accepted.*

6. The phrase صيغة الحزب الواحد *lit. the one-party format* can be translated as *single-party rule.* The phrase أو التنظيم الواحد provides a synonymous term that can be left out.

7. We can apply lexical substitution and reconstruction to translate ليس بسبب إلغائه الديموقراطية والتعدد الحزبي as *not because it suspended democracy and multiparty rule.*

8. In this context, the preposition قبل *before* has a rhetorical function; it encodes priority, rather than the semantic function of temporal sequence. We can translate it using the frozen expression *let alone.*

9. The proper noun الاتحاد الاشتراكي is *the Socialist Union.*

10. وجود is *presence* or *existence.* We can leave it out to avoid the redundancy of *in addition to the existence/presence of the national security laws.*

11. We can translate the modifier phrase المقيدة للحريات *lit. freedom restricting* as the relative clause *that curtail civil liberties.*

12. The topicalized quantified phrase كل ذلك *all of this* is inside the scope of the negation marker لم, and therefore, it is functionally equivalent to *none of this.*

13. The idiomatic phrase عقبة في سبيل التعاون *lit. an obstacle in the road /way of cooperation* can be rephrased as *stopped these parties from cooperating.*

14. The relative clause الذي ظهر في السنوات الأخيرة *lit. which appeared in the past few years* is ambiguous. It can modify التوجه الإسلامي *the Islamist orientation* or النظام *the regime.* The context strongly supports the former interpretation, which requires structuring the translation in a way that does not separate the relative clause from the noun it modifies—for example, *the regime's Islamist orientation, which emerged in the past few years.*

15. The relative clause in الذي عبر عنه الصادق المهدي *lit. which Al-Sadiq Al-Mahdy expressed* modifies with the demonstrative phrase هذا الموقف *this position.* However, there are two structurally ambiguous prepositional phrases, namely, باعتباره بداية المصالحة and في لقاء بورتسودان, which can modify the verb in the main clause (يقول) or the one in the relative clause (عبر). The context makes it clear that these phrases modify the verb in relative clause, but we need to make sure this ambiguity does not affect

the translation. We can achieve this goal by changing the order of the prepositional phrases, which also helps us keep the verb and its complement together. We can also apply lexical substitution and translate عبر عنه as *described* rather than *expressed*. These strategies give us *this position, which Al-Sadiq Al-Mahdy described as a "starting point for reconciliation" at the Port Sudan meeting*.

16. The adverbial phrase وكعادته *and as it is his habit* is functionally equivalent to *as usual*.

17. The clause أن يرمي بطعمه لما حسب صيدا ثمينا *lit. to throw his bait when he thought there was a good catch* is an idiom used to describe Numeri as a shrewd politician who uses religion to gain power. The idiom is transparent enough to include in the translation, but we can also use a functionally equivalent fishing idiom, such as *bait and switch*.

18. The clause أن ينتقص ذلك شيئا من إسلامه أو إسلامية أهل السودان is equivalent to *detracting from his faith or that of the Sudanese people*.

19. The interaction of negation and quantification (encoded by إلا *except*) results in a construction that means *all Mr. Al-Sadiq did was*, which can be rephrased as *Mr. Al-Sadiq's only response was*.

20. The Classical Arabic idiom أثلج صدرنا *lit. cooled our chests*, along with the first-person plural reference, makes this sentence highly formal. We might have to lose the figurative language to maintain the formal tone of the source sentence, as in *we are pleased*.

21. The preposition على *on* functions as a modal of necessity in this context, whereas the perfective verb كان sets time reference to the past. The phrase كان على السيد الصادق is functionally equivalent to *Mr. Al-Sadiq had to*.

22. The Form II causative verb يسبب does not mean *cause* in this context. Rather, it means *to present/provide reasons*, which is the same thing as يبرر *justify*. We can leave out this verb to avoid redundancy. The object phrase قبوله المصالحة *lit. his acceptance of the reconciliation* can be reconstructed using ellipses to get *had to justify/explain why he accepted reconciliation*.

23. This phrase repeats the same information presented in the previous clause; therefore, we can delete it. The only additional information is the year, which we can incorporate in the previous clause, as in *until 1976, a year before the reconciliation*.

24. The verb انتفت *was negated* constitutes a functional gap, but it lexically entails the meaning of negation. Therefore, we can translate it as *are no longer relevant*.

25. الإرادة السودانية الذاتية is *Sudanese sovereignty.*

26. This noun phrase needs to be translated as a full sentence to have a parallel structure with the previous sentence, as in *It is necessary to coordinate national efforts.*

Annotated Text 9

العرب وحوار الثقافة والتقانة

يا له من مخاض عسير!! نهايات ومابعديات

1. The semantically noncompositional frozen expression يا له من marks exclamatory sentences, as in *what a painful birth,* but these constructions are not common in English titles, especially when there is a subtitle. We can reduce the exclamatory sentence to a simple noun phrase, such as *the birth pains,* followed by a colon and the subtitle.

2. The compound مابعديات is made up of the relative pronoun ما *which,* the preposition بعد *after,* the attributive adjective suffix ـي, and the feminine plural suffix. The word is plural because it refers to other compounds with ما بعد, such as ما بعد الحداثة *postmodernism* and ما بعد الاستعمارية *postcolonialism.* This expression is equivalent to *post- isms.*

3. The verb يكون *be* is used here as an intransitive verb without a complement. Together with the discourse marker prefix ـل, we have a construction that means *let the talk of the end be* (as in *come into being*), but *let be* is not a functional equivalent in this context. We can reconstruct the sentence as *let's talk about the end.* The problem now is that the phrase *the end* is vague (the end of what?). We can avoid this issue by substituting *end* with *conclusion,* as in *let us start with the conclusion.*

4. The existential marker ثمة is equivalent to *there is,* whereas ليس encodes sentential negation. Together, they are equivalent to *there is no* or *there is not.* This clause has two prepositional phrases: في ذلك *in that,* and مع عصرنا *with our time.* The first prepositional phrase is a modifier in which the demonstrative ذلك *that* refers to the previous sentence (starting with the conclusion). The second one is a complement specifying the second element in the hypothesized contradiction. Therefore, this clause literally means *there is no contradiction in that (starting with conclusions) with our time,* which we can revise as *which is not a contradiction in our time.*

5. The figurative phrase يلهث فيه قادمه يكاد يلحق بسابقه is a relative clause with an embedded clause, and it involves various lexical and structural

gaps, including the verb يكاد *almost* and the active participles with the possessive pronouns. In a case like this, it is more productive to approach the phrase holistically rather than getting stuck in the details. The active participles قادم *that which is coming* and سابق *that which precedes* are used in a generic way to refer to the past and the future. Therefore, we use temporal domain expressions, as in *a time where the future quickly becomes past.*

6. مرأى is a locative noun derived from the verb رأى *see*; therefore, it is equivalent to *vantage point*. However, the phrase على مرأى من بدايتها *lit. from the vantage points of their beginnings* is used figuratively. It represents time as space where ideas and systems can be seen collapsing from a position that is very close to the point in time when they start. In other words, the phrase is equivalent to *as soon as they appear.*

7. أوج is an archaic borrowing from Persian that means *the highest point*, and it is used with the preposition في *in* to form a superlative open collocation. The phrase في أوج جدتها literally means *at the highest of its newness*, which we can reduce to *new* because candidate collocations such as *brand new* and *spic and span* do not fit in this context. We can make other changes to maintain the superlative interpretation, as in *new things immediately become outdated.*

8. The phrase تمرير قراراتها literally means *passing its resolutions/decisions*, but this is not what it means in this context because power does not propose resolutions that pass through a voting process. Rather, the passing figure of speech has to do with the ability to impose changes on the world. We can apply lexical substitution and translate this phrase as *exercising its will*. Because this phrase is conjoined to others, it needs to have the same grammatical structure. If we translate لخدمة أغراضها وتبرير ممارستها as *to serve its purposes/interests and justify its practices*, we need to translate تمرير قراراتها using the infinitive form, as in *to exercise its will.*

9. The preposition بعد *after* encodes the temporal relation of sequence, but there is a problem using *after* to connect two sentences that describe present states. The clause المعلومات مال *information is money* has a present-tense interpretation by default, whereas the perfective inchoative verb أصبح has a present simple or perfect interpretation. To avoid a translation such as *information is money after it is/has become a developmental resource*, we can translate بعد using a conjunction that encodes the causal relation expressed by the temporal sequence, as in

information is money, as it has become a developmental resource. A better solution is to add a sentential adverb, as in *information is money, now that it has become a developmental resource.*

10. The verb أوشك constitutes a lexical gap, but this is not a complicated issue because we can translate it as *almost*. The problem is the verb يكون, which is often translated as *be*, as in *money is almost data*. In this context, يكون is an inchoative verb that means *become* rather than *be*. The phrase أوشك أن يكون is equivalent to *has almost become/turned into*.

11. The adjectival phrase المعرفي–المعلوماتي is made up of two attributive adjectives, one derived from معرفة *knowledge* and one derived from معلومات *information*. Both adjectives have English equivalents, namely, *epistemic* and *informatic* (rather than *informational*). The problem is that when Arabic adjectives are separated by a hyphen, they are functionally equivalent to English blends, but *epistemo-informatic* is not a common expression. More important, these adjectives do not describe the referent of the head noun, التضاد *contrast*, but the elements that are in *contrast*. In other words, the contrast is between knowledge and information, or, more specifically, data. This issue can be resolved by translating these adjectives as nouns while reconstructing the phrase as *the knowledge /data dichotomy*.

12. The sentence اقتربت الثقافة من أن تصبح هي علم المستقبل describes a figurative situation in which time is represented as space with culture moving closer to a point where it becomes a science. The main function of the metaphor is a semantic one that has to do with temporal structure. We do not need this metaphor in the translation because the English present progressive entails all of its temporal features, as in *culture is becoming the science of the future.*

13. يطوي في عباءته is an idiom that literally means *folds in its cloak*. The function of this idiomatic expression is to describe a hierarchical structure with the referent of the subject phrase at the top. In this particular context, we can translate the whole idiom as *subsume, incorporate,* or another equivalent.

14. The sentence دعنا نستطرد في حديث الأضداد *let us elaborate on the contradictions issue* states the rhetorical function of the second paragraph. We have two options here. We can leave it out completely, or we can convert it into an adverbial phrase, such as *in the same vein*. The final translation will depend on what we do with the next sentence, which presents the thesis statement of this paragraph. The second sentence, which is an

exclamation, can be translated as a statement with a sentential adverb of emphasis, such as *indeed*, to make up for the loss of the exclamatory structure. To avoid having two sentential adverbs, we can go with the deletion option for the first sentence.

15. مثلما is a sentential conjunction that means *just like*. The problem here is that we expect the new information to precede this conjunction, which is why the close translation *younger generations learn from older generations, just like older generations learn from younger generations* is rather odd. We can improve the translation by reversing the order of the conjoined clauses, but the translation still involves some repetition, which we can avoid by reducing it to a single clause, as in *younger and older generations learn from each other.*

16. The prepositional phrase بمعدل يفوق في سرعته معدل اكتسابه لها and the embedded relative clause along with its modifiers form an adverbial structure that modifies the verb تتهالك. Instead of translating it as *at a rate that exceeds the rate of their acquiring it*, we can simplify the structure, using only a comparative phrase with a passive verb, as in *because knowledge is outdated faster than it can be acquired.*

17. *Michel Foucault's "reverse history."*

18. The conjunction و *and* here has the discourse function of encoding contrast with the preceding negated clause. This function is expressed in English with the contrastive *but*. Alternatively, we can express this contrast by starting a new sentence with the sentential adverb *rather* and an *it*-cleft construction, as in *Rather, it is the present that gives meaning to the past.*

19. In this context, the adverbial حتى *until* encodes the discourse function of contrasting degree rather than temporal structure, and therefore, it is functionally equivalent to the *so . . . that* construction or the adverbial phrase *to the point*. جان بودليار is *Jean Baudrillard.*

20. The philosophical term طابع المكان is *the concept of space.*

21. The phrase الصغير متناهي الصغر is made up of a generic adjective الصغير *that which is small* and the modifying collocation متناهي الصغر *very small*, which would sound quite redundant in English. The whole phrase can be translated using a superlative construction, such as *the smallest of things*, which we can substitute with *atoms and particles*, depending on what we do with the rest of the sentence.

22. جزيئات البيولوجيا الجزيئية can be morphologically packaged as *bioparticles.*

23. This phrase is equivalent to *the 0/1 dichotomy.*

24. The adjectival frozen expression الساحقة الماحقة is made up of two words that sound the same except for the first stem consonant, a construction that adds emphasis. In this particular context, the phrase is equivalent to *all-powerful*.

25. The problem in this sentence has to do with the interaction between negation and quantification, encoded in the adverbial إلا *except*. This issue can be resolved by leaving out both negation and quantification, while changing the translation to the passive voice to get *economic growth matched only by the increase/surge in poverty*.

26. The adjective محتملة *possible* expresses possibility, but so does the modal ربما *may*. Having two modals of possibility would be redundant in the translation. The verb يقدم means *to take a step toward*, which does not necessarily mean that the action is complete. To avoid the possibility of changing this meaning, we can reconstruct this phrase using the passive *by*, as in *to avoid a possible nuclear attack by the Soviet enemy*.

27. وليدة *infant* is used in this context metaphorically to describe the relation between the internet and the Cold War: The internet is an outcome of the Cold War. We can maintain the figurative language using expressions such as *the prodigy of the Cold War* or *the baby of the Cold War*, but each of these expressions adds new elements of meaning that are not expressed in the source text. Alternatively, we can apply literalization to get *the internet, a product of the Cold War*. This phrase corresponds to the complement of the verb يروجون *promote*. The issue now is that the subject of this verb is vague because it is not clear who "they" are. To avoid vagueness while maintaining "the internet" in the topic position, we can use the passive voice, as in *here is the internet, a product of the Cold War, promoted as*.

28. The classical phrase ونشر الوفاق والوئام بين الأنام does not add much to the content of the text because it is a paraphrase of the previous phrase. However, it hints to the author's sarcasm while adding stylistically motivated features, such as alliteration and rhyme. This whole phrase can be left out, and sarcasm can be preserved by adding *love* to the preceding phrase to get *love and peace*.

29. The phrase هوايتها الأبدية *lit. its eternal hobby* can be reconstructed as *its age-old habit*.

30. The noun الأمر *the matter* is a placeholder that provides the grammatical structure needed to add the relative clause, starting with الذي *which*. This is a structural gap that can be dealt with by deleting the placeholder

along with the relative pronoun, and starting a new sentence with *it seems as though*.

31. The plural adjectives كبار *big* and صغار *small* are used here as nouns in a fashion similar to *the rich* and *the poor*. Because we cannot translate them as *the big* and *the small*, we can apply lexical substitution, as in *the powerful players in our world are exporting their conflicts to the powerless*.

32. تتبدى is a reflexive verb derived from يبدو *appear*, and it is equivalent to *manifest itself*. In this sentence, the verb تتبدى is used in a superlative construction that can be translated using *most*, as in *manifest itself most clearly*.

Appendixes

Arabic Abbreviations

Ms./Mr.	أستاذة/أستاذ	أ
Associated Press (AP)	أسوشيتد برس	أ ب
Professor (Prof.)	أستاذ دكتور	أ د
Middle East News Agency (MENA)	وكالة أنباء الشرق الأوسط	أ ش أ
United Arab Emirates (UAE)	الإمارات العربية المتحدة	إ ع م
Agence France-Presse (AFP)	وكالة الأنباء الفرنسية	أ ف ب
etcetera (etc.)	إلى آخره	إلخ
L'Union du Maghreb Arabe (UMA)	اتحاد المغرب العربي	ا م ع
the end/finished	انتهى	ا هـ
telephone (tel.)	تليفون	ت
died [followed by the date of death]	توفي	ت
Greenwich Mean Time (GMT)	توقيت غرينتش	ت غ
local time (LT)	توقيت محلي	ت م
Agence Tunis Afrique Presse (TAP)	وكالة تونس إفريقيا للأنباء	تاب
International Standard Book Number (ISBN)	الترقيم الدولي الموحد للكتاب	تدمك
a second (sec.)	ثانية	ث
gram (g)	جرام	ج
volume (vol.)	جزء	ج
pound [currency]	جنيه	ج
Sudanese pound [currency]	جنيه سوداني	ج س
United Arab Republic (UAR)	الجمهورية العربية المتحدة	ج ع م
Arab Republic of Egypt (ARE)	جمهورية مصر العربية	ج م ع
gram (g)	جرام	جم

Egyptian pound [currency]	جنيه مصري	جم
Hamas (Islamic Resistance Movement)	حركة المقاومة الإسلامية	حماس
versus [sports] (vs.)	خصم	خ
doctor (Dr.)	دكتور	د
minute (min.)	دقيقة	د
Emirati dirham [currency]	درهم إماراتي	د ا
Jordanian dinar [currency]	دينار أردني	د ا
Bahraini dinar [currency]	دينار بحريني	د ب
Tunisian dinar [currency]	دينار تونسي	د ت
Algerian dinar [currency]	دينار جزائري	د ج
Iraqi dinar [currency]	دينار عراقي	د ع
Kuwaiti dinar [currency]	دينار كويتي	د ك
Libyan dinar [currency]	دينار ليبي	د ل
Moroccan dirham [currency]	درهم مغربي	د م
zip code	رمز بريدي	ر ب
Saudi riyal [currency]	ريال سعودي	ر س
Omani riyal [currency]	ريال عماني	ر ع
Qatari riyal [currency]	ريال قطري	ر ق
Yemeni riyal [currency]	ريال يمني	ر ي
International Standard Book Number (ISBN)	الرقم الدولي الموحد للكتاب	ردمك
hour (hr.)	ساعة	س
Syrian Arab News Agency (SANA)	الوكالة العربية السورية للأنباء	سانا
Business registration number	سجل تجاري	س ت
Questions and answers (Q&A)	سؤال وجواب	س ج
centimeter (cm.)	سنتيمتر	سم
Sudan News Agency (SUNA)	وكالة السودان للأنباء	سونا
street (st.)	شارع	ش
Limited liability company (LLC)	شركة ذات مسؤولية محدودة	ش ذ م م
publicly traded company	شركة مساهمة	ش م
ante meridien (a.m.)	صباحا	ص
page (P.)	صفحة	ص
Peace be upon him (PBUH)	صلى الله عليه وسلم	ص
carbon copy [CC in business letters and emails]	صورة	ص
post box (P.O. box)	صندوق بريد	ص ب
Peace be upon him (PBUH)	صلى الله عليه وسلم	صلعم
sales tax	ضريبة مبيعات	ض م

Federation of Arab News Agencies (FANA)	اتحاد وكالات الأنباء العربية	فانا
Fatah (Palestinian Liberation Movement)	حركة تحرير فلسطين	فتح
Before Christ (BC)	قبل الميلاد	ق م
Qatar News Agency (QNA)	وكالة الأنباء القطرية	قنا
kilogram (kg.)	كيلو جرام	كجم
kilogram (kg.)	كيلو غرام	كغم
kilogram (kg.)	كيلو جرام	كلج
kilogram (kg.)	كيلو غرام	كلغ
kilometer (km.)	كيلومتر	كلم
kilometer (km.)	كيلومتر	كم
Kuwait News Agency (KUNA)	وكالة الأنباء الكويتية	كونا
liter	لتر	ل
Syrian lira (SYP)	ليرة سورية	ل س
Lebanese lira (LL)	ليرة لبنانية	ل ل
post meridien (p.m.)	مساء	م
meter	متر	م
Engineer [title/term of address]	مهندس	م
subject [in business letters]	موضوع	م
Anno Domini (AD)	ميلادية	م
milligram (mg.)	ملليجرام	ملجم
milliliter (ml.)	ملليلتر	مل
millimeter (mm.)	ملليمتر	ملم
millimeter (mm.)	ملليمتر	مم
Anno Hijrah (AH)	هجرية	هـ
telephone (tel.)	هاتف	هـ
Algerian News Agency	وكالة الأنباء الجزائرية	وأج
Saudi Press Agency	وكالة الأنباء السعودية	واس
Emirates News Agency	وكالة أنباء الإمارات	وام
Palestine News and Information Agency (WAFA)	وكالة الأنباء والمعلومات الفلسطينية	وفا
Maghreb Arabe Presse (MAP)	وكالة المغرب العربي للأنباء	ومع

Conjunctive Frozen Expressions

on the other hand	على الجانب الآخر
in contrast	على النقيض
provided/on condition	على أن
anyway	على كل حال
anyway	على كل
nevertheless	غير أنه
in addition	فضلا عن هذا
meanwhile	في تلك الأثناء
whereas	في حين
on the other hand	في مقابل ذلك
by the same token	قس على ذلك
especially	لا سيما
no sooner . . . than	لم يكد . . . حتى
since, because	لما كان
not only . . . but also	ليس فحسب . . . بل
no sooner . . . than	ما أن . . . حتى
no sooner . . . than	ما كاد . . . حتى
no sooner . . . than	ما لبث حتى
even though	مع أن
yet, however	مع ذلك/هذا
therefore, consequently	من ثم

last but not least	أخيرا وليس آخرا
in addition, moreover	إضافة إلى ذلك
nevertheless	إلا أن
besides	إلى جانب هذا
as for	أما عن
consequently	بالتالي
even though	بالرغم من
instead of	بدلا من
thus	بذلك
regardless of, disregarding	بصرف النظر عن
in other words	بعبارة أخرى
regardless of, disregarding	بغض النظر
thanks to, due to	بفضل
since	بما أن
as soon as	بمجرد أن
accordingly	بناء على ذلك
nevertheless	بيد أن
since	حيث إن
whether	سواء أكان
additionally, moreover	علاوة على ذلك

nevertheless	مهما يكن من أمر	on one hand	من ناحية
nevertheless	مهما يكن	on the other hand	من ناحية أخرى
therefore	نظرا لذلك	accordingly, therefore	من هذا المنطلق
accordingly	وعليه	hence, therefore	من هنا

Adverbial Frozen Expressions

indefinitely	إلى أبد الآبدين
indefinitely	إلى أجل غير مسمى
etcetera	إلى آخره
to a large extent	إلى حد كبير
to some extent	إلى حد ما
until further notice	إلى حين إشعار آخر
infinitely, indefinitely	إلى ما لا نهاية
as they come, in order	أولا بأول
first and foremost	أولا وأخيرا
first and foremost	أولا وقبل أي شيء
no matter who/what	أيا كان
retroactively	بأثر رجعي
first and foremost	بادئ ذي بدء
in its entirety	بأسره
verbatim, to the letter	بالحرف الواحد
hardly, barely	بالكاد
at all, never/ever	بالمرة
in any shape or form	بأي شكل من الأشكال

down to the last detail	بحذافيره
somehow or other	بشكل أو بآخر
to put it bluntly	بصريح العبارة
somehow or other	بطريقة أو بأخرى
including	بما في ذلك
over night	بين عشية وضحاها
every now and then	بين فنية وأخرى
sometimes . . . and at other times	تارة . . . وتارة أخرى
one after another	تلو أخرى/الأخرى
completely, at all	جملة وتفصيلا
side by side	جنبا إلى جنب
until further notice	حتى إشعار آخر
back and forth, round trip	ذهابا وإيابا
upside down	رأسا على عقب
slowly	رويدا رويدا
in large groups	زرافات زرافات
in groups and as individuals	زرافات ووحدانا

(memorize) by heart	عن ظهر قلب	equally	سواء بسواء
instead of, in lieu of	عوضا عن	whether we like it or not	شئنا أم أبينا
let alone, not to mention	فما بالك بـ	similarly to, just like	شأنه شأن
immediately	في التو واللحظة	gradually	شيئا فشيئا
in the first place	في المقام الأول	year round, all the time	صيف شتاء
in its own right	في حد ذاتها	sooner or later	عاجلا أو آجلا
over night	في ليلة وضحاها	in cash	عدا ونقدا
as it is the case	كما هو الحال	at all, never, ever, whatsoever	على الإطلاق
at will	كيفما ومتى شاء	respectively, consecutively	على التوالي
no more and no less	لا أكثر ولا أقل	publicly	على الملأ
God forbid	لا سمح الله	equally	على حد سواء
inevitably	لا محالة	as far as I know	على حد علمي
in and of itself	لذاته وبذاته	according to, quoting	على حد قول
perhaps (low probability)	لعل وعسى	publicly	على رؤوس الأشهاد
unless (low possibility)	اللهم إذا	to name only a few	على سبيل المثال لا الحصر
except for	اللهم إلا	for example	على سبيل المثال
if necessary	لو لزم الأمر	in other news	على صعيد آخر
all the time	ليل نهار	all along, all the time	على طول الخط
pros and cons, one's rights and obligations	ما له وما عليه	as is	على علاته
taking in consideration	مع الأخذ بعين الاعتبار	similar to	على غرار
		by the way	على فكرة
from A to Z	من الألف إلى الياء	seriously	على محمل الجد
from now on	من الآن فصاعدا	around the clock	على مدار الساعة
on the other hand	من الناحية الأخرى	along the same lines	على نفس المنوال
from time to time	من آن لآخر	along the same lines	على نفس الوتيرة
out of	من باب	along these lines	على هذا النحو
all over again, anew	من جديد		

face to face	وجها لوجه	from time to time	من حين لآخر
so be it	وليكن ما يكون	in vain	من دون طائل
and so on and so forth	وهكذا دواليك	let alone, not to mention	ناهيك عن
and so on and so forth	وهلم جرا	and vice versa	والعكس بالعكس
		and vice versa	والعكس صحيح

Exocentric Compounds

general mobilization	التعبئة العامة	godfather	الأب الروحي
passport	جواز سفر	martial laws	أحكام عرفية
curiosity	حب استطلاع	latest fashion	آخر صيحة
vote of no confidence	حجب الثقة	pseudonym	اسم حركي
cornerstone	حجر الزاوية	shooting	إطلاق نار
quarantine	حجر صحي	house arrest	إقامة جبرية
minimum of subsistence	حد الكفاف	the canons of literature	أمهات الكتب
war of attrition	حرب استنزاف	secretary general	الأمين العام
university campus	الحرم الجامعي	executive director	أمين سر
vicious circle	حلقة مفرغة	police officer	أمين شرطة
direction	خط سير	treasurer	أمين صندوق
disappointment	خيبة أمل	librarian	أمين مكتبة
feasibility study	دراسة جدوى	by oneself	بأم عين
phonebook	دليل الهاتف/التليفون	patent	براءة اختراع
		all of them	بكرة أبيهم
astronaut	رائد فضاء	humans	بني آدم
money capital	رأس المال	infrastructure	البنية التحتية
homemaker	ربة منزل	hibernation	البيات الشتوي
the average person	رجل الشارع	the crux of the matter	بيت القصيد
		settling scores	تصفية حسابات

knockout	الضربة القاضية	reaction	رد فعل
traitors, fifth column	الطابور الخامس	doctoral dissertation	رسالة دكتوراه
shrines	العتبات المقدسة	record (unsurpassed measurement)	رقم قياسي
mastermind	العقل/الرأس المدبر		
foreign currency	عملة صعبة		
spare part	قطعة غيار	national anthem	السلام الوطني
rainbow	قوس قزح	menopause	سن اليأس
password	كلمة سر	misunderstanding	سوء تفاهم
situation, condition	لسان حال	the masses of the public	السواد الأعظم
the Arabic language	لغة الضاد	resume, curriculum vitae	سيرة ذاتية
dormitories	المدينة الجامعية	resume, curriculum vitae	سيرة مهنية
career	مستقبل مهني	honeymoon	شهر العسل
trustworthy	موضع ثقة	employer	صاحب العمل
stereotype	نظرة نمطية	tabloids	الصحف الصفراء
point of view, perspective	وجهة نظر	criminal record	صحيفة سوابق
heir	ولي العهد	the crux of the matter	صلب الموضوع

Noun–Adjective Collocations

APPENDIX

E

Noun–Adjective Collocations

loud explosion	انفجار مدوي	bright, brilliant white	أبيض ناصع
considerable importance	أهمية كبيرة	brutal occupation	احتلال غاشم
biting/severe cold	برد قارس	strong will	إرادة حديدية
open defiance	تحد سافر/صارخ	sharp increase	ارتفاع حاد
in-depth analysis	تحليل عميق	serious crisis	أزمة حادة
minor modifications	تعديلات طفيفة	warm welcome	استقبال حار
radical change	تغيير جذري	serious injury	إصابة بالغة
notable progress	تقدم ملحوظ	extensive damage	أضرار جسيمة
false accusation	تهمة ملفقة	heavy responsibilities	أعباء جسيمة
sincere repentance	توبة نصوحة	massive numbers	أعداد هائلة
to be filthy rich	ثراء فاحش	overwhelming majority	أغلبية ساحقة
exuberant price	ثمن باهظ	self-sufficiency	اكتفاء ذاتي
enormous wealth	ثروة طائلة	overwhelming majority	أكثرية ساحقة
futile debate	جدل عقيم	severe pain	آلام مبرحة
heinous crime	جريمة نكراء	heavy rain	أمطار غزيرة
breathtaking beauty	جمال أخاذ	giant waves	أمواج عاتية
overflowing crowd	جمع غفير	crashing waves	أمواج متلاطمة
all-out effort	جهد جهيد	free and fair elections	انتخابات حرة ونزيهة
painstaking efforts	جهود مضنية		
satisfying answer	جواب شافي		

the current month	الشهر الجاري
a barren desert	صحراء جرداء
a barren desert	صحراء قاحلة
mere coincidence	صدفة محضة
close friend	صديق حميم
bitter conflict	صراع مرير
great difficulty	صعوبة بالغة
dead silence	صمت مطبق
fatal blow	ضربة قاتلة
knockout	ضربة قاضية
honorable guest	ضيف كريم
blind obedience	طاعة عمياء
extenuating circumstances	ظروف قاهرة
pitch dark	ظلام دامس
pitch dark	ظلام كاحل
severe storm	عاصفة هوجاء
deep-rooted enmity	عداوة متأصلة
arch enemy	عدو لدود
blatant aggression	عدوان غاشم
iron will	عزيمة صلبة
deep relationship	علاقة وطيدة
ancient times	العهود السحيقة
disastrous consequences	عواقب وخيمة
dreamy eyes	عيون ناعسة
utter stupidity	غباء مستحكم
overwhelming joy	فرحة غامرة
miserable failure	فشل ذريع
abject poverty	فقر مدقع
overwhelming victory	فوز ساحق
utter chaos	فوضى عارمة
thorny issue	قضية شائكة
slender physique	قوام ممشوق
brute force	قوة غاشمة

dire need	حاجة ماسة
pressing need	حاجة ملحة
impenetrable barrier	حاجز منيع
lame excuse	حجة واهية
horrible accident	حادث مروع
massive fire	حريق هائل
naked truth	حقيقة عارية
fierce campaign (negative)	حملة شعواء
constructive dialogue	حوار بناء
comfortable life	حياة كريمة
extensive damage	خسائر فادحة
energetic steps, making strides	خطى حثيثة
colossal mistake	خطأ جسيم
grave mistake	خطأ فادح
eminent danger	خطر داهم
eloquent orator /speaker	خطيب مفوه
wild imagination	خيال جامح
unyielding defense	دفاع مستميت
open invitation	دعوة مفتوحة
irrefutable proof	دليل قاطع
massive destruction	دمار شامل
piled-up debts	ديون متراكمة
live ammunition	ذخيرة حية
sharp mind	ذهن متقد
crushing reply	رد مفحم
firm refusal	رفض قاطع
firm refusal	رفض بات
deep desire	رغبة دفينة
burning desire	رغبة ملحة
regular customer	زبون دائم
compelling reason	سبب وجيه
terrific speed	سرعة فائقة

casual observation	ملاحظة عابرة	excessive force	قوة مفرطة
bitter argument	مناقشة حادة	impending	
beautiful scenery	منظر خلاب	disaster	كارثة محققة
horrible death	موتة شنيعة	outright lie	كذب محض
resounding		nonsense	كلام فارغ
success	نجاح باهر	broken language	لغة ركيكة
urgent call	نداء عاجل	coarse/vulgar	
profuse bleeding	نزيف حاد	language	لغة سوقية
overwhelming joy	نشوة عارمة	horrible night	ليلة ليلاء
emphatic denial	نفي قاطع	desperate attempts	محاولات مستميتة
scathing criticism	نقد لاذع	incurable disease	مرض عضال
crushing defeat	هزيمة ساحقة	bright future	مستقبل زاهر
fresh air	هواء طلق	serious problem	مشكلة عويصة
permanent job	وظيفة ثابتة	fierce battle	معركة طاحنة
solemn oath	يمين غليظ	prominent position	مكانة بارزة

Verb–Object Collocations

misuse	أساء استعمال	give his opinion	أبدى رأيه
ill-treat	أساء معاملة	clear someone's	
eavesdrop	استرق السمع	name	أبرأ ذمته
overthrow a		make a deal	أبرم اتفاقا
government	أسقط حكومة	ratify a treaty	أبرم معاهدة
declare		make ineffective,	
bankruptcy	أشهر إفلاسه	diffuse	أبطل مفعول
brandish a weapon	أشهر سلاحا	give	أتاح الفرصة
set something		follow	
on fire	أضرم النار في	instructions	اتبع تعليمات
listen intently	أطرق السمع	make someone	
fire/discharge		angry	أثار حفيظة
(a weapon)	أطلق الرصاص	inflame the	
fire/discharge		conflict	أجج الصراع
(a weapon)	أطلق النار	foil an attempt	أحبط محاولة
release a statement	أطلق تصريحا	make progress	أحرز تقدما
launch a campaign	أطلق حملة	release (from jail)	أخلى سبيل
release (from jail)	أطلق سراح	clear from	
spread a rumor	أطلق شائعة	responsibility	أخلى مسئوليته
launch a missile		put out a fire	أخمد حريقا
/rocket	أطلق صاروخا	lead the discussion	أدار الحوار
let out a cry	أطلق صرخة	shed blood	أراق دم
launch an		make a mistake	ارتكب خطأ
initiative	أطلق مبادرة	commit a sin	ارتكب معصية

rehabilitate	رد اعتبار	declare war	أعلن الحرب
adjourn a session	رفع جلسة	reveal a secret	أفشى سرا
lift a siege off	رفع الحصار عن	hold a party	أقام حفلا
file a lawsuit	رفع دعوى	lay down his	
shake his belief	زعزع إيمانه	weapon	ألقى سلاحه
set a record	سجل رقما قياسيا	assume a name	انتحل اسم
score a goal	سجل هدفا	seize the	
draw blood	سحب دم	opportunity	انتهز الفرصة
pay debts	سدد ديون	violate the law	انتهك القانون
leak out the news	سرب الخبر	invade one's	
make/pass a law	سن قانونا	privacy	انتهك خصوصية
wage war	شن حربا	exert effort	بذل جهدا
launch a campaign	شن حملة	survive a crisis	تجاوز أزمة
defame	شوه سمعة	be on top of a list	تصدر قائمة
ring the bell	ضرب الجرس	play a character	تقمص شخصية
defy his parents	عق والديه	sustain losses	تكبد خسائر
pass away	فارق الحياة	assume	
defy description	فاق الوصف	responsibility	تولى مسئولية
whet one's		take pulse	جس النبض
appetite	فتح شهيته	bring disgrace	جلب العار
inflame an issue	فجر قضية	hold his breath	حبس أنفاسه
make a surprise	فجر مفاجأة	finalize the matter	حسم الأمر
break up a protest	فرق مظاهرة	achieve justice	حقق العدالة
break a contract	فسخ عقدا	make a wish	
gone mad	فقد صوابه	come true	حقق أمنية
lift a siege off	فك الحصار عن	edit a manuscript	حقق مخطوطا
decipher, break		spare the lives of	حقن دماء
a code	فك شفرة	make a wise	
take the place of	قام مقام	decision	حكم عقله
receive his salary	قبض راتبه	dissolve a political	
offer condolences	قدم التعازي	party	حل حزب
offer		replace	حل محل
congratulations	قدم التهاني	break the law	خرق القانون
render a service	قدم خدمة	breach a treaty	خرق معاهدة
file a complaint	قدم شكوى	slow down	خفف السرعة
curb, suppress	كبح جماح	break a promise	خلف وعدا
keep a secret	كتم سرا	disappoint	خيب أمل
dedicate one's life	كرس حياته	reconcile	رأب الصدع

distort the truth	مسخ الحقيقة	heed the call	لبى النداء
set aside	نحى جانبا	fulfill a wish	لبى رغبة
set a trap	نصب فخا	fulfill a request	لبى طلبا
breach a covenant	نكث عهدا	stayed at home	لزم بيته
face difficulty	واجه صعوبة	gamble	لعب القمار
criticize	وجه انتقادا	draw attention	لفت انتباه
accuse	وجه تهمة	have sex	مارس الجنس
make a plan	وضع خطة	pursue a hobby	مارس هواية
		beg	مد يده

Light Verbs

make a decision	أخذ قرارا	adopt a measure	اتخذ إجراء
take as an example	أخذ مثلا	use as an excuse	اتخذ ذريعة
take its course	أخذ مداه	make a call, contact	أجرى اتصالا
take a direction	أخذ منحى	hold a referendum	أجرى استفتاء
take a position	أخذ موقفا	hold elections	أجرى انتخابات
take a breath	أخذ نفسا	run an experiment	أجرى تجربة
take time	أخذ وقتا	hold an investigation	أجرى تحقيقا
salute	أدى التحية	make changes	أجرى تعديلات
take oath of office	أدى اليمين	perform surgery	أجرى جراحة
perform rituals	أدى مناسك	do a study	أجرى دراسة
do one's duty	أدى واجبه	hold discussions	أجرى مباحثات
render a service	أسدى خدمة	hold talks	أجرى محادثات
do a favor	أسدى معروفا	perform rituals	أجرى مراسم
give advice	أسدى نصيحة	hold negotiations	أجرى مفاوضات
give priority	أعطى الأولوية	take a rest	أخذ استراحة
put one's trust in	أعطى الثقة	take precautions	أخذ الحيطة
give the floor	أعطى الكلمة	take the initiative	أخذ المبادرة
make it possible	أعطى المجال	take one's turn	أخذ دوره
give an impression	أعطى انطباعا	take the shape/form	أخذ شكلا
pay attention	أعطى أهمية	take the shape/form	
give authority	أعطى صلاحيات	take the shape/form	أخذ صورة
yield profits/results	أعطى مردودا	get guarantees	أخذ ضمانات
yield results	أعطى نتائج		

give an example	ضرب مثلا	make a promise	أعطى وعدا
make an appointment	ضرب موعدا	greet	ألقى السلام
make an agreement	عقد اتفاقا	shed light on	ألقى الضوء على
hold a meeting	عقد اجتماعا	arrest	ألقى القبض على
pin one's hopes on	عقد الأمل على	put the blame on	ألقى اللوم على
be intent on	عقد العزم	give a speech	ألقى خطبة
be intent on	عقد النية	read/recite poetry	ألقى شعرا
forge alliances	عقد تحالفات	give a speech	ألقى كلمة
hold a session	عقد جلسة	give a lecture	ألقى محاضرة
make peace	عقد سلاما	take a look	ألقى نظرة
make a deal	عقد صفقة	give a sermon	ألقى وعظة
get married	عقد قران	catch one's breath	التقط أنفاسه
hold a conference	عقد مؤتمرا	take a picture	التقط صورة
form a court	عقد محكمة	receive treatment	تلقى العلاج
draw a comparison	عقد مقارنة	take an exam	دخل اختبارا
complete a journey	قطع رحلة	convert to Islam	دخل الإسلام
lose hope	قطع الأمل	go down in history	دخل التاريخ
cross the street	قطع الطريق	break into the market	دخل السوق
buy a ticket	قطع تذكرة	enter a competition	دخل مسابقة
go a distance	قطع شوطا	enter a competition	دخل منافسة
make an oath	قطع عهدا	fall victim	سقط ضحية
cover a distance	قطع مسافة	fall prey	سقط فريسة
die	لقي حتفه	fortune telling	ضرب الودع
die	لقي مصرعه	lay siege	ضرب حصارا
		break a record	ضرب رقما قياسيا
		seal off (for security reasons)	ضرب طوقا أمنيا

Common Expressions in Business Correspondence

Dateline

Date	التاريخ:
Date (*lit. written/issued on* . . .)	حرر في . . .
Date (adverbial form: *written/issued on* . . .)	تحريرا في . . .
Date (*lit. the date* . . . *[Gregorian/Syriac], which coincides with* . . . *[Hijra]*)	التاريخ . . . الموافق . . .

Reference Line

This is a combination of numbers and letters (e.g., Ref: X123) used to identify the letter or memo in future correspondence or for internal archiving purposes. It is usually written flush right a line below the date:

Reference	الإشارة:
Reference number	رقم:
Reference number	العدد:

References

Unlike the reference line, which refers to the letter itself, this is a comprehensive list (similar to a bibliography) of all the documents, previous correspondence, laws, and policies mentioned in the letter or memo. It is written flush right a line below the reference line:

Reference	المرجع:
References	المراجع:

Attention Line

This line is used when addressing a company, but the letter is directed to a specific individual within the company:

Attention (*lit. Party*)	طرف:
Attention (*lit. Care of* [not to be confused with c/o])	عناية:

Subject Line

This line provides the gist of the letter for the reader's convenience:

Subject	الموضوع:
Subject	م/

Action Required

This line specifies the response that is expected from the addressee:

Action required	المطلوب: الإجراء
considering and advising	الرأي وإبداء النظر
responding before November 26, 2010	الرد قبل ٢٦ نوفمبر ٢٠١٠

Salutations

To Whom It May Concern	إلى من يهمه الأمر
Dear Mr. . . .	السيد الأستاذ / . . .
Dear Dr. . . . / Dear Prof. . . .	الأستاذ الدكتور / . . .

Dear Ms. . . . (*lit. Honorable Madam . . .*)	السيدة الفاضلة / . . .
Dear Mr. . . . (*lit. Honorable Sir . . .*)	السيد الفاضل / . . .
Dear Ladies and Gentlemen	حضرات السيدات والسادة
Dear Colleagues	السادة الزملاء الأعزاء
Respected Mr. . . .	السيد المحترم . . .
Dear . . . (*lit. Your Kindness*)	عطوفة . . .
Dear Colleague (*lit. Brother Colleague*)	الأخ الزميل

Religious and Official Formulas

These formulaic expressions can be used anywhere in the letter before the message:

In the Name of Allah, Most Gracious, Most Merciful	بسم الله الرحمن الرحيم
Peace Be Upon You and the Mercy of God and His Blessing!	السلام عليكم ورحمة الله وبركاته
Phrase used to separate formalities and greetings from the message	
(*lit. Kind Greeting and after[that]*)	تحية طيبة وبعد
(*lit. After the greeting*)	بعد التحية
(*lit. As for [what is] after [the greeting]*)	أما بعد
(*And after [the greeting]*)	وبعد

Openings

following up on	عطفا على
in reference to	إشارة إلى
we inform you that	نفيدكم بأن
we inform you that	نحيطكم علما بأن
we would like to inform you that	نود إحاطتكم علما بأن
we inform you that [*polite and formal*]	نحيط سيادتكم علما بأن
Please, be informed that	
Please, be informed that	برجاء التفضل بالعلم بأن
(*lit. I am honored to inform you that*)	أتشرف بالإفادة
Please, accept	برجاء التكرم بقبول

I, the undersigned, hereby certify   أقر أنا الموقع أدناه
I, the above named, hereby certify   أقر أنا المذكور أعلاه

Complimentary Closings

These are formulas that are usually translated as *Sincerely* or similar closings:

lit. This (letter) and please accept
abundant respect and appreciation   هذا وتفضلوا بقبول وافر الاحترام والتقدير
lit. And please accept the utmost respect
and appreciation   وتفضلوا بقبول فائق الاحترام والتقدير
lit. This (letter) and much gratitude and
appreciation to you   هذا ولكم منا جزيل الشكر والتقدير
lit. Many thanks to you   ولسيادتكم جزيل الشكر
lit. Accept our greetings, Sir [Tunisia]   تقبلوا سيدي تحياتنا
lit. With kindest wishes   مع أطيب التمنيات
lit. With our kindest greetings   مع أطيب تحياتنا
lit. And peace is the closing   والسلام ختام
lit. With gratitude   مع الشكر
lit. And peace   والسلام

Directives

If a letter does not specify the expected response in the "Action Required" line, it can be summarized at the end:

This is for your information   هذا للعلم والإفادة
This is for your information and compliance   هذا للعلم والالتزام
This is for your information and necessary action   هذا للعلم واتخاذ اللازم
Please, acknowledge receipt   رجاء الإفادة بالاستلام
Please, consider and advise   رجاء التكرم بالنظر والإفادة
to be implemented   للعمل بموجبه
effective immediately (*lit. effective from its date*)   نافذ من تاريخه
effective on . . . (*lit. To be considered from [date]*)   ... اعتبارا من

Notations

enclosures/attachments	الملحقات
enclosures/attachments	المرفقات
enclosures/attachments [Tunisia]	المصاحيب
enclosures/attachments (*lit. this [letter] and you find enclosed*)	هذا، وتجدون مرفقا
enclosures/attachments (*lit. enclosed in its fold*)	مرفق طيه
carbon copy	نسخة
carbon copy	صورة
carbon copy	ص
carbon copy	صورة.مبلغة
note/postscript (NB/PS)	ملحوظة
note/postscript (NB/PS)	ملاحظة
over (*lit. to be followed/continued*)	يُتبع
over (*lit. Please, look at its reverse side*)	انظر خلفه من فضلك

Signature

signature	إمضاء
signature	توقيع
name of signatory	اسم الموقع
Yours faithfully/Sincerely	المخلص
authorized signatory	المفوض بالتوقيع
requester [Lebanon/Jordan]	المستدعي
presented/submitted by	مقدمه لسيادتكم
on behalf of . . .	بالنيابة عن . . .

Bibliography

Abdul-Raof, Hussein. *Arabic Rhetoric: A Pragmatic Analysis*. London: Routledge, 2006.

"ArabiCorpus." Brigham Young University, 2015. http://arabicorpus.byu.edu.

Baker, Mona. *In Other Words: A Coursebook on Translation*. New York: Routledge, 1992.

Bateson, Mary. *Arabic Language Handbook*. Washington, DC: Georgetown University Press, 2003.

Biguenet, John, and Schulte Rainer. *The Craft of Translation*. Chicago: University of Chicago Press, 1989.

Buckwalter, Tim, and Dilworth Parkinson. *A Frequency Dictionary of Arabic: Core Vocabulary for Learners*. New York: Routledge, 2010.

Carter, Ronald. *Vocabulary: Applied Linguistic Perspectives*. New York: Routledge, 2012.

"Corpus of Contemporary American English." Brigham Young University, 2015. http://corpus.byu.edu/coca.

Eco, Umberto, and Alastair McEwen. *Experiences in Translation*. Toronto: University of Toronto Press, 2008.

Faiq, Said. *Cultural Encounters in Translation from Arabic*. Buffalo: Multilingual Matters, 2004.

Fromkin, Victoria, Robert Rodman, and Nina Hyams. *An Introduction to Language*, 10th edition. Independence, KY: Cengage Learning, 2013.

Gee, James. *How to Do Discourse Analysis: A Toolkit*. New York: Routledge, 2014.

Green, Georgia. *Pragmatics and Natural Language Understanding*, 2nd edition. New York: Routledge, 1996.

Hatim, Basil. *Communication across Cultures: Translation Theory and Contrastive Text Linguistics*. Exeter: University of Exeter Press, 1997.

Hatim, Basil, and Jeremy Munday. *Translation: An Advanced Resource Book*. New York: Routledge, 2005.

Johnstone, Barbara. *Repetition in Arabic Discourse: Paradigms, Syntagms, and the Ecology of Language*. Philadelphia: John Benjamins, 1991.

Lakoff, George, and Mark Johnson. *Metaphors We Live By*. Chicago: University of Chicago Press, 2003.

Langacker, Ronald. *Cognitive Grammar: A Basic Introduction*. New York: Oxford University Press, 2008.

McCarus, Ernest. *English Grammar for Students of Arabic: The Study Guide for Those Learning Arabic*. Ann Arbor, MI: Olivia and Hill Press, 2007.

Parkinson, Dilworth. *Using Arabic Synonyms*. Cambridge: Cambridge University Press, 2005.

Robinson, Douglas. *Becoming a Translator: An Introduction to the Theory and Practice of Translation*. New York: Routledge, 2012.

Ryding, Karin. *Arabic: A Linguistic Introduction*. Cambridge: Cambridge University Press, 2014.

Strauss, Susan, and Parastou Feiz. *Discourse Analysis: Putting Our Worlds into Words*. New York: Routledge, 2013.

Tassini, Adriana. *The Translator Training Textbook: Translation Best Practices, Resources & Expert Interviews*. North Charleston, SC: Adriana Tassini, 2011.

Watson, Janet. *The Phonology and Morphology of Arabic*. New York: Oxford University Press, 2002.

Venuti, Lawrence. *The Translation Studies Reader*. New York: Routledge, 2012.

———. *The Translator's Invisibility: A History of Translation*. New York: Routledge, 2008.

Index